The Voegelinian Revolution

ERIC VOEGELIN

THE VOEGELINIAN REVOLUTION

A Biographical Introduction

Ellis Sandoz

Louisiana State University Press
Baton Rouge and London

DESIGNER: Patricia Douglas Crowder
TYPEFACE: VIP Trump
TYPESETTER: G & S Typesetters, Inc.

Published with the assistance of the Council on Research,
Louisiana State University

LIBRARY OF CONGRESS CATALOGING IN PUBLICATION DATA

Sandoz, Ellis, 1931–
  The Voegelinian revolution.

  Bibliography: p.
  Includes index.
    1. Voegelin, Eric, 1901–   . 2. Political scientists—
United States—Biography.   I. Title.
JA93.V63S25   320'.092'4 [B]   81-12344
ISBN 0-8071-0870-7   AACR2

For my wife

A foolish consistency is the hobgoblin of little minds, adored by little statesmen and philosophers and divines. With consistency a great soul has simply nothing to do. He may as well concern himself with his shadow on the wall. Speak what you think now in hard words and tomorrow speak what tomorrow thinks in hard words again, though it contradict every thing you said today. —"Ah, so you shall be sure to be misunderstood."—Is it so bad then to be misunderstood? Pythagoras was misunderstood, and Socrates, and Jesus, and Luther, and Copernicus, and Galileo, and Newton, and every pure and wise spirit that ever took flesh. To be great is to be misunderstood.

RALPH WALDO EMERSON

Contents

Abbreviations Used in Text

A   *Anamnesis*
AM   "Autobiographical Memoir"
ER   *From Enlightenment to Revolution*
NSP   *The New Science of Politics*
OH   *Order and History*
SPG   *Science, Politics, and Gnosticism*

Acknowledgments

In attempting to say what it seems to me most needs to be said about Eric Voegelin by way of introducing his work to a larger audience, I have been immeasurably assisted by Eric Voegelin himself, and I have greatly enjoyed Mrs. Voegelin's charming hospitality and stimulating conversation during my many visits to their home to talk and collect materials. Time to do my writing and financial aid have been provided through summer research grants from East Texas State University's Division of Organized Research and from the Earhart Foundation. This work was also supported by a research grant from the National Endowment for the Humanities. My colleague Miroslav John Hanak read a portion of a draft of the manuscript and made a number of valuable suggestions. Chapter 5 is a revision of "Voegelin's Idea of Historical Form," originally published in *Cross Currents*, XII (1962), 41–67, and Chapter 6 is a revision of "The Foundations of Voegelin's Political Theory," originally published in the *Political Science Reviewer*, I (1971), 30–73. I am grateful to these journals for permission to republish here. I also wish to acknowledge, with thanks, permission to quote extensively from Eric Voegelin, *From Enlightenment to Revolution*, ed. John H. Hallowell (Durham, N.C.: Duke University Press, 1975), and Eric Voegelin, "Reason: The Classic Experience," *Southern Review*, n.s., X (1974), 237–64.

I am most appreciative for all the assistance I have received in bringing this book to completion. None of its shortcomings are attributable to any of my benefactors, however. Finally, the typescript was prepared by my assistant, Susan Eckerle Willbern, a graduate student in zoology, whose expert stenographic help, research assistance, intelligent collaboration, and sense of humor lightened the burden of authorship and are acknowledged with pleasure. Beverly Jarrett, Executive Editor and Assistant Director of the Louisiana State University Press, copy-edited the typescript and, by her talent, skill, and patience, not only eliminated many imperfections but made the onerous editorial process almost enjoyable.

The Voegelinian Revolution

Introduction

My dual purpose in writing this book is to provide a general introduction to Eric Voegelin's thought and to do so in such a way as to demonstrate its revolutionary character. Academic interest in Voegelin has steadily increased in recent years. But the work he has done has importance far beyond the confines of the academy, and it is this wider audience that I have addressed. The volume, it is hoped, will be of value to persons seriously interested in the abiding questions of human existence as they have been explored by a ranking thinker over the past half-century. It is intended to bridge the considerable gulf that separates Voegelin from other thinkers and from the general public to whom he is an obscure figure. Voegelin belongs neither to a school of thought nor to the prevailing orthodoxies which compose the current climate of opinion. His uniqueness as a thinker and the complexity of his work justify an attempt, such as the present one, to supply a guide for those who wish to understand and appreciate his significance.

Introducing an intellectually demanding body of writing now pyramided into some fifteen books and over ninety published articles may well be justification enough for an evaluative study. But my acquaintance with the man and pursuit of his work over three decades, together with my reflections on the history of political theory from antiquity onward, lead me to conclude that Voegelin's achievement is truly extraordinary. While caution is doubtless in order in assessing the long-term significance of contemporary events, including the stature of intellectual achievement, the evidence in Voegelin's case is persuasive, indeed, compelling. By all the pertinent criteria of scholarly attainment, technical mastery of materials and philosophical analysis, and breadth of vision, Voegelin's work is of epochal importance.

Apart from the biographical and expository presentation of the subject, then, it is the argument of this book that Voegelin's thought constitutes a revolution in philosophy and political science, one sufficiently noteworthy in its sphere to justify this book's title. It is, of course, my premise that any revolution occurs with the events themselves, not when everyone discerns their revolutionary proportions at a sometimes-distant later time. At least an inkling of the character and extent of the present revolution emerges in the course of the following presentation, and the final two chapters are devoted to its summary.

This book is an interpretive introduction, not a definitive commentary or a critical evaluation. It could not be the former, because it introduces work still in progress. Nor could it, in all honesty, be the latter, because I have been for many years, and remain, Eric Voegelin's student and his friend. I have not felt the discomfort of having to choose truth above friendship in studying his works, prepared though I am to do so, because I have found them illuminative of every subject they touch upon and scientifically of the highest order of cogency and validity. What follows is an interpretation, not merely an appreciation. As a scholar and teacher Voegelin has strenuously avoided making disciples of his students, believing it to be of utmost importance that both he and they serve truth as the fundamental requirement of the Weberian intellectual honesty which is the lodestar of all scientific inquiry. Hence, though I have paid scrupulous attention to what the sources say, have utilized extensive tape-recorded interviews with Voegelin, and have benefited from his comments in revising the manuscript for publication, he is not to blame for the approach taken, the lines of material selected as central, or the interpretation given.

A further word about my approach to and organization of the materials dealt with will perhaps be useful. Voegelin has always identified himself as a political scientist and philosopher of politics. Although this is not an intellectual biography, it is organized more or less chronologically, apart from the stage-setting of the first chapter.

The second and third chapters are biographical; they sketch the subject's life and work from the beginning to the present, and they contain the most elaborate discussion of the five German books to appear so far in English. The prime source for these chapters is what I have called Voegelin's "Autobiographical Memoir." This important document resulted from a series of tape-recorded interviews with Voegelin over a period of several weeks in the summer of 1973. Some twenty-seven hours of recorded responses to questions I posed to him were transcribed and then edited by Voegelin to form a narrative which is at once autobiographical and a running commentary on key facets of his own work as he sees it himself. The bulk of this document is published herewith as an integral part of the book, as it was originally intended to be.

In undertaking this study of Voegelin's thought, attentive to its development over the decades to the present, I have favored recent work and the current state of his philosophy. My method of first sketching the whole of the work thus far (with an initial emphasis on publications through 1938) and of then concentrating more detailed attention at four subsequent crosscuts in the intellectual horizon so as to show the stages of his inquiry, entails some repetitiveness. Displaying a "horizon" at successive stages down to 1938, then at 1952, 1957, 1966, and 1981 required successive consideration of the same problems as seen in the moving perspectives of the enlarging horizons. Moreover, the horizons could not be treated comprehensively in single chapters; they had, thus, to be treated selectively on the basis of what was changed or accented or new by comparison with the earlier horizon, so that a topical selectivity was required. The topical selectivity itself, then, necessitated going back and moving forward among the works in the several time periods. A "neater" introduction to Voegelin's thought might have devoted chapters to such key topics as Man, Politics, History, and Being. But this kind of organization of the material does, in fact, defy the interrelatedness of each of the topics. Such a dissection could no more give an accurate understanding of the content, not to mention its movement and vitality, of Voegelin's inquiry into the reality of man's political existence in history and the Whole than the autopsy of a corpse provides an understanding of the man whose body it was.

Voegelin's thought is to be seen as the pilgrimage of a philosophizing man in quest of truth, not in isolation from the realities of politics and the exigencies of contemporary life, but in constant and responsive interplay with them. The depth of his immersion in political reality and his resistance to its corruption is of key importance to his thought. I have sought to stress the pragmatic and commonsensical dimensions of his thought, even as it rises to the extraordinary complexities of theoretical analysis and meditation. This approach to the work originates in Voegelin's own understanding of reason and human rationality as forming a continuum from common sense as its foundation to philosophic and scientific insight, and that notion of rationality is displayed in all his work, from the 1920s onward. But this scarcely prepares one for the complexity that is, in fact, encountered in the study of Voegelin's thought. A knowledgeable scholar and friend remarked to me that *The Ecumenic Age* is as complicated as Hegel's *Phenomenology of Spirit*, a fair candidate in anybody's contest for the most difficult book ever written. I don't agree with the assessment: Voegelin is clear, Hegel is cunningly ambiguous. Still, the point is made, and the last chapter of this book, which deals with *The Ecumenic Age*, will perhaps suggest the reasons for it.

I, too, have tried to be clear, to introduce the material by gradations, in a sequential way, so that the chief features of Voegelin's theories will emerge, enabling attentive readers to understand them and to share with me the excitement of that illumination. For the pilgrimage Voegelin undertakes, and which we join at our various levels, arrives at new horizons for us as well as for him; and I have merely tried, as a sort of custodian of the compass, to map his progress from peak to peak through rugged terrain. In this mapping operation, I have kept mainly (if not exclusively) to the high ground of Voegelin's thought through which he unfolds a new analysis of reality and ultimately provides us with a new science of human affairs. I have thus omitted virtually all of his splendid detailed treatment of the numerous documentary sources from which his insights arise, only briefly considering the analyses of the defective and "deformed" accounts of reality (such as Gnosticism and modern ideology) with which his investigation critically interacts repeatedly and against the evils of which it is a therapy. My objective has been to illumine the core of Voegelin's thought through a process of exposition that leads the reader into its heart, showing in the process not only the decisive insights but also their integral connection with the method of inquiry itself. The tensions with the defective accounts of reality come to light in this procedure, to be sure. But the details and the full-scale arguments showing the why and how of deficiency are largely left aside. To have done otherwise would have subverted my purpose of providing a concise yet searching and balanced account of the uniqueness of the work before us and its place in the panorama of Western political philosophy. Because the *language* of inquiry is critically important to Voegelin's whole effort, I have permitted him to speak for himself on every important issue as far as that could feasibly be done.

CHAPTER I

A Starting Point: Common Sense
and the New Science

To convince oneself of Jascha Heifetz' greatness
as a violinist one has only to hear him play; a similar test of the profundity of Eric Voegelin as a philosopher is most convincing. Accordingly, a bibliography of Voegelin's writings is provided at the end
of this volume as an index of a scholar's production which is in
every way the equivalent of the artist's achievement, if range and
virtuosity be accepted as common criteria. Of course, if one dislikes
violin-playing on principle—or if one is exclusively a fan of Emerson, Lake, and Palmer and responds with "Jascha Who?"—then hearing Heifetz play will offer less-than-cogent proof of his brilliance.
Still: the proof of the pudding is in the eating (to change metaphors),
and a perusal of Voegelin's own work is the best demonstration of its
significance.

I

Another way of documenting the unique significance of Voegelin is
by consulting experts, the jury technique widely used in academe
whenever a qualitative judgment is wanted. A sampler of such expert opinions might begin with the statement of a distinguished Old
Testament scholar, Princeton's Bernhard W. Anderson:

The great merit of Voegelin's work is that he seeks to recover "the whole"
by penetrating to the dynamic of human existence. . . . The field of Old Testament studies, like other scholarly disciplines, is currently the victim of
specialization. Hence, it is refreshing to read the work of a philosophical

"layman" in the field who has taken it upon himself to master the original sources and the secondary literature up to the time of his writing. . . . This [*Israel and Revelation*] is one of the few books on the Old Testament which has so engrossed my interest that I have eagerly wondered what would be on the next page.[1]

James L. Wiser has commented: "Voegelin has attempted much more than simply rigorous intellectual history. Important as the understanding of the Greek science of order is in itself, the greater achievement of this study becomes clear only within the larger horizon constituted by Voegelin's own theoretical intentions. . . . Voegelin's attempt to understand philosophy as a form of existence-intruth is simultaneously a presentation of those historical events in which the opening of existence towards transcendence was seen as disclosing the very nature of humanity itself."[2]

John H. Hallowell has written: "This analysis of Plato and Aristotle reflects a brilliant, subtle mind and displays an erudition that few scholars can match. It is a remarkable intellectual achievement but more importantly it is, along with his other writing, an adventure in philosophy not unlike the one undertaken by Plato himself."[3] Dante Germino has written:

With the publication of the long-awaited fourth volume to his *magnum opus*, *Order and History*, Eric Voegelin has established himself as the leading political philosopher of our time. The virtues apparent in previous volumes—enormous erudition, openness to the evidence wherever it leads, masterful use of sources, exceptional interpretive gifts, penetration to the key philosophical issues—abound in the present one also, but another dimension of the argument is more powerfully present: Voegelin no longer stands forth principally as the interpreter of the thought of past philosophers but presents his own original and profound philosophy of history. What we have before us, then, is not another book but a masterpiece.[4]

Theologian Thomas J. J. Altizer, has called Voegelin "one of the major thinkers of our time, and major religious thinkers," going on

---

1. Bernhard W. Anderson, "Politics and the Transcendent: Eric Voegelin's Philosophical and Theological Analysis of the Old Testament in the Context of the Ancient Near East," *Political Science Reviewer*, I (Fall, 1971), 3.
2. James L. Wiser, "Philosophy and Human Order," *ibid.*, II (Fall, 1972), 158.
3. John H. Hallowell, "Existence in Tension," *ibid.*, 180.
4. Dante Germino, "*Order and History*, Volume Four: *The Ecumenic Age*," *Journal of Politics*, XXXVII (August, 1975), 847.

to say, "Eric Voegelin may well be historically unique in having mastered the worlds of both Athens and Jerusalem: *Order and History* is surely unique in its project of unveiling the coinherence [*sic*] of noetic [rational] understanding and biblical faith as the primary and indispensable ground of Western civilization."[5] Political scientist R. Bruce Douglass has commented: "*Order and History* . . . elaborate[s] a history of the symbolization of order, out of which a philosophy of history begins to emerge. This development of a philosophy of history rooted in detailed, catholic study of the history of symbolisms of order is Eric Voegelin's distinctive contribution to political theory. . . . The logic of his work would seem to be that the only way to challenge effectively a defective view of history is to provide an alternative that is philosophically sound."[6]

In 1956, when *Order and History* first began to appear, Crane Brinton of Harvard said, "This whole work seems to me clearly to take rank with the works of Toynbee, Spengler, Sorokin, and Collingwood." And Roger Shinn called *Israel and Revelation* "one of the great intellectual works of our generation. . . . A masterful combination of scientific scholarship with theological and poetic insight." As Shinn later wrote: "It is evident that the lavish praise Voegelin has won from many critics is not extravagant. His is one of the monuments of scholarship of our time."[7] Distinguished historian C. A. Robinson of Brown University said of Voegelin's analysis of Hellenic antiquity: "The true strength of these volumes, and it is a very great and remarkable strength, lies in the penetrating and significant analysis of the ancient Greek writers."[8] James B. Pritchard and W. F. Albright were two among many others who lauded Voegelin's achievements. Albright went so far as to say that Voegelin's "use of Hebrew is almost impeccable."[9] And Notre Dame's Gerhart

5. Thomas J. J. Altizer, "A New History and a New But Ancient God? A Review Essay," *Journal of the American Academy of Religion*, XLIII (1975), 757.

6. R. Bruce Douglass, "The Gospel and Political Order: Eric Voegelin and the Political Role of Christianity," *Journal of Politics*, XXXVIII (February, 1976), 44.

7. Roger L. Shinn in *Saturday Review*, XLI (March 8, 1958), 27; *Christian Century*, LXXV (September 17, 1958), 1053.

8. C. A. Robinson in *American Historical Review*, LXIII (1957–1958), 940.

9. James B. Pritchard, *ibid.*, 640–41; William F. Albright, "Eric Voegelin's *Order and History*, with Special Reference to Vol. I," in *Theological Studies*, XXII (1961), 275.

Niemeyer found the initial three volumes of *Order and History* "a great deed of the spirit, one which will stand as a monument of this mid-century."[10]

Voegelin's *The New Science of Politics* excited such interest that *Time* magazine seized upon it for the feature article of its thirtieth anniversary issue, entitled "Journalism and Joachim's Children."[11] Michael Oakeshott's anonymous review for the London *Times Literary Supplement* included the statement that "this book must be considered one of the most enlightening essays on the character of European politics that has appeared for half a century."[12] Arnold Brecht wrote elsewhere that the "mid-century revolt against positivism, scientific method, and relativism in political science is making headway. It has now found what may easily come to be considered its leading expression in a small and difficult, but rich and important book by Professor Eric Voegelin."[13] And a Yale political scientist, Robert A. Dahl, while expressing nearly total disagreement with Voegelin, grudgingly conceded the author to be "a writer of such massive erudition [that he] uses a third-century document with more skill than most of us use the *New York Times*."[14]

II

In response to such a series of comments from authority—and those observations represent only a fraction of the published commentary—one might reasonably argue that Voegelin is not obscure at all. It was, after all, to Voegelin that *Newsweek* turned for a comment when Toynbee died in 1975. And he has lectured and served as visiting professor throughout this country and abroad at such leading universities as Oxford, London, Chicago, Harvard, Johns Hopkins, Yale. He maintains a staggering correspondence with scholars in dozens of disciplines in all corners of the world. He has been the subject of two panels of the American Political Science Association,

10. Gerhart Niemeyer in *Review of Politics*, XXI (July, 1959), 596.
11. *Time Magazine* (March 9, 1953), 57–60.
12. *Times Literary Supplement* (London), (August 9, 1953), 504.
13. Arnold Brecht in *Social Research*, XX (1953), 230.
14. Robert A. Dahl, "The Science of Politics: Old and New," *World Politics*, VII (1955), 486.

and his work has been honored by the Association with the Benjamin E. Lippincott Award. He was appointed in 1958 to fill the chair in political science at the University of Munich left vacant since the death of Max Weber in 1930. And he served as Salvatori Distinguished Scholar in the Hoover Institution on War, Revolution, and Peace at Stanford University after retirement from Munich in 1969.

This is not exactly obscurity. Still, Voegelin is not nearly so famous as, say, Herbert Marcuse or Angela Davis, nor even so well known as those with whom he is most frequently compared: Spengler, Toynbee, Sorokin, or perhaps Collingwood. Why this absence of popular appreciation despite the aforementioned praises? The answer is not simple; it goes to the heart of the body of thought before us. Parts of the answer are implied by the commentators I have quoted. To begin with, much of Voegelin's work has focused on antiquity, a far remove from the workaday concerns of the general public and even of social scientists. Moreover, Voegelin steadily moves at the frontier of knowledge. Hence, full appreciation of his work requires the attentive response of an accomplished scholar. As a reviewer of *The Ecumenic Age* expressed it: "Voegelin's brilliant work rests on a mastery of considerable ancient history, philosophy, and religion. . . . This author attempts to create a universally significant philosophy of history on a scale superseding Spengler, Toynbee, Hegel, and Marx. . . . Only advanced scholars in the realms of philosophy of history, intellectual history, and religion will exert the effort required to understand this book."[15] No D. C. Somervell has appeared to edit and popularize *Order and History* as occurred with Toynbee's *A Study of History*[16]—nor would Voegelin permit such a thing to be done.

Addressing the man's evident obscurity even within the restricted horizon of professional political scientists, William C. Havard, Jr., and Gregor Sebba pondered the question of what has "prevented the appropriate recognition of the emergence of a new theory of politics" as that is provided in Voegelin's thought and writings. They concluded that two things were decisive. "The first is that the

15. Philip D. Jordan in *History*, III (1975), 233.
16. Arnold J. Toynbee, *A Study of History*, abridgment edited by D. C. Somervell (2 vols.; New York & London: Oxford University Press, 1947–1957).

advancement of that theory '. . . is largely the work of one independent thinker . . . who published his first book four decades ago and
is still forging ahead at a pace which leaves his best readers behind.' The second is the enormous demand which the [Voegelinian]
achievement makes on the 'newcomer to such studies.' Not only
must the reader be able to follow abstract reasoning at its highest
level, but he must know the history of ideas, philosophy (in all its
dimensions), theology, the full sweep of history from prehistory to
modernity, and the present development of scholarship in fields as
widely separated as anthropology, biblical criticism, comparative literature, psychology, and others. . . . 'All this is very far from the concerns of the practicing political scientist today.'"[17]

These explanations for Voegelin's relative obscurity are surely
valid. But there is another, perhaps more fundamental explanation.
As a philosopher and scientist devoted to the exploration of the human condition in all its dimensions, Voegelin's work is revolutionary. Thus, he must be approached on his own terms; he cannot be
"explained" in terms either of the variegated subject matter he deals
with or the source materials he utilizes. The decisive dimension of
his achievement lies in the sphere of imaginative insight. New insights are always difficult to appreciate, doubly so when they neces-
sitate a major shift in the structure of scientific thinking itself. Yet
just this kind of Copernican revolution is present in Voegelin's work.

A lesser, but more obvious, effect of Voegelin's revolutionary
originality is that he is (in varying degrees) at odds with all schools of
thought. He does not fit any of the convenient intellectual pigeon-
holes. Hence, he has no applauding claque, no automatic clientele,
either academic or political. He is a genuinely independent thinker.
His work is strikingly free of polemics, yet it clearly entails a rejection of all of the dearest Idols of the Cave of modern intellectuals
here and abroad, most especially of positivism, Marxism, and Freudianism. And these are not merely the idols of the intellectuals, but
of a substantial segment of the educated public which has itself been
educated at the hands of such intellectuals, not a few of whom are

17. William C. Havard, "The Changing Pattern of Voegelin's Conception of History and Consciousness," *Southern Review*, n.s., VII (1971), 50; internal quotations
from Gregor Sebba, "The Present State of Political Theory," *Polity*, I (1968), 259–70.

university professors and publicists, shapers of the climate of opinion more generally. In stressing that he was partisan of no cause, Voegelin once made the point this way:

I have in my files the documents according to which I am a Communist, a Fascist, a National Socialist, an old Liberal, a new Liberal, a Catholic, a Protestant, a Platonist, a neo-Augustinian, a Thomist, and of course an Hegelian. Not to forget that I was strongly influenced by Huey Long. This list I consider of some importance, because the various characterizations of course always name the pet *bête noire* of the respective critic and give therefore a very good picture of the intellectual corruption and destruction which characterizes the contemporary academic world. Understandably I have never answered criticisms of this kind; critics of this type can become objects of inquiry but they cannot be partners in a discussion.[18]

"To be great is to be misunderstood," Emerson once said,[19] and misunderstood Voegelin has assuredly been. For it is evident that he could not belong to all of the persuasions with which he has been identified, but it is scarcely comprehensible even to persons of considerable sophistication that he belongs to none of them.

This is so much a source for the misunderstanding of Voegelin's work, as well as for the muting of its resonance among the educated public, that another illustrative example may not be amiss. Thus the following humorous detail in Voegelin's recounting of the grim life-and-death drama of his escape from Austria into Switzerland after the Nazi *Anschluss* and his immediate firing from the law faculty of the University of Vienna in 1938. Having narrowly eluded the Gestapo and fleeing by train with two bags, leaving his wife at her parents' home to follow a week later, he crossed the Austrian border and presented himself at an American consulate in Switzerland.

In Zurich I had to wait for a nonquota immigration visa extended to scholars who had been offered jobs in the United States. My friends at Harvard— [Gottfried von] Haberler, [Joseph A.] Schumpeter, and in a very decisive

18. Eric Voegelin, "Autobiographical Memoir," unpublished transcript of taped interviews with the author (1973), p. 46; hereinafter cited parenthetically in text as AM. For the Huey Long in Voegelin see the ascerbic review of the first three volumes of *Order and History* by Moses Hadas in the *Journal of the History of Ideas,* XIX (June, 1958), 444, and my comments in *Social Research,* XXVIII (Summer, 1961), 233–34.

19. Ralph Waldo Emerson, "Self-Reliance," in Brooks Atkinson (ed.), *The Complete Essays and Other Writings of Ralph Waldo Emerson* (New York: Modern Library, 1950), 152.

function as head of the Department of Government, Arthur Holcombe— had provided a part-time instructorship. But I had not yet received an official letter, and I had to wait for that in Zurich in order to get the American visa. In waiting for the visa I had dealings with the American vice-consul in Zurich, a very nice Harvard boy, who had grave suspicions about me. He explained that I was neither a Communist, nor a Catholic, nor a Jew and therefore had no reason whatsoever not to be in favor of National Socialism and be a National Socialist myself. Hence, if I was obviously in flight the only reason must be some criminal record; and he did not want to give me the visa before the matter of my criminality was cleared up. Fortunately, in due course the letter of Holcombe arrived, advising me of my appointment as a part-time instructor, and with the signature of Holcombe on the letter the Harvard boy in the consulate was convinced that I was in the fold, and I got my visa.

I am telling this incident not in order to be critical of this particular vice-consul, who was as innocent of political problems, and especially human problems, as such people happen to be. . . . That anybody could be anti-National Socialist without being motivated by an ideological counter-position, or because he was a Jew, is, indeed, as far as my experience goes, inconceivable to most people in the academic world whom I know. (AM, 43–44)

By his own interpretation, Eric Voegelin is a philosopher and scientist whose primary commitment is to serve truth, a task to which he has unreservedly devoted his entire mature life. It is the single-minded devotion to that purpose that has supplied yet a third source of his obscurity and contributed to his being misunderstood: he has created a new language of philosophical discourse. As the anecdote just recounted suggests, there is something incredible about the life of reason in devotion to truth, and lesser explanations for personal and academic activities may be suspected. Sometimes the suspicions are dark, as the various attempts to classify Voegelin themselves indicate. There is, in principle, nothing unique in this. In antiquity dark suspicions cost Socrates his life. In the mid-eighteenth century David Hume reflected on the plight of his own devotion to "Sceptical philosophy" in these words:

Every passion is mortified by it, except the love of truth; and that passion never is, nor can be, carried to too high a degree. It is surprising, therefore, that this philosophy . . . should be the subject of so much groundless reproach and obloquy. But, perhaps, the very circumstance which renders it so innocent is what chiefly exposes it to the public hatred and resentment. By flattering no irregular passion it gains few partizans [*sic*]: By opposing so many vices and follies, it raises to itself abundance of enemies, who stigmatize it as libertine, profane, and irreligious.[20]

While the lists of complaints against it may differ, Voegelin's new philosophy has emerged through a critical process that carries with it the articulation of a new language. The process of critique has left as casualties along the way not only the several "isms" already noticed, but to a considerable degree the received conceptions of philosophy and science themselves. No vested interest has been left untouched, a fact not lost on some readers. Thus the thoroughness of the critical revisions present in his thought provoked a leading political scientist, commenting on *The New Science of Politics* in 1955, to petulantly conclude that Voegelin "has not only 'undefined' science; he has un-scienced it."[21] From the standpoint of the positivist-behavioralist conception of science, no doubt he had. Things were little better from the standpoint of contemporary academic philosophy whose brotherhood was confronted toward the end of his analysis of Classical philosophy in 1957 by Voegelin's startling conclusion "that the history of philosophy is in the largest part the history of its derailment" (OH, III, 277). In 1973 he invoked Whitehead's judgment that "modern philosophy has been ruined."[22] Hardly the stuff with which to win friends and placate professors of philosophy! Without at this point exploring the details, it can be said that these and similar judgments reflect the sober and painstaking

20. David Hume, *Enquiries Concerning the Human Understanding and Concerning the Principles of Morals*, ed. by L. A. Selby-Bigge (2nd ed.; Oxford: Clarendon Press, 1902), 41.
21. Dahl, "The Science of Politics: Old and New," 489.
22. Eric Voegelin, "On Classical Studies," *Modern Age* (Winter, 1973), 3. The statement occurs in Alfred North Whitehead, *Science and the Modern World: Lowell Lectures, 1925* (New York: Free Press Paperback Edition, 1967), 55. In context it reads as follows: "The enormous success of the [seventeenth century's] scientific abstractions, yielding on the one hand *matter* with its *simple location* in space and time, on the other hand *mind*, perceiving, suffering, reasoning, but not interfering, has foisted onto philosophy the task of accepting them as the most concrete rendering of fact.
"Thereby, modern philosophy has been ruined. It has oscillated in a complex manner between three extremes. There are the dualists, who accept matter and mind as on an equal basis, and the two varieties of monists, those who put mind inside matter, and those who put matter inside mind. But this juggling with abstractions can never overcome the inherent confusion introduced by the [fallacious] ascription of *misplaced concreteness* to the scientific scheme of the seventeenth century."

study of voluminous source materials and are far from cavalier. Voegelin's linguistic precision is a mark of the demands made by the enterprise of putting philosophy back on the tracks again, of rethinking the character and foundations of the science of man. But this language is itself a substantial barrier to the general reader's appreciation of Voegelin just because it is technically precise, as it must be if it is to be adequate to its high task. Recovery of the language of science is a major dimension of Voegelin's entire work from the 1930s onward. Hence, to understand him one must master his language, a demanding but rewarding requirement.

And finally, both obscurity and misunderstanding arise from the drift of Voegelin's philosophy, for it firmly addresses the whole history and hierarchy of human existence with special emphasis upon the modes of man's participation in the divine as reflected in documented experience. In a world heavily encumbered by immanentist ideologies and secularist presumptions, this distinctive feature of his thought is as unpalatable as were similar features, for example, in the later thought of both Henri Bergson and George Santayana. A standard history of American philosophy dismissed with a sneer Santayana's valedictory statements in *The Idler and His Works* (published in 1957, five years after his death): "In my various books I have discussed things at very unequal removes from the function of spirit within me. But that center was truly philosophical. I can identify my self heartily with nothing in me except with the flame of spirit itself. Therefore the truest picture of my inmost being would show none of the features of my person, and nothing of the background of my life. It would show only the light of understanding that burned within me and, as far as it could, consumed and purified all the rest."[23] The passage was introduced by Herbert Schneider with these two sentences. "As his senses and memories began to fail him in his Italian seclusion, [Santayana] imagined his 'real' being to be that of his spirit. In this mood he wrote, near the end of his bodily career, these words, which seem pathetically false to his naturalistic realist friends."[24] But of course, Schneider's readers had already been

---

23. George Santayana, *The Idler and His Works* (New York: Books for Libraries, 1957), 20.
24. Herbert W. Schneider, *A History of American Philosophy* (3rd ed.; New York and London: Columbia University Press, 1963), 508.

prepared some pages earlier for the aberration of Santayana's unseemly celebration of the spirit as the flame of the divine in man (on
the Christian pattern at that) when the historian wrote: "Santayana
was never more than a half-hearted realist and less than a half-
hearted American."[25] Voegelin is not the first modern philosopher to
run against the brick wall of secularist dogmatism.

But Voegelin's work has also found misunderstanding among the
spiritual dogmatists. After greeting the first volume of *Order and
History* with enthusiasm in 1959, and speaking of its author's "tren-
chant and even delphic expression" and his "unique achievement,"
the Roman Catholic philosopher-theologian Frederick D. Wilhelmsen wrote in thinly veiled rage against the infirmities of the fourth
volume of that work in 1975. What was the trouble? The Christ of
dogmatic Christianity was missing.

Christianity is represented through the prism of the experience of St. Paul
and exclusively through that prism. The historical figure of Jesus is totally
by-passed and the only "Christ" to emerge in Voegelin's pages is "The Resurrected" of Paul's experience. . . . This omission is likely to disappoint a
number of Voegelin's Catholic "conservative" followers. . . . To speak, as
[Voegelin] does, of the "fallacy . . . entertained by doctrinaire theologians,
metaphysicians, and ideologists" indicates a kind of precious washing of the
hands by a latter-day Pilate who is too pure to enter the Golgotha of history.
. . . But, Dr. Voegelin, "if He is not risen"—in the words of St. Paul—then I
for one don't give a damn about St. Paul's experience of Him. . . . Professor
Voegelin's understanding of the structure of history fails.[26]

In sum, then, any explanation for Voegelin's comparative obscurity is complex, but above all it results from his philosophical independence and originality. His books are no harder to read than many
others that are regular fare to political science, sociology, and philosophy students. The language is of some novelty and sprinkled
with Greek words, true, but it is essentially clear—even aphoristic
and sometimes poetic—despite its stylistic compression. It subtly
explores and illuminates matters of intrinsic interest to those open
to the perennial quest for a better understanding of their own hu-

25. *Ibid.*, 503; cf. p. 509, and the comments on Santayana's address, "Ultimate
Religion."
26. Frederick D. Wilhelmsen, "The Achievement of Eric Voegelin," *Modern Age*
(Spring, 1959), 182; Wilhelmsen, "The New Voegelin," *Triumph* (January, 1975),
32, 35.

manity. But for all his indebtedness to modern scholarship (and it is very great indeed) Voegelin has marked out new territory for exploration by new means. The continuities of his work with that of earlier philosophers and of the leading lights of modern natural science are pronounced. He has steadily sought to prosecute his studies in full recognition of the best and latest insights into all of the problems with which he deals. A glance at his works immediately demonstrates this. That critics regularly fail to notice it supplies evidence to support Voegelin's contention that massive illiteracy pervades the educated stratum of society. Such illiteracy, parading as its opposite, reinforces the inhospitable climate of opinion and fosters the kind of warfare of contending dogmatisms hinted at in the foregoing paragraphs and termed by Voegelin the "dogmatomachy" (A, 328–33)[27] of the contemporary scene—a welter of "positions" and strife within which he has resolutely declined to become submerged.

On the one hand, he has added, as a gloss to Whitehead's assertion that modern philosophy is ruined, the statement: "The life of Reason, the ineluctable condition of personal and social order, has been destroyed."[28] But on the other hand, he has stressed repeatedly that this is only one side of things:

> While modernity in the pejorative sense is undeniably a characteristic of the modern period, there goes on, at the same time, the resistance to the disorder, as well as efforts to regain the reality lost or distorted. However one wishes to construct the concept of modernity, it will have to cover both the destruction of reality, committed by alienated human beings, the ideological thinkers, for the purpose of their aggrandizement, and the countermovement of the philosophers and scholars which in our time culminates in the splendid advance of the historical sciences, revealing as grotesque the ideological constructions which still dominate the scene. (AM, 107)

The latter point also was emphasized in connection with Voegelin's celebrated analysis in *The New Science of Politics* which concluded that "the essence of modernity [is] the growth of Gnosticism" (NSP, 126). After noting that the continuity of Gnosticism from antiquity into the modern period was still a matter of common knowledge among scholars of the eighteenth and nineteenth centuries, and es-

27. Also see Eric Voegelin, "Equivalences of Experience and Symbolization in History," (1970), 218–20.
28. Voegelin, "On Classical Studies," 3.

pecially noting Ferdinand Christian Baur's[29] tracing in 1835 of the Gnostic element throughout Western history and into the works of Jakob Boehme, F. W. J. von Schelling, F. E. D. Schleiermacher, and Hegel, he added:

I want to stress that Gnosticism, as well as its history from antiquity to the present, is the subject of a vastly developed science, and that the idea of interpreting contemporary phenomena as Gnostic phenomena is not as original as it may look to the ignoramuses who have criticized me for it. Generally I should like to remark: if I had discovered for myself all the historical and philosophical problems for which I am criticized by intellectuals, I would be without a doubt the greatest philosopher in the history of mankind. [Thus] before publishing anything on the applicability of Gnostic categories to modern ideologies I consulted with our contemporary authorities on Gnosticism, especially with [Henri Charles] Puech in Paris and [Gilles] Quispel in Utrecht. Puech considered it a matter of course that modern ideologies are Gnostic speculations, and Quispel brought the Gnosticism of Jung in which he was especially interested to my attention. (AM, 67; *cf.* SPG, 3–7)

III

Our excursion through the list of ways in which Voegelin's obscurity may be explained has also surveyed how he has been misunderstood. The question, then, is how is he best approached and understood. The difficulty of finding a starting point here brings to mind the sobering reflections of Sir Frederick Pollock and Frederic William Maitland at the beginning of their great *History of English Law*: "Such is the unity of all history that any one who endeavors to tell a piece of it must feel that his first sentence tears a seamless web. . . . The web must be rent; but, as we rend it, we may watch the whence and whither of the severed and ravelling threads which have been making a pattern too large for any man's eye."[30]

Even though there may be some tearing of the seamless web involved here, too, I have no doubt that the right starting point for one

29. Baur's book is entitled *Die christliche Gnosis oder die christliche Religionsphilosophie in ihrer geschichtlichen Entwicklung* (Tuebingen: C. F. Osiander, 1835).

30. Sir Frederick Pollock and Frederic William Maitland, *The History of English Law, Before the Time of Edward I* (2 vols.; 2nd ed.; Cambridge: Cambridge University Press, 1968), I, 1.

COMMON SENSE AND THE NEW SCIENCE 19

who wishes to understand Eric Voegelin is an appreciation of the centrality of common sense and ordinary experience in his work. Despite all its complexities, no less than was Whitehead's, Voegelin's entire "philosophy [is] adapted to the requirement of science and to the concrete experience of mankind." Hence, regardless of what "traverses our naive experience," to contradict it is suspect on principle: "I hold that the ultimate appeal is to naive experience and this is why I lay such stress on the evidence of poetry."[31] The matter is not left to mere inference. The recovery of commonsense understanding, the exploration of its dimensions and continuity with theoretical reason and science, its application as the starting point for Everyman's grasp of truth and order, and its centrality to any critique of received doctrines—all are regularly displayed in Voegelin's work. This is a key to his remarkable power as a teacher and to his writing and thought more generally, one which accounts for its vigor, robustness, independence, and manliness.

Common sense has its philosophical representation preeminently in the eighteenth-century Scottish school of that name. Thomas Reid then defined it as that "certain degree" of rationality "which is necessary to our being subjects of law and government, capable of managing our own affairs, and answerable for our conduct towards others. This is called common sense, because it is common to all men with whom we can transact business, or call to account for their conduct."[32] Voegelin added: "Common sense is a compact type of rationality." Its insights cannot be directly made into propositions that can become principles of science. But it has solid merit and theoretical promise, and it is both the presupposition and starting point of noetic (or philosophic) experience and reason. "The civilized *homo politicus* does not need to be a philosopher, but he must have common sense" (A, 352–53).[33]

That all of Voegelin's mature work issues from this perspective can be confirmed from his direct statements. In 1924 the young

31. Whitehead, *Science and the Modern World*, 89; cf. 90–94.
32. Thomas Reid, *Essays on the Intellectual Powers of Man* (1785; repr. ed., Cambridge, Mass.: M.I.T. Press, 1969), 559, quoted in Eric Voegelin, *Anamnesis* (Munich: Piper, 1966), 352.
33. For further discussion of common sense and rationality, see Chapter 6 below and pp. 214–16.

Voegelin was awarded one of the first Laura Spellman Rockefeller Memorial Fellowships and came to the United States from Austria for two years of study at Columbia, Harvard, and Wisconsin.

These two years in America brought the great break in my intellectual development. . . . At Columbia University I had courses with [Franklin Henry] Giddings the sociologist, John Dewey, and Irwin Edman, John Wesley the economist, [John Whittier] Macmahon in public administration, and I was overwhelmed by a new world of which hitherto I had hardly suspected the existence. The most important influence came from the library. During the year in New York, I started working through the history of English philosophy and its expansion into American thought. My studies were strongly motivated and helped by Dewey and Edman. I discovered English and American commonsense philosophy. More immediately the impact came through Dewey's recent book on *Human Nature and Conduct* [1922] which was based on the English commonsense tradition. From there I worked back to Reid and [Sir William] Hamilton. This English conception of common sense as a human attitude which incorporates a philosopher's attitude toward life without the philosopher's technical apparatus, and inversely the understanding of Classic and Stoic philosophy as a technical, analytical elaboration of the commonsense attitude, has remained a lasting influence in my understanding both of common sense and Classic philosophy. I got the first inkling of what the continued tradition of Classic philosophy on the commonsense level, without necessarily the technical apparatus of an Aristotle, could mean for the intellectual climate and the cohesion of a society. The tradition of common sense I now recognized to be the factor that was signally absent from the German social scene, and not so well developed in France as it was in England and America. . . . In this year in New York I began to sense that American society had a philosophical background far superior in range and existential substance, though not always in articulation, to anything that I found represented in the methodological environment in which I had grown up.

During the year at Columbia, when I took courses with Dewey and Giddings and read their work, I became aware of the categories of social substance in the English-speaking world. John Dewey's category was "likemindedness," and I found that "likemindedness" was the term used by the King James Version to translate the New Testament *homonoia*. That was the first time I became aware of the problem of *homonoia* about which I knew extremely little at the time, because my knowledge of Classic philosophy was still quite insufficient and my knowledge of Christian problems practically nonexistent. Only later, when I had learned Greek and was able to read the texts in the original, did I become aware of the fundamental function of such categories for determining what the substance of society really is. The term of Giddings was the "consciousness of kind." Though I did not know very much about the background of these problems, I remember already becoming aware that Giddings was intending the same problem as John Dewey but preferred a terminology that would not make visible the connection of the problem with the Classic and Christian traditions. It was an attempt to transform the *homonoia,* in the sense of a community of the spirit, into something innocuous like a community of kind in a biological sense.

The first year at Columbia was then supplemented by the second year in which the strongest impression was, at Harvard, the newly arrived Alfred North Whitehead. Of course I still could understand only a very small portion of what Whitehead said in his lectures, and I had to work myself into the cultural and historical background of his work that came out at the time, *Science and the Modern World* [1925]. But it brought to my attention that there was such a background into which I had to work myself more intensely if I wanted to understand Anglo-Saxon civilization. The occasion for expanding my knowledge offered itself in the second semester of the year 1925–26 when I went to Wisconsin. I had become aware of the work of John R. Commons at Columbia, as during that year his *Human Nature and Property* was published. . . . In Wisconsin I got into what I considered at the time, with my still limited knowledge, to be the real, authentic America: It was represented by John R. Commons, who took on for me the shape of a Lincolnesque figure, strongly connected with the economic and political problems, both on the state and national level, and with particular accents on the labor problem. . . .

The account of the American experience would be incomplete without mentioning the strong influence of George Santayana. I have never met him, but I got acquainted with his work in New York, partly through the suggestion of Irwin Edman. I studied his work with care and still have in my library the copies which I bought in that year in New York. Santayana was a revelation concerning philosophy to me comparable to the revelation I received at the same time through commonsense philosophy. Here was a man with a vast background of philosophical knowledge, sensitive to the problems of the spirit without accepting a dogma, and not interested at all in neo-Kantian methodology. . . .

The results of these two years in America precipitated my book *On the Form of the American Mind.* . . .[34]

This literary work in which I assembled the results of the two American years does not, however, give a full understanding of the importance which these two years had in my life. The great event was the fact of being thrown

34. Eric Voegelin, *Ueber die Form des amerikanischen Geistes* (Tuebingen: J.C.B. Mohr, 1928).

into a world for which the great methodological debates of the neo-Kantian type, which I considered the most important thing intellectually, were of no importance. Instead, there was the background of the great political foundation of 1776 and 1789, and of the unfolding of the founding act through a political and legal culture, primarily represented by the lawyers' guild and the Supreme Court. There was the strong background of Christianity and Classical culture which was so signally fading out, if not missing, in the methodological debates in which I had grown up as a student. In brief, here was a world in which this other world that I had grown up in was intellectually, morally, and spiritually irrelevant. That there should be such a plurality of worlds had a devastating effect on me. The experience broke for good, at least I hope it did, my provincialism of a Central European or generally European kind without letting me fall into an American provincialism. I gained an understanding through these years of the plurality of human possibilities realized in various civilizations, as an immediate experience, an *expérience vécue*, which hitherto had been accessible to me only through the comparative study of civilizations, as I found them in Max Weber, in Spengler, and later in Toynbee. The immediate effect was that upon my return to Europe certain phenomena which were of the greatest importance in the intellectual and ideological context of Central Europe, as for instance the work of Heidegger, whose famous *Sein und Zeit* I read in 1928, no longer had any effect on me. It just ran off, because I had been immunized against this whole context of philosophizing through my time in America and especially in Wisconsin. The priorities and relations of importance between various theories had been fundamentally changed, and as far as I can see for the better. (AM, 28–33)

I have quoted this long passage, not only because it is apt, but also because I wish here to apply to Voegelin's thought one of its own convincing, commonsense principles. This is that a thinker himself best knows what it is he is doing: the self-interpretation of the human beings to whom experiences happen (and who therewith articulate these in the symbolisms of philosophy, prophecy, poetry, and the rest) is decisive for their comprehension. As Voegelin has more succinctly expressed the principle: "The reality of experience is self-interpretive. The men who have the experiences express themselves through symbols; and the symbols are the key to understanding the experience expressed. . . . What is experienced and symbolized as reality, in an advancing process of differentiation, is the substance of history. . . . [This is the] principle that lies at the basis of all my later work" (AM,81). But this principle was implanted in Voegelin's mind very early, even before his sojourn in America. He attributes its origin to his study in Berlin in 1922–1923 with the great historian of antiquity, Eduard Meyer: "I like to believe that Meyer's technique of understanding a historical situation through the self-understanding of the persons involved has entered my own work as a permanent factor" (AM, 15).

We shall have occasion to trace out many of the implications of these statements in pages that follow. The point for the present is the simple one that, however high his head may be in the clouds, Voegelin's feet are always firmly on the ground. He takes the attitude to be a preeminently American one. It means, crudely stated, that Voegelin generally means just what you think he means. He methodically seeks to pursue the problems of human existence back to the points of their original articulation in the concrete personal experiences of concrete individuals. The quintessentially human, or existential dimension is sought and savored in the specific places and times of particular events, on the assumption that what is critically true for a man is no less true for men. This is the root of his own version of William James's "radical empiricism."[35] As Gregor Sebba stated the principle: "For Voegelin, the first thinker to see a problem clearly and in its entire structure established the analytical vocabulary which embodies the new insight. This vocabulary remains authoritative so long as the analysis stands. Hence the need to return to the first appearance of a verbal symbolism: the water is clearest at the source, as he explained to me in 1933."[36]

Multiple consequences follow from this approach to the exploration of the human condition. Obviously, it means that abstract general statements are suspect on principle. No positivist ever insisted more steadily than has Voegelin that experience must guide thought, that general terms can have as real referents only individual concrete objects or events.[37] Yet the antipositivist twist comes at once, in Voegelin's amplification of *experience* so that, in his pages, it em-

35. See Voegelin's discussion of James's radical empiricism already, *ibid.*, 41–52.
36. Gregor Sebba, "Prelude and Variations on the theme of Eric Voegelin," *Southern Review*, XIII (Autumn, 1977), 658n.
37. Cf. Leszek Kolakowski, *The Alienation of Reason: A History of Positivist Thought*, trans. Norbert Guterman (Garden City, N.Y.: Doubleday & Co., Inc., Anchor Books, 1969), Chapter 1 and *passim*.

braces the whole range of human awareness and is not reduced to mere sensory perception.

A general term like *philosophy*, for instance, means what those persons meant who coined the term to name their activity: Voegelin turns to the empirical "materials" and explores the emergence and flowering of philosophy from Thales to Aristotle, seen within the context of the whole of Hellenic experience and writing. The life of Socrates, he finds, is then the empirical evidence of the true order of the soul; and philosophy in its climax in Plato and Aristotle is an *imitatio Socratis*. Such a life is not a mere pursuit of abstract truth through the advancement of speculative propositions. Rather it is, above all, existential and combative; it arises and flourishes as a man's resistance to the forces in society which seek to corrupt him and alienate him from the true order of existence and reality. Note the commonsensical drift of this view as Voegelin states it:

Plato was supremely conscious of the struggle and its polarity. Philosophy is not a doctrine of right order, but the light of wisdom that falls on the struggle; and help [as provided by Socrates and Plato to those around them] is not a piece of information about truth, but the arduous effort to locate the forces of evil and identify their nature. For half the battle is won when the soul can recognize the shape of the enemy and, consequently, knows that the way it must follow leads in the opposite direction. Plato operates in the *Republic*, therefore, with pairs of concepts which point the way by casting light on both good and evil. His philosopher does not operate in a vacuum, but in opposition to the sophist. (OH, III, 43, 62–63)

The opposing pairs of concepts developed by Plato "must be understood in their aggregate as the expression of a man's resistance to a social corruption which goes so deep that it affects the truth of existence under God. Philosophy, thus, has its origin in the resistance of the soul to its destruction by society. Philosophy . . . [is] an act of resistance illuminated by conceptual understanding." Concretely, the motivating experience of the man who becomes the philosopher is "opposition to the sophist" (OH, III, 68, 70). Philosophy in antiquity, that is to say philosophy par excellence, is existential in the sense of being a life lived in resistance to untruth out of a love of wisdom experienced as divine, for only God is wise.

The implications of the insight, at the point where resistance is first illuminated by concepts, are all but lost in our modern interpretations of Plato's work. Today Plato has become a philosopher among others; and our modern term even includes the philodoxers [lovers of opinion] to whom he was opposed. For Plato the philosopher is literally the man who loves wisdom, because wisdom puts substance into the freedom of his Arete [excellence, virtue] and enables the soul to travel the road toward salvation. In the philosopher who resists the sophist lives a soul which resists the destruction of Arete. The philosopher is man in the anxiety of his fall from being; and philosophy is the ascent toward salvation of Everyman, as the pamphylic components of the myth [of Er which concludes the *Republic*] suggest. Plato's philosophy, therefore, is not *a* philosophy but *the* symbolic form in which a Dionysiac soul expresses its ascent to God. If Plato's evocation of a paradigm of right order is interpreted as a philosopher's opinion about politics, the result will be hopeless nonsense, not worth a word of debate. (OH, III, 70)

So understood, Voegelin is at one with Emerson in acknowledging that "Plato is philosophy, and philosophy, Plato," and with Whitehead in concluding that "the European philosophical tradition is . . . a series of footnotes to Plato."[38] But the *so understood* must be stressed, for neither Emerson nor Whitehead understood the core of Plato's philosophy, or philosophy simply, as has Voegelin. In that sense Voegelin's conception of philosophy is new.

Yet there is the paradox that a further consequence of Voegelin's approach to the exploration of the human condition is its studied "unoriginality."[39] What does this mean? We have just glimpsed his highly original interpretation of the nature of philosophy. Sebba explains: "Unoriginal thinking is a difficult art to learn. It is not free to invent but forced to recognize. Is there anything new under the sun?"[40] Voegelin's retort might well be a counter question: Have you considered everything under the sun? His method entails just such an enterprise, and for this reason his work is filled with detailed comparative analyses of materials drawn from very nearly everywhere under the sun. Thus he might deny that his interpretation of Plato—and of Hellenic philosophy generally—is new. Rather, he has only recovered, by scrupulous attentiveness to the sources, Plato's own self-understanding of philosophy. It is only new to us. Indeed, it

38. Ralph Waldo Emerson, "Plato; Or, the Philosopher," in Atkinson (ed.), *Complete Essays*, 471; Alfred North Whitehead, *Process and Reality: An Essay in Cosmology* (1929; repr. ed.; New York: Free Press, 1969), 53.
39. See Sebba, "Prelude and Variations on the Theme of Eric Voegelin," 658–59.
40. *Ibid.*

is the loss of this original understanding of philosophy through social amnesia that has made its history largely the story of its derailment during the past two millennia (OH, I, ix; III, 274–79). To combat this amnesia, not to propound novelties, is the business of the
scholar and philosopher. The task is explicitly announced on the
first page of *Order and History*. Voegelin is mindful as few others
have been of the range, diversity, and extent of man's intellectual
history. He is chastened by Aristotle's observation: "For scientific
insights do not occur among men only once, or twice, or a small
number of times; but they recur an infinite number of times" (OH,
III, 289–90).[41] Modesty about one's discoveries is both seemly and
prudent; immodesty is damnfoolishness or worse. Whoring after
novelty, especially the modern ideological variety, is a pathology of
thought, a leading source of social disorders and of the amnesia that
fosters them. The principle of unoriginality is formulated radically:
"The test of truth, to put it pointedly, will be the lack of originality
in the propositions."[42] This is a further dimension of Voegelin's reliance on common sense, whereby the test of validity is conformity
with the received opinions of mankind, or where "the memory of
man runneth not to the contrary," or where the lover of myth (*philomythos*) and the lover of wisdom (*philosophos*) can be seen to intend the same reality on a scale of theoretical penetration that runs
from the compact to the more differentiated (OH, I, 60).

In stressing unoriginality Voegelin has in the foreground, among
other things, the not-so-minor problem of shoddiness of scholarship
among professional academicians who, too often, are blissfully ignorant of the subjects they speak about with supposed expertise. Thus
he remarked that he was forced to learn Greek in the mid-1930s by
the recognition that, as a political scientist engaged in opposition to
and critique of the Nazi ideology and its racism, a knowledge of
Plato and Aristotle was imperative.

The acquisition of that knowledge was of course fundamental for my later
work, not only as far as my knowledge of Greek philosophy was concerned,
but for understanding fundamentally that one cannot deal with materials
unless one can read them. That sounds trivial but, as I later found out, it is a
truth not only neglected but hotly contested by a good number of persons

41. Aristotle, *Meterologica* I, 3.
42. Voegelin, "Equivalences of Experience," 222; cf. p. 226.

who are employed by our colleges and who, with the greatest of ease, talk about Plato and Aristotle, or Thomas and Augustine, or Dante and Cervantes, or Rabelais or Goethe, without being able to read a line of the authors on whom they pontificate. (AM, 39)

More emphatically, Voegelin suggests that the best-known novelties of modern ideological thought have been attained at the expense of science and honesty, to a degree of human detriment that becomes monotonously murderous in practice. The treatment accorded Karl Marx is the best example, because of Marx's enormous influence and popularity.

When Marx says that his rational dialectics [of materialism] stands Hegelian dialectics on its feet, he does not correctly describe what he is doing. Before the actual inversion begins, he has done something much more fatal: he has abolished Hegel's problem of reality. . . . [H]e has by this act abolished the philosophical approach to the problem of reality on principle. The Marxian position is not anti-Hegelian, it is antiphilosophical; Marx does not put Hegel's dialectic on its feet, he refuses to theorize. . . .

Did Marx know what he was doing? . . . If we turn to [his] early work, we find that Marx had an excellent understanding of Hegel's problem of reality but preferred to ignore it. Marx understood Hegel perfectly well. . . . [W]as Marx being intellectually dishonest?

As the editor of Marx's early writing phrased the matter: "Marx—if we may express ourselves in this manner—misunderstood Hegel as-it-were deliberately." They do not dare outrightly call Marx an intellectual faker. . . . After all, Marx was not a common swindler. . . . Unless we want to give up at this point, we must transfer the problem to the level of pneumapathology. Marx was spiritually diseased and we have localized the most glaring symptom of his disease, that is, his fear of critical concepts and of philosophy in general. . . . We shall coin the term "logophobia" for this symptom. . . . The Marxian spiritual disease . . . consists in the self-divinization and self-salvation of man; an intramundane *logos* of human consciousness is substituted for the transcendental *logos*. What appeared on the level of symptoms as antiphilosophism and logophobia, must etiologically be understood as the revolt of immanent consciousness against the spiritual order of the world. This is the core of the Marxian idea.

. . . .

At the root of the Marxian idea we find the spiritual disease, the Gnostic revolt. . . . Marx is demonically closed against transcendental reality. . . . His spiritual impotence leaves no way open but derailment into Gnostic activism. Again we see the characteristic combination of spiritual impotence with mundane lust for power, resulting in a grandiose mysticism of Paracletic existence. And again we see the conflict with reason, almost literally in the same form as in [Auguste] Comte, in the dictatorial prohibition of metaphysical questions concerning the ground of being, questions that might disturb the magic creation of a new world behind the prison walls of the revolt. Marx, like Comte, does not permit a rational discussion of his principles—you have to be a Marxist or shut up. We see again confirmed the correlation between spiritual impotence and antirationalism; one cannot deny God and retain reason.

Spiritual impotence destroys the order of the soul. Man is locked in the prison of his particular existence. It does not, however, destroy the vitality of intellectual operations within the prison. The *Theses on Feuerbach* . . . are an unsurpassed masterpiece of mystical speculation on the level of a demonically closed existence. Marx knew that he was a god creating a world. He did not want to be a creature. He did not want to see the world in the perspective of creaturely existence—though he admitted that man has difficulties in getting out of the rut. . . . By the standards of mystical speculation, the construction [of the *Theses*] is impeccable. It is probably the best world fetish ever constructed by a man who wanted to be God. (ER, 257–59, 276, 298–99)[43]

Hard words? Indeed, they are hard enough even for an Emerson who advocated hard words. Truth sometimes requires hard words, as every man of common sense knows, and it is the task of a philosopher to serve truth and to do so in unmistakable language. The sense of philosophy as a love of wisdom arising in opposition to untruth lies just beneath the surface of such hard words. Voegelin states that the "motivations of my work are simple; they arise from the political situation" (AM, 96). The political situation of Voegelin's early adult life was that of post–World War I with the collapse of the Austro-Hungarian Empire, the triumph of Bolshevism in Russia, the burgeoning of ideological politics in Central and Western Europe with contending Socialist and Communist factions, emergent fascism, national socialism, and the consolidation with murderous resolve of totalitarian regimes by Stalin and Hitler. He did his political and intellectual apprenticeship in the hardest of schools. He hammered out his scientific outlook by picking his way through the minefields of conflicting methodological positions and by standing

43. Reprinted from *From Enlightenment to Revolution*, by Eric Voegelin (edited by John H. Hallowell), by permission of Duke University Press. Copyright 1975, Duke University Press (Durham, N.C.), hereinafter cited textually as ER.

in steady opposition to ideologues of the left and right, ultimately at substantial personal risk. In short, Voegelin's hard words arise from personal experience as well as from close textual analysis, and they should no more astonish us than do those of Plato or of Aleksandr Solzhenitsyn. The cases are analogous in signaling an Aschylean wisdom born of suffering.

IV

Common sense and tough-mindedness go hand in hand. Our illustrations of the significance of common sense as the best starting point for understanding Voegelin led us to stress the principles of self-interpretation—of understanding a thinker as he understood himself—and of studied unoriginality in the explication of the texts wherein philosophers and prophets articulate their experiences of reality. In the course of these reflections, the character of philosophy has been clarified in its oppositional dimension as a reflex of the love of wisdom which is its core. That example, and the illustration of the critique of Marx's thought, showed in specific terms the manner in which opposition to disorder in the contemporary world serves philosophic truth. Along the way the matter of language showed its importance as technical terms floated to the surface of the discussion and hard words were found in Voegelin's assertion of the scientific validity of Plato's elaboration of the paradigms of order and in his analysis of Marx's rebellion as a deliberate swindle. These ravelling threads only hint at large subject matters to be considered more fully in subsequent chapters.

This is to supply no more than a starting point, however. Even if we agree with Aristotle that "a good beginning is thought to be more than half of the whole, and many of the questions we ask are cleared up by it,"[44] to complete the beginning we must outline the balance of the study.

Voegelin is no system builder, and he regularly deprecates thinkers who are systematizers as representatives of the derailment of philosophy. Hence, while we have no system to explore, we do have continuities of reflection on salient problems of human existence.

44. Aristotle, *Nicomachean Ethics*, Bk. 1, Chap. 7, 1098b7–8, trans. W. D. Ross.

The drift of this large corpus of writing is intimated in the epigraph to *Order and History*, taken from Saint Augustine's *De Vera Religione*: "In the study of creature one should not exercise a vain and perishing curiosity, but ascend toward what is immortal and everlasting." In his pursuit of the immortal and everlasting as experienced by men in history, Voegelin is not haunted by the foolish consistency which is a hobgoblin of little minds. Rather his work shows a process of steady revision, backtracking, and reformulation as study of the materials necessitates new perspectives and insights. The principle underlying these operations is that the truth of existence can only be validated by the empirical evidence in William James's sense. It is the obligation of the philosopher-scientist to follow the evidence wherever it leads at whatever the cost.

The truth to be delivered out of this meditative process is not ultimate truth, the truth to end the search for all truth, a system to end all systems. Rather it is the illumination of the *process* of reality by bringing to bear the reflective consciousness of a man in community with other men, past and present, who devoted themselves to the reflective search of reality as an indispensable part of the quest for their true humanity. The truth to be delivered, then, is representative truth. Its claim to scientific validity rests on "the belief in the premise that a truth concerning the reality of man found by one man concretely does, indeed, apply to every man."[45] Hence, it is representative in two senses: in the sense of its being representative of divine truth itself, and in the sense of its being a truth experienced and symbolized by a concrete person who therewith becomes representative of all men. The epistemological and ontological consequences of the view will be of concern later. At the outset, it is imperative to secure this perspective as informing Voegelin's search of the trail of symbolisms in history as the chief means of recovering the engendering experiences which have given rise to them. For therein appears to lie the only "constant" of history. Truth lies at the level of experience, not of the symbols. Hence, "the constants of engendering experience are the true subject matter of our studies."[46]

The comparative study of symbolisms and engendering experi-

45. Voegelin, "Equivalences of Experience," 234.
46. *Ibid.*, 216.

ences comprises the basis of Voegelin's procedure. It takes form in the discernment of equivalences of both by "a philosopher who has become conscious of the time dimension of his own search of truth and wants to relate it to that of his predecessors in history." A result is that "the comparative study of symbols attains to an understanding of itself as a search of the search." The exploration of the symbols and their underlying experiences yields the insight that the search in which the philosopher is engaged today is, indeed, the same search in which his predecessors were engaged in their day.[47]

Yet the apperception of experiences-symbolisms as equivalent dissolves the apparent constant in history: equivalence is not identity; the apperception of equivalence occurs in the process of the search when actively conducted by a philosopher, and the truth of reality is simultaneously differentiated into a recognizably superior insight emerging from the depth of consciousness. The constant that remains, then, is only "the process in the mode of presence"; that is, the constant—if there is one at all—is pushed back into the depth beyond experience-symbolization as the process of reflection, the structure of the search itself. Thus, says Voegelin:

There is no constant to be found in history because the historical field of equivalents is not given as a collective of phenomena which could be submitted to the procedures of abstraction and generalization. History originates in the presence of the process when a truth of reality emerging from the depth recognizes itself as equivalent but superior to a truth previously experienced. If anything that has turned up in the course of our search deserves the name of a constant, it is the process in the mode of presence. The search, thus, has not been futile but the result subverts the initial question. For we have not found a constant in history but the constancy of a process that leaves a trail of equivalent symbols in time and space. To this trail we can, then, attach the conventional name of "history." History is not a given . . . but a symbol by which we express our experience of the collective as a trail left by the moving presence of the process.

Beyond constancy and equivalence there remains the problem of the process itself. We have immediate knowledge of the process only in its presence. A man whom we can name concretely—a Heraclitus, Plato, Plotinus, or St. Augustine—experiences the process in its mode of presence. The historical field that is left by the process, however, is not left by the confrontation of truth in the psyche of one concrete man but results from the pres-

47. *Ibid.*, 216, 223.

ence of the process as it moves through the multitude of concrete beings who are members of mankind. The process as a whole that leaves the trail is not experienced by anybody concretely. In our time, this problem is rarely faced with critical awareness, though it is a fundamental problem of philosophy. When a philosopher explores the nature of man and arrives at the sweeping statement: "All men by nature desire to know," one may take exception to its general form. For the statement may apply to the philosopher whose experience of his own psyche has engendered it, but there is no empirical justification for the extension of the insight to "all men." Still, we do not discard the statement as fanciful, because we share with Aristotle the belief in the premise that a truth concerning the reality of man found by one man concretely does, indeed, apply to every man. The faith in this premise, however, is not engendered by an additional experience of man's nature, but by the primordial experience of the reality as endowed with the constancy and lastingness of structure that we symbolize as the Cosmos. The trust in the Cosmos and its depth is the source of the premises—be it the generality of human nature or, in our case, the reality of the process as a moving presence—that we accept as the context of meaning for our concrete engagement in the search of truth. The search for truth makes sense only under the assumption that the truth brought up from the depth of his psyche by man, though it is not the ultimate truth of reality, is representative of the truth in the divine depth of the Cosmos. Behind every equivalent symbol in the historical field stands the man who has engendered it in the course of his search as representative of a truth that is more than equivalent. The search that renders no more than equivalent truth rests ultimately on the faith that, by engaging in it, man participates representatively in the divine drama of truth becoming luminous.[48]

These passages announce the principal problems to be addressed in this volume. Their subtlety and complexity are evident from a cursory reading. Our concern is with the core of Voegelin's thought. At that core is the task of rendering human existence less opaque, more meaningful, through the process of philosophical enquiry, *i.e.*, through the search of truth.

48. *Ibid.*, 233–34.

CHAPTER 2

Biography and the Course
of Thought to 1938

I

Born in Cologne, Germany, on January 3, 1901, the
son of Otto Stefan Voegelin, a civil engineer, and Elisabeth Ruehl
Voegelin, Erich Hermann Wilhelm Voegelin lived in Cologne and in
Koenigswinter in the Rhineland until 1910, when he moved with his
family to Vienna, Austria. He was a resident of Vienna until his
flight to Switzerland and, then, the United States in the summer of
1938. He remained in the United States for twenty years and became
an American citizen in 1944. He lived for a semester in Cambridge,
Massachusetts, for a few months in Bennington, Vermont, two and a
half years in Tuscaloosa, Alabama, and settled for sixteen years in
Baton Rouge, Louisiana. In 1958 Voegelin returned to Europe, this
time to Munich, West Germany, where he remained until 1969 when
he returned to the United States. Since 1969 he has resided in Stanford, California. He and Lissy Onken were married on July 30, 1932;
they have no children.

Against the background of this basic chronology, certain features
of his education and career as a teacher and scholar may be sketched.
After the move from Germany to Austria in 1910, Voegelin finished
the last year of elementary school and entered a modified Classical
high school (or *Realgymnasium*) which required eight years of Latin, six years of English, two years of Italian, and otherwise stressed
mathematics and physics. He studied French with a private tutor
during this same period. He recalls as a high point of this period the
study of *Hamlet*, during one semester, interpreted on the basis of Al-

fred Adler's psychology of superiority (*Geltung*). After Einstein's "Theory of Relativity" came out in 1917, Voegelin and a classmate studied it during the final year of high school with their mathematics and physics teacher, Philip Freud. "We studied it, and at first could not understand it, but then discovered that our difficulty was caused by the simplicity of the theory. We understood it perfectly well but could not believe that something so simple could arouse such a furor as a difficult new theory. The mathematical apparatus, of course, was entirely at our disposition" (AM, 8), since studies in that field were required through differential calculus and Voegelin went on to an introduction to the theory of matrices and group theory.

After completing the examination marking graduation from high school, Voegelin entered the University of Vienna in 1919 and completed his doctorate in 1922. During the summer vacation after high school graduation, however, and spurred by the excitement following the Communist revolution in Russia, he read Marx's *Capital* and became a convinced Marxist for a time—from August, 1919, until December! "By Christmas the matter had worn off, because in the meanwhile I had attended courses in both economic theory and the history of economic theory and knew what was wrong with Marx. Marxism has never been a problem for me after that."

Voegelin's politics have been steadfastly antiideological. As a young man, perhaps under the influence of one of the prominent faculty members of the university and party stalwart, Carl Gruenberg, he, like most of his young friends, voted for the Social Democratic party in the 1920 election—the first in which he participated—although he never formally affiliated with that party. We have here to picture Voegelin as "a slim young man with blond hair and sharp eyes behind his glasses, his Pascalian nose jutting out in a metaphysical curve" and already possessing a reputation with his associates "for fiendish erudition and the ability to take off vertically from any question whatever, to disappear within minutes in the theoretical ionosphere, leaving a trail of recondite references behind."[1]

Voegelin had hesitated between doctoral programs in mathemat-

---

1. The characterization is by his friend and colleague of the time, Gregor Sebba, from his article "Prelude and Variations on the Theme of Eric Voegelin," *Southern Review*, XIII (Autumn, 1977), 649.

ics and physics, in law, and a new program in political science offered in the faculty of law, ultimately choosing the last but continuing his interest in the former subjects. His decision turned on a
lack of real enthusiasm for mathematics, an unwillingness to become a civil servant (which the program in law probably would have
led to), and economic considerations: he was very poor, and the political science degree was attainable in three years, but the law degree would have required four. In addition, he was strongly attracted
to the study of politics and to the distinguished faculty in that field
at Vienna. Voegelin's range of studies was wide; he completed his
doctorate with Hans Kelsen, the author of the 1920 Austrian Constitution and famed for his "Pure Theory of Law," and with Othmar
Spann as joint "doctor-fathers." This was a considerable feat, since
Kelsen's and Spann's philosophical positions were viewed as incompatible. Spann's seminars introduced Voegelin to the serious study
of the Classic philosophy of Plato and Aristotle and to the German
idealist systems of Johann Gottlieb Fichte, Hegel, and Schelling. Of
equal if not greater importance were the economics seminars with
Ludwig von Mises and the lifelong friendships there formed with
F. A. von Hayek, Oscar Morgenstern, Fritz Machlup, and Gottfried
von Haberler.

The intellectual horizon of the University of Vienna at the time,
and down to the rise of national socialism in the early 1930s, was
enormous. It was still the university of the capital of the empire and
a leading center of science in a number of fields. In addition to Kelsen, there were a number of younger scholars in the fields of law and
politics trained by him, especially Alfred von Verdross in international law and Adolf Merkl who specialized in administrative law.
The Austrian school of marginal utility in the field of economics had
been built by Eugen Boehm-Bawberk, already dead when Voegelin
matriculated, and continued to be represented by Friedrich Weiser,
the grand old man who delivered the principal lectures on economic
theory at the time, as well as by the younger Mises who was already
famous because of his money theory. Joseph Schumpeter was at
Graz, but his work was studied. Theoretical physics, which also interested Voegelin, went back to Ernst Mach at Vienna and was represented by Moritz Schlick at the time. Ludwig Wittgenstein was a
force in this circle, more by his writings than personal presence. Dis-

tinguished historians included Alfons Dopsch, who was internationally famed for his study of Carolingian economics, and Otto Brunner was a rising star. The history of art was well established at the university through the work of Max Dvořák, who had died by the time Voegelin enrolled; but Josef Strzygowski still was active, and Voegelin attended his lectures in Renaissance art and was attracted to his great work in the history of Near Eastern art. The Institute for Byzantine Music, headed by Egon Wellesz, lay more on the periphery of Voegelin's interest, but he became acquainted with Wellesz before the latter's going to Oxford after the Nazi takeover. The massive influence of the psychologists was, of course, present, and the young Voegelin studied with Sigmund Freud's friend Hermann Swoboda and thereby became conversant with the work of both Freud and Otto Weininger. He did not know Freud personally, but did have as friends many of Freud's students, such as Heinz Hartmann, Robert Waelder, and Ernst Kries.

The law faculty was the center of Voegelin's interest and work after 1922 and until his flight from Austria in 1938. Through the years, he regularly attended the seminars, especially the private seminars, of Spann, Kelsen, and Mises. His young associates in the Spann seminar dropped out of his life after national socialism became virulent, because many of them became Nazis or joined other radical movements, having been attracted to Spann partly because of his devotion to romanticism and German idealism. Kelsen's private seminar brought together men with whom Voegelin formed lasting friendships, especially Alfred Schutz, Felix Kaufmann, and Fritz Schreier. Several of these friends relocated in America after Hitler's rise.

A separate and enduring circle developed from these friendships. Nicknamed the *Geistkreis*—or Intellectual Circle—somewhat ironically, it met once each month over a period of a decade and a half and was held together by the participants' various intellectual interests and pursuits of this or that science. In addition to many of the people so far mentioned, the *Geistkreis* also included Herbert Fuerth, Johannes Wilde the art historian, Georg Schiff, and Friedrich Engel-Janosi the historian, although the membership fluctuated over the period. The monthly meetings were held in the home of one of the participants and papers were read and criticized. The rule of the circle was that the host might not read a paper, since his wife was entitled to attend the meeting in her home (women were otherwise excluded), and it was thought uncivilized for a wife to see her husband torn to pieces. Some of the members of the *Geistkreis* were affected by the change of policy respecting Jews after the imperial government was supplanted by the Republic. When Voegelin enrolled in 1919, many of the full professors in the university were Jewish, but a rule against promoting younger Jews to such positions was established. Since Jews thereafter could never rise above the level of unpaid lecturers, such excellent men, for example, as Alfred Schutz and Felix Kaufman had to pursue private business occupations.

II

What influences are decisive for understanding Voegelin's intellectual development? A plausible question, but not one that can be answered with any precision. Voegelin simply cannot be traced back to this or that source for the headwaters, as it were, of his own intellectual development. Certainly he cannot be reduced to earlier sources from which he is derivative. That said, however, certain important influences can be identified during the period between 1922 and 1938. As already noted, the American experience of 1924 to 1926 was by his own estimate a turning point in that development. From the welter of Vienna's intellectual activity in the twenties and thirties, three other events and/or personalities stand out: the early discovery of Max Weber, the influence of the Stefan George Circle and its augmentation by Karl Kraus, and the association with Hans Kelsen (AM, 1–10). A more detailed discussion of the various Viennese "circles" and Voegelin's role in them is given by Friedrich Engel-Janosi. For example, Voegelin gave a dozen papers to the *Geistkreis* (its most industrious member) over the years from 1921 to 1938, his topics ranging far and wide: "Methods in the Social Sciences," "Philosophy of Judaism," "Meaning of Art History," "England," "Shakespeare," "Paul Valéry," "Age of Augustine," "Concept of the State," and "Mongol Letters" among them. J. Herbert Fuerth (a founder of the Circle and a member throughout its seventeen years), writing from Washington, D.C., in 1972, gave this estimate: "Voegelin is perhaps the greatest living political scientist (and I believe the only one of us who can most nearly be called a real genius)."[2]

Voegelin's doctoral dissertation, entitled *Wechselwirkung und Gezweiung* (*Reciprocal Influence and Doubling*, 1922) was a comparative study of the key categories of Georg Simmel's and Othmar Spann's sociology. It dealt with the ontological problem of the difference between constructing social theory on the assumption of reciprocal relations among autonomous individuals or on the assumption of a preexistent spiritual bond among human beings that would be realized in their interpersonal relations, *i.e.*, the difference between Simmel's individualistic and Spann's universalistic theories of community.

By 1925 Voegelin had studied Max Weber thoroughly enough to publish an essay on his work.[3] Weber was of great importance for consolidating Voegelin's attitude toward science and sharpening his resistance to ideologies of all descriptions. His study of the *Sociology of Religion* and *Economics and Society* buttressed his rejection of Marxism as scientifically untenable. Earlier work in economics and the history of economic theory already had established this in his mind. Later lectures by Weber (published as *Science and Politics*) clarified the point that the ideologies supply the values premised by action, but are not themselves scientific propositions. The matter became troublesome through Weber's distinction between the ethics of intention and the ethics of responsibility, the problem of taking responsibility for one's actions whatever one's intentions in acting may be. "Weber was on the side of the ethics of responsibility . . . so that if you, for instance, establish a government that expropriates the expropriators, you are responsible for the misery which you cause for the people expropriated. No excuse for the evil consequences of moralistic action could be found in the morality or nobility of your intentions. The moral end does not justify immorality of action. . . . Ideologies are not science and ideals are no substitute

2. Cf. Friedrich Engel-Janosi, . . . *aber ein stolzer Bettler: Erinnerungen aus einer verlorenen Generation* (Graz, Vienna, Cologne: Verlag Styria, 1974), pp. 108–28 and *passim*.

3. Eric Voegelin, "Ueber Max Weber," *Deutsche Vierteljahrsschrift fuer Literaturwissenschaft und Geistesgeschichte*, III, pp. 177–93.

for ethics" (AM, 11). Voegelin firmly adopted these principles. He later discovered the connection between Weber's views and the teachings of the neo-Kantian methodology of the historical sciences developed by the so-called Southwest German School of Heinrich Rickert and Wilhelm Windelband. From Weber's perspective, if social science is to be science, then it must be value-free. This, in turn, restricted social science to the exploration of causes and effects within social processes, leaving the underlying values out of account but for an acknowledgment of their use in selecting the materials. Value judgments were excluded from science, which meant that basic premises could not be critically examined, either in the realm of action or in the realm of science.

The areas could not be analysed by Max Weber. The external symptom of this gap in Max Weber's theory is the fact that in his sociology of religion, wide as it ranged, there was no treatment of early Christianity nor of Classic philosophy. That is to say, the analysis of experience that would have supplied the criteria for existential order and responsible action remained outside his field of consideration. If Weber nevertheless did not derail into some sort of relativism or anarchism that is due to the fact that even without the conduct of such analysis he was a staunch ethical character and in fact, as the biography of his nephew, Eduard Baumgarten, has brought out, a mystic. So he knew what was right without knowing the reasons for it. But of course as far as science is concerned that is a precarious position, because students after all want to know the reasons why they should conduct themselves in a certain manner; and when the reasons and the rational order of existence are excluded from consideration, emotions are liable to carry you away into all sorts of ideological and idealistic adventures in which the ends become more fascinating than the means. Here is the gap in Weber's work constituting the great problem with which I have dealt during the fifty years since I got acquainted with Max Weber. (AM, 12)

Finally, Weber established once and for all for Voegelin the indispensability of a wide range of comparative knowledge for anyone who claims to be a scholar in the field of social and political science: "And that means the comparative civilizational knowledge, not only of modern civilization but also of Near Eastern and Far Eastern civilizations, and to keep that knowledge up to date in contact with the specialist sciences in the various fields." To do otherwise is, in his view, to forfeit the claim to being an empiricist and to be defective in scholarship (AM, 13). This same view was underlined by his acquaintance with Oswald Spengler's *Decline of the West* and with the person and work of Eduard Meyer. And it was reinforced by the example of such other leading scholars as Alfred Weber, with whom he studied in Heidelberg for a semester in 1929. Even citing Auguste Comte's good example in this regard, Voegelin stresses: "The necessary empirical range of knowledge is still the basis of all serious science in these matters," *i.e.,* in the fields of philosophy, politics, sociology, and history (AM, 14).

The acquisition of a range of comparative knowledge was pursued in many ways by Voegelin and, as one can easily see from perusing his bibliography, has remained a constant factor in all his work. It was abetted by a summer spent in Oxford in 1922 where he attended the lectures of the distinguished Classicist Gilbert Murray, and it received major impetus from the early American experience. His Rockefeller Fellowship was extended for a third year (1926/1927), during which Voegelin studied in Paris at the Sorbonne. While there, he perfected his command of French and read extensively in French literature and philosophy, economics and law. He attended Léon Brunschvicg's lectures on Pascal and studied literature, acquiring for his personal library almost a complete set of major French prose writings from the *La Princesse de Clèves* by Comtesse de La Fayette to the work of Marcel Proust whose *À la Recherche du temps perdu* was the current rage. He discovered the French history of consciousness as a parallel phenomenon to the English and American theory of consciousness that ran from the eighteenth century into the present. Albert Thibaudet's and René Lalou's work especially directed his attention to Stéphane Mallarmé and Paul Valéry.

He collected Valéry's works, including many first editions, for his library and heard the famous poet speak on one occasion. The poet's Lucretian philosophy reminded him of George Santayana's Lucretianism, and he so fell in love with the poem "Cimetière marin" that he paid a nostalgic visit to the place of its setting on a later trip to France. He read with fascination the French memoirs literature; and the memoirs of the Cardinal de Retz, especially, provided an introduction to the politics of the seventeenth century. The great conspiracy recounted therein brought Voegelin to a comparative study of the Wallenstein conspiracy, of the conspiracy of the Fiesco in Genoa, and of the conspiracy of the Spaniards in Mexico. The memoirs of the Duc de la Rochefoucauld provided a transition to the philosophy of the *moralistes*, and by reading the Marquis de Vauvenargues he learned about the line of influence that runs from the *moralistes* to Nietzsche. Against the background of his study of legal theory, especially of Léon Duguit, Voegelin became acquainted with the French theory of *solidarité* as the substance of society.

Voegelin traveled into the French countryside, to Chartres and in the summer to the remnants of the monasteries in Normandy. Moreover, he discovered the community of Russian exiles living in Paris and took that occasion to interest himself in the study of the Russian language with Konstantin V. Mochulsky and G. Lozinsky as teachers for most of the year. By the time of his return to Vienna he was able to read Dostoevsky.

Although he was acquainted with Henri Bergson's *Matter and Memory* and *Essai sur les données immédiates de la conscience* (*Time and Free Will*) in 1927, it was not until publication of *The Two Sources of Morality and Religion* in 1932 that Voegelin became seriously interested in that thinker. In the same year, Voegelin made another trip to France and England. He was interested at the time in the politics of the sixteenth century, especially in the work of Jean Bodin, and collected materials for an extensive essay on Bodin which he subsequently wrote for his "History of Political Ideas" but has not so far been published. "I worked through the catalogue of the Bibliothèque Nationale on French publications in history and politics of the sixteenth century. As far as I remember I had every single item in the catalogue in hand at least once" (AM, 36). It was during this time that he became aware of the tremendous influence the Mongol invasions of the fifteen century, and especially the temporary victory of Tamerlane over Bayazid, had as a model of the political process as reflected in the writers of the following century. Virtually every important author treated these events as being outside the normal experience of Western politics and as introducing the phenomenon of an inexplicable rise to power, one affecting the very existence of Western civilization, as a new factor in world history. The humanists' portrayal of the Ottoman threat, and its brief interruption by Tamerlane, was seen by Voegelin to enter into the conception of the man who can rise to power by his virtue as reflected in Machiavelli's *Prince* and in his fictitious biography of Castruccio Castracani.

Voegelin subsequently published from the research materials gathered at the time an essay on the humanists' picture of Tamerlane (1937) and another on the background of Machiavelli (1951).[4]

The study of Bodin was of cardinal importance for Voegelin's subsequent theory of politics. There he found Bodin, a great political philosopher, living and writing against a background of political turmoil erupting from a warfare of contending doctrinal positions that triggered eight religious civil wars in France alone during the sixteenth century. This "dogmatomachy," as Voegelin would later term it, arose at least partly because of the split between experience and symbolism, which permitted doctrines to lead an uncontrolled life of their own and, thereby, become a source of disruption in human affairs. Four centuries earlier the French philosopher had clearly understood the derivative nature and secondary importance of doctrine (ideas) in relation to their engendering experiences.

Jean Bodin recognized that the struggle between the various theological truths on the battlefield could be appeased only by understanding the secondary importance of doctrinal truth in relation to mystical insight. He wanted his sovereign, the king of France, to be, if not a mystic, at least someone advised by a mystic like himself in order to stand above the dogmatomachy. My careful study of the work of Bodin in the early thirties gave me my first full understanding of the function of mysticism in a time of social disorder. I still remember Bodin's *Lettre à Jan Bautru* [ca. 1562] as one of the most important documents to affect my own thought. In the twentieth century, when the dogmatomachy is no longer that of theological but of ideological sects, a similar understanding of the problem has again been reached by Henri Bergson in his *Les deux sources de la morale et de la religion*. I doubt that Bergson has the same stature as a mystic that Bodin has. Still, these two French spiritualists are for me the representative figures for the understanding of order in times of spiritual disorder. (AM, 118–19)[5]

Voegelin's few weeks in London in 1934 were spent exploring the resources of the Warburg Institute, which introduced him to the prominence of alchemy, astrology, and Gnostic symbolisms in Re-

4. Eric Voegelin, "Das Timurbild der Humanisten: Eine Studie zur politischen Mythenbildung," *Zeitschrift fuer Oeffentliches Recht*, XVII, 5, pp. 545–82. Voegelin, "Machiavelli's Prince: Background and Formation," *Review of Politics*, XIII, (1951), pp. 142–68.

5. See Jean Bodin, *Colloquium of the Seven about Secrets of the Sublime*, trans. with intro. by Marion Leathers Daniels Kuntz (Princeton, N.J.: Princeton University Press, 1975), xxi*n*.

naissance thought. He subsequently discerned the continuities of these matters from the Middle Ages through the Renaissance into the modern period and wrote a chapter on astrological politics for his unpublished "History of Political Ideas." These discoveries sensitized him to dimensions of modern politics amply represented in his later studies of modernity, the *philosophes*, Marx, Hegel, the role of magic in Old Testament prophecy (such as Isaiah's metastatic faith), and thematic to his 1977 lecture on "The Sense of Imperfection" at the Eranos Symposium in Switzerland.

The comparative and interdisciplinary thrust of Voegelin's scholarship, as mentioned earlier, was enhanced by the so-called Stefan George Circle and by the influence of Karl Kraus from the early 1920s onward. George was a great German symbolist poet whose work Voegelin absorbed and through whom he became aware of symbolist lyrics and began the study of Mallarmé and Valéry. But George's influence lay chiefly in the prominence of many of his adherents, friends, and students who determined the climate of the German universities for the more alert students there. Voegelin absorbed intensely Friedrich Gundolf and his books on *Goethe*, on the *History of Caesar's Fame*, and on *Shakespeare und der Deutsche Geist*; Max Kommerell and his *Jean-Paul* and his volume on the German classic and romantic literature, *Der Dichter als Fuehrer*; Ernst Bertram's study of Nietzsche; Wilhelm Stein's study of Raphael; and Ernst Kantorowicz's study, *Kaiser Friedrich II*. Of particular influence were the works of Classical scholars, beginning with that of Heinrich Friedemann (who was killed in World War I) on Plato and continued by Paul Friedlaender's and Kurt Hildebrandt's work on Plato which became fundamental for Voegelin, whose own studies were carried out in their spirit (OH, III, 6n).

Because the debauchery of the German language was a major phenomenon in the period leading up to Hitler, the influence of Stefan George was complemented by that of the well-known publicist Karl Kraus whose importance was "of the first magnitude" to Voegelin beginning in the early 1920s and especially after his return from America and France in 1927 (AM, 17). Kraus's magazine *Die Fackel* (*The Torch*) was read by all of Voegelin's contemporaries. It and Kraus's other literary work provided a critical understanding of the politics of the times, most especially of the press's role in the process of social disintegration in Germany and Austria which prepared the way for national socialism. Both George and Kraus were artists who defended the standards of language against the destruction of it worked in the imperial period after 1870. Nothing comparable had happened in England, France, or America. The task of "regaining language" became a matter of deliberate effort on the part of the younger generation of the time. Voegelin's deliberate schooling on this point can be seen in his adoption of the Stefan George Circle's style in his early books, *Ueber die Form des amerikanischen Geistes* (1928) and more especially in *Die Rassenidee in der Geistesgeschichte* (1933).

Regaining language meant recovering the subject matter to be expressed by language and that meant getting out of what one would call today the false consciousness of the petty bourgeois (including under this head Positivists and Marxists) whose literary representatives dominated the scene. Hence, this concern with language was part of the resistance to ideologies that destroy language inasmuch as the ideological thinker has lost contact with reality and develops symbols for expressing not reality but his state of alienation from it. To penetrate this phony language and to restore reality through the restoraton of language was the work of Karl Kraus as much as of Stefan George and his friends at the time. Particularly influential in the work of Karl Kraus was his great drama of the First World War *Die Letzten Tage der Menschheit*, with its superb sensitivity to the melody and vocabulary of phoniness in politics, war patriotism, denigration of enemies, ochlocratic name-calling, etc. Karl Kraus's work, with its first climax in *Die Letzten Tage der Menschheit*, was continued throughout the 1920s in his criticism of the literary and journalistic language of the Weimar Republic in Austria and Germany. It increased in importance with the gradual emergence of national socialism to dominance on the public scene. His second great work dealing with the major catastrophes of the twentieth century was his *Dritte Walpurgisnacht*, treating the phenomenon of Hitler and national socialism. . . . I would say that a serious study of national socialism is still impossible without recourse to the *Dritte Walpurgisnacht* and to the years of criticism in the *Fackel*, because here the intellectual morass that must be understood as the background against which a Hitler could rise to power becomes visible. The phenomenon of Hitler is not exhausted by his person. His success must be understood in the context of an intellectually or morally ruined society in which personalities who otherwise would be grotesque marginal figures can come to public power, because they superbly represent the people who admire them. . . . The study of this period by Karl Kraus, and especially his astute analysis of the dirty detail (that part of it that Hannah Arendt has called the banality of evil), is still of the greatest importance, because parallel phenomena are to be found in our Western society though fortunately not yet with the destructive effects that led to the German catastrophe. (AM, 17–19)[6]

Voegelin's relationship with Hans Kelsen, his major professor and subsequent colleague in the law faculty at Vienna, was equally influential. A distinguished lawyer, the technical author of the Austrian Constitution of 1920, and the founder of the important "Pure Theory of Law," Kelsen was also a prominent jurist and member of the Austrian Supreme Court. His commentary on the Austrian Constitution shows his juridical acumen at its best. In Vienna during the time under consideration, the intellectual climate was dominated by Immanuel Kant and neo-Kantianism. In the circle of the "Pure Theory of Law" to which Voegelin belonged a philosopher was someone who based his methodology on Kant. If one read books written before Kant then he was a historian. "Hence," Voegelin states, "my interest in Classic philosophy, which was already marked at that time, was interpreted by my colleagues as historical interest and an attempt to escape from true philosophy represented by the neo-Kantian thinkers" (AM, 99–100).

Kelsen's work was inseparable from the "Pure Theory of Law." "It was the splendid achievement of a brilliant analyst, and it was so good that it could hardly be improved upon. What Kelsen did in this respect stills stands as the core of any analytical theory of law. I later used this core, with some improvements of my own, in the courses in jurisprudence that I gave [in the Law School at Louisiana State University in the 1950s.] I should like to stress that there never has been a difference of opinion between Kelsen and myself regarding the fundamental validity of the 'Pure Theory of Law'" (AM, 20–21).[7] The principal thing Voegelin learned from his long association

6. Cf. Hannah Arendt, *The Origins of Totalitarianism* (New York: Harcourt, Brace, 1951); Arendt, *Eichmann in Jerusalem: A Report on the Banality of Evil* (New York: Viking Press, 1965).

7. See Hans Kelsen, *Reine Rechtslehre: Einleitung in die rechtswissenschaftliche Problematic* (Leipzig and Vienna, 1934); *Pure Theory of Law* (Berkeley: University of California Press, 1967); *General Theory of Law and the State*, trans. Anders Wedberg (1945; repr. ed.; New York: Russell & Russell, 1961). See also the following articles by Voegelin, for which full bibliographical data is given at pp. 254–55 herein: "Reine Rechtslehre und Staatslehre" (1924); "Kelsen's Pure Theory of Law," (1927);

with Kelsen, from his numerous works and from his seminar discussions, was the technique of conscientiously and responsibly reading and analyzing texts. But differences with Kelsen were evolving even before Voegelin's completion of the doctorate. That he was never simply an adherent was suggested by the fact that both Kelsen and Othmar Spann were his "doctor-fathers" in 1922. The differences arose principally from Voegelin's unwillingness to accept the ideological components imposed on the core of the "Pure Theory of Law" and separable from it. The ideology in question was, of course, the neo-Kantian methodology, which was superimposed upon the field of science—in this case the logic of the legal system. Through this restriction, political science (*Staatslehre*) was coterminous with legal theory (*Rechtslehre*), and that reduction was untenable for Voegelin. He felt, even if he did not immediately see why, that it was impossible to deal with the problems of the state, and with political problems at large, while omitting consideration of everything except the logic of legal norms.

Signs of a divergence appeared in 1924 when Voegelin published an early essay which confronted the pure *Rechtslehre* with the materials dealt with in the early nineteenth-century German *Staatslehre*. Already Voegelin was projecting for political science (and as the task of the political scientist of the future) the reconstruction of the full range of politics beyond its arbitrary restriction to the *Normlogik* of the "Pure Theory of Law."[8]

Kelsen's version of neo-Kantian methodology was that of the so-called Marburg School of Hermann Cohen. Cohen's interpretation of Kant's *Critique of Pure Reason* concentrated upon the constitution of science in the categories of time, space, and substance, *science* thereby meaning Newtonian physics as understood by Kant. Kelsen used this model in constructing the "Pure Theory of Law"; that is, he constituted a science by applying these categories to a body of materials. Whatever did not fit into the categories of *Normlogik* could not be considered science.

There were other neo-Kantian schools, however, above all the Southwest German School represented by Windelband and Rickert.

"Die Souveraenitaetstheorie Dickinsons und die Reine Rechtslehre," (1928); "Die Einheit des Rechts und das soziale Sinngebilde Staat," (1930).
   8. Voegelin, "Reine Rechtslehre und Staatslehre" (1924).

This school came to the constitution of science in the sense of the historical and social sciences by "values." This feature of neo-Kantian methodology originated in the 1870s when the Protestant theologian Albrecht Ritschl first drew a distinction between sciences of facts and sciences of values. The origin of this distinction lay in the beginning dominance of the natural sciences as the model of science simply. In the face of prestige of the natural sciences, the theologians, historians, and social scientists had to show that theirs was science, too, and so "values" were invented. By Rickert's conception, the values were various cultural forces of indisputable reality—such as the state, art, religion, and the like—each of which designated an area of reality to be explored by the appropriate science of politics, aesthetics, and theology. This was called the constitution of science by "reference to a value" (the *wertbeziehende Methode*) and the sciences so constituted themselves could then claim to be "value-free" (AM, 22–23).[9]

This technique of reconstructing the historical and social sciences by the so-called *wertbeziehende Methode*, however, suffered from the defect that the values were highly complex symbols, dependent for their meaning on the established "culture" of Western liberal society. It was very well to assume the *Staat* to be a value which determined the selection of materials, but this selection would run into all sorts of difficulties because the model of the *Staat* was the Western *Nationalstaat*, and it would be difficult to bring the Greek polis under this head and still more difficult to bring an Egyptian empire under it. Moreover, the values had to be accepted: and what did one do if somebody did not accept them, as for instance certain ideologists who wanted to establish a science by relating materials not to the value of the state but to the value of its withering away? The apocalyptic, metastatic dreams of, for instance, the Marxist ideology, going back to Fichte's Johannine conception of the withering away of the state, simply did not fit into the constitution of a political science under the value of the "state." (AM, 23)

III

The first inkling of problems such as those just sketched anticipated a break with Kelsen, but that did not occur for a number of years.

9. Cf. Voegelin, *The New Science of Politics*, 17 (hereinafter cited textually as NSP). Cf. Alfred Weber, *History of Philosophy*, trans. by Frank Thilly, with "Philoso-

And the magnitude of the problems themselves became apparent to Voegelin only as his horizon broadened through the various ways already suggested, and the assimilation of those influences, and through the increasing prominence of ideological politics as a stimulus to his thought.

Upon his return to Vienna in 1927 Voegelin wrote *On the Form of the American Mind* (1928) and, therewith, satisfied the *Habilitation* requirement to become a lecturer in political science and sociology (*Privatdozent*) in the law faculty beginning in 1929. In order to convincingly establish his credentials in political science, he published *The Authoritarian State* in 1936 and was promoted to associate professor. It was a section of that book (to be more fully considered shortly) which finally precipitated the rift with his old professor. In its third part he rejected not the "Pure Theory of Law" as such, but Kelsen's claims to providing an adequate account of political reality. "I had to stress the inadequacy of a theory of law for understanding political problems and the destructive consequences of the claim that one should, or could, not deal scientifically with political problems. The relation with Kelsen was never the same after that" (AM, 54).[10]

Voegelin's teaching career had started in high school, when he worked as a tutor for fellow pupils whose parents were more affluent than his own as a means of earning pocket money. After he entered the university he was employed as a volunteer assistant in the Handelsvereinigung-Ost, an Austrian-Ukrainian trading company that began after the occupation of the Ukraine during World War I by the Central European powers. He obtained the job, permitting him to pay his expenses at the university, through the father of one of the pupils he had tutored who happened also to be secretary general of the Vienna Chamber of Commerce. Through contacts with professors at the university, he later secured a very low-paying teaching position at the Volkshochschule Wien-Volksheim.

It was in this rough-and-tumble atmosphere that Voegelin learned to discuss and debate. The school was an adult education institution

phy Since 1860" by Ralph Barton Perry (rev. ed.; New York: Charles Scribner's Sons, 1925). Sec. 79, pp. 552–62.

10. For the detailed critique of Kelsen's theory see Voegelin, *Der Autoritaere Staat* (1936), Chap. 6, esp. pp. 143–50.

sponsored by the Socialist government of the city of Vienna. Its students were the more intellectually alert and industrious young radical workers. By the time Voegelin stood facing in his classes these rather radical Socialists, many of them outright Communists, his three-month Marxist phase of 1919 was well behind him. His subjects at the Volkshochschule were political science and the history of ideas. He taught there before going to America, after his return in 1927, and right down to the *Anschluss* in 1938 when the Nazis removed him. Frequently, there were heated debates in which the young teacher dared not give in lest he lose his authority. Over the years personal relations warmed and friendships grew, however, despite ideological conflicts and despite Voegelin's steadfast resolve to be a conscientious teacher and scientifically oriented scholar.

After the lecture and seminar hours in the evening, after nine o'clock, we continued the discussion in one of the numerous coffee houses of the neighborhood. I remember still a scene in the 1930s when, after a wild debate resulting in disagreement, one of these young fellows, not so very much younger than I was myself, with tears in his eyes told me: "And when we come to power we will have to kill you!" The good relations with these young radicals lasted well into the Nazi period; they became even more intense in the thirties because everybody knew that, if I was not a Communist, I was still less a National Socialist. When the blow of the occupation fell, I was able to help some of them with letters of recommendation on their flight to safer areas, like Sweden. (AM, 88)

Voegelin's situation in the university was quite different. By 1929, when Voegelin became a lecturer, the university classrooms were already filled with tension. The students there came from middle-class homes, and the more intellectually alert ones were substantially affected by German nationalism and anti-Semitism. "There were no open conflicts but the relations were not warm. In 1938, when the National Socialist occupation came, I had to observe that quite a number of the students whom I had in my seminar on administrative procedure donned the black uniform of the SS" (AM, 89).

Neither the appointment as lecturer nor the one as associate professor carried a salary. Through these years Voegelin was also an assistant for constitutional and administrative law in the law faculty. Working with first Kelsen and later with Adolf Merkl, he secured a very modest income. His salary started at S 100 and reached S 250 by

1938, or $50 per month, from which taxes had to be paid. Everything else necessary to support himself and his wife Voegelin earned from free-lance writing, teaching, and the like.

Voegelin's publications down to 1938 reflect his responses to the political climate of the time. His groping for ways to come to grips with the rise of Communist, Fascist, and Nazi totalitarian politics provide the common ground for four of the five books he wrote prior to emigration to America. The exception was the first one, *On the Form of the American Mind*, which has already been discussed (See pp. 20 ff.).[11]

With Austria sandwiched between Germany to the north and Italy to the south, the rise of Hitler and Mussolini and the impact of these developments on Austrian politics drove Voegelin to study major issues posed by the rapidly changing politics of Germany and Austria upon his return from the three years abroad. His two companion volumes of 1933, *Rasse und Staat* (*Race and the State*) and *Die Rassenidee in der Geistesgeschichte* (*The Race Idea in Intellectual History*), show the results of his study of national socialism, among other things, particularly the biological theory underlying the Nazi race doctrine. Voegelin's interest in the natural sciences had persisted from high school days onward. He continued the study of mathematics at Vienna (including the theory of functions with Philipp Furtwaengler), and he undertook intensive study of biology during his year in New York (1924–1925). A number of his friends were biologists, including Kurt Stern who was at work on *Drosophila* genetics in the laboratory of Thomas Hunt Morgan at Columbia University. Frequent visits to the Morgan laboratory and numerous evenings spent in the company of young American biologists provided an invaluable basis for Voegelin's critique of the complicated biological problems presented by the race question in Nazi ideology. The analytical results did little to confirm Nazi claims, of course, and the second of these two books (which traced the idea from its beginnings in the eighteenth century) was withdrawn from circula-

11. By the time he wrote *On the Form of the American Mind*, the industrious young Voegelin had already published nine articles on a wide variety of subjects and six others were published during the same year. His first English-language publication was "Kelsen's Pure Theory of Law," *Political Science Quarterly*, in 1927.

tion by the Berlin publisher (Junker and Duennhaupt); the remainder of the edition was destroyed. By the end of 1933 both books were "unavailable."[12] Hence, they are virtually unknown.

These two books must be seen against the turbulence of the times. On January 30, 1933, Hitler became chancellor of the German Reich, a parliamentary government; and on March 23, following passage of the "Enabling Act" by the Reichstag and Reichsrat, he proclaimed himself master of Germany, therewith firmly establishing Nazi dictatorship. The Preface to *The Race Idea in Intellectual History* was dated "Vienna, October, 1933." *Race and the State* had appeared during the summer of that year through Voegelin's publisher for the book on American thought, a leading scientific house, J. C. B. Mohr–Paul Siebeck of Tuebingen. *Race and the State*'s argument was presented against the background of the historical analysis provided in the other volume. Both the race theory and the race idea were analyzed, with detailed attention to the contemporary political meaning posed by their propagation through the Nazi movement and ideology. Despite this backdrop, however, neither book is a mere tract for the times; both are solid scientific work of a high order of scholarship and great analytical power. Voegelin himself remarked in 1973: "I consider *The Race Idea in Intellectual History* to be one of my better efforts." And Sebba speaks of its "magisterial . . . calm, uncompromising stance" (AM, 25).

The opening sentences of that work set the tone for the whole volume: "The knowledge of man has come to grief. . . . The race theory of our time is characterized by an uncertainty of perspective for the essential and by the decline of the technical art to grasp it through a thought process." Later in the Introduction Voegelin adds: "The present state of race theory, in contrast to its Classical form, is a state of decay. . . . With few exceptions, race theory today moves within inauthentic (*unechtem*) thinking about man."[13] The book goes on to argue that the "theoretical" biologists and anthropologists who are the leading proponents of such so-called race theory display a vacuous ignorance of the thought decisive for understanding the problems with which they are dealing, particularly of Ger-

12. Sebba, "Prelude and Variations on the Theme of Eric Voegelin," 653.
13. Eric Voegelin, *Die Rassenidee in der Geistesgeschichte von Ray bis Carus* (Berlin: Junker & Duennhaupt, 1933), 1, 17.

man scientific thought. Why their investigations of heredity are a fiasco is unclear to the uneducated persons who hang on their every word and who—because of their own ignorance of the historical exploration of the question of race from the perspective of the Christian and Classical Greek philosophers through Leibniz, Wolff, Herder, Kant, and Schiller—readily embrace the utterly destructive reduction of the human essence to the material factors of "blood" and genetics. Such reductionism is fallacious, concluded Voegelin. The physical dimension of man cannot be treated as the total man, discounting his mind and spirit. Above all, the individual human being is to be literally and historically understood as an indivisible whole, each in his essence a living unity and "not the puzzle-pieces of hereditary factors that he appears to be in genetics."[14]

The book reminds its readers that leading scientists and thinkers of earlier times have always seen the human form as a unity, a physical and spiritual entity; never did they dare to mutilate this unity by locating the essence of man in the body divorced from the spirit. Yet just this deplorable spectacle is presented in the contemporary "theory." As Plato has established for all time, great history is to be found only where the exacting reciprocity of physical prowess and spiritual nobility is held in proper balance. Contemporary race theory, wrote Voegelin, is a picture of destruction in which nothing at all remains of this original view of man; this is a result of the liberal and Marxist ideas which emerged at the turn of the century and which have given rise to the Nazi doctrines. Voegelin continues, with emphasis, "*What links race theory, which is rooted in this time period, with liberalism and Marxism*, is the will to make the state ahistorical (*geschichtslos*), to deliver it to the masses, to destroy the historic substance of history, and to destroy primordial man in his capacity to generate society."[15] The race theory twists the liberal doctrine of equality so that it comes to mean that everyone is equal who possesses a certain complex of physical characteristics. It adapts Marxist materialism by substituting for economic relationships biological ones as keys to the spiritual superstructure of society. And it sets forth a "theory" of man to "explain" his nature

14. *Ibid.*, 19.
15. *Ibid.*, 22.

through biology—thus reducing the phenomenon of man to the animal or to inorganic material. "Man as a spiritual-bodily (corporeal) and historical substance cannot be 'explained' through that."[16]

In the final paragraph of the Introduction Voegelin remarks that his purpose is not only to widen the historical horizon but also to restore and reintroduce the original and philosophically developed fundamental questions that had disappeared from the contemporary science and to explore these as a practical scientific matter. Of course, he concedes, such work is not easy. To penetrate the thought processes of a Leibniz, a Kant, and a Schiller requires industry, knowledge of the facts, and a certain spiritual breadth and readiness to which not everybody will condescend—"above all, so far as I see, not every race theorist of our day." Hence, such persons should confine themselves to performing suitably those small tasks for which they are equipped—and remain silent about the larger questions of men and the state. "Whoever makes it easy on himself in matters of the spirit is not entitled to take part in the discussion."[17]

Voegelin's language is caustic, his contempt patent. Sebba in 1977 commented on his own early reading of these two early books:

When I read these two books I knew that Voegelin would be on the Nazi list when Austria fell. I still wonder how he had the nerve to publish both books in Hitler's Germany, and how two German publishers could be blind enough to accept them.

Race and the State maintains its stance of theoretical objectivity only with the greatest difficulty. Voegelin savages the leading German race biologist [Fritz Lenz], he cannot bring himself to use the word "National Socialism" even when he refers to it, yet he attempts to write his way around the censor without budging from the truth. For me the book still evokes the nightmare of these critical years when it first dawned on us that the freedom of expression was becoming lethal to its practitioners.[18]

In Race and the State Voegelin measured the inadequacies of contemporary race doctrine against the best thinking in the biological sciences and against the Classical and Christian science of man. He adopted especially Max Scheler's recent *Die Stellung des Men-*

16. *Ibid.*
17. *Ibid.*, 23. "Wer es sich in geistigen Dingen leicht macht, der hat nicht mitzureden."
18. Sebba, "Prelude and Variations on the Theme of Eric Voegelin," 652.

schen im Kosmos as the basis of his philosophical anthropology: the root of the state is to be sought in the nature of man.[19] An adequate philosophical anthropology must be grounded in the fundamental experiences (*Grunderfahrungen*) of men. These experiences form the basis of the science of man as it has been developed, especially by Plato, Aristotle, Descartes, Kant, and the young Fichte. Voegelin first explored the validity of the philosophers' analysis of man, re-establishing it as the foundation of the critique that followed.

According to that philosophical foundation, man's essence possesses a stratified structure by virtue of which men participate in, and thereby epitomize, all the realms of being. Yet man is emphatically an ontological unity, a whole essence. Because his ontic structure belongs to the several realms of being, human reality may be explored through the several sciences appropriate to each particular dimension of reality, such as physics, chemistry, biology, and the spiritual sciences. Thus, although it is possible (and legitimate) to explore human beings as animals through biology, one difficulty of the Nazi race doctrine was that it presumed this partial approach to man to suffice for assertions about the whole of man. Such a procedure was empirically and theoretically unwarranted and, hence, fallacious: it presumed the part to be the whole of man when, in fact, it was not even the decisive part. Such a natural science of race, Voegelin argued, could say nothing whatsoever about the whole of man's being and the complex of body, soul, and spirit of which it is ontologically composed. "The human being's collective essence as a single entity is everyman's everyday experienced reality of this composite."[20]

A related further difficulty with the Nazi race theory was that it did not arise from the fundamental experiences, but rested upon a set of dogmas that Voegelin called "the dogma system of natural science superstition."[21] The two fundamental dogmas of this system

19. Eric Voegelin, *Rasse und Staat* (Tuebingen: J.C.B. Mohr, 1933), 2, 10, 19, 35, 64, 71. See Max Scheler, *Man's Place in Nature*, trans. Hans Meyerhoff (1928; New York: Noonday Press, 1962) and the brief account of his thought given in I. M. Bochenski, *Contemporary European Philosophy*, trans. Donald Nicholl and Karl Aschenbrenner (1947; 2nd ed.; 1951; Berkeley: University of California Press, 1969), 140–51.
20. Voegelin, *Rasse und Staat*, 11.
21. *Ibid.*, 9–10, 13–14.

were: (1) The only truly "scientific" method is that of the natural sciences, and it alone is to be applied to resolve all problems encountered in the human horizon. All other methods, especially those of the sciences of the spirit, are merely vestiges of a useless past "metaphysical" period of human intellectual development now overcome. Any problems that cannot be mastered through application of the scientific method are illusory problems that can be disregarded. (2) Science advances on a line of steady progress. Thus the investigator is adequately prepared for his scientific task when he knows the contemporary content and boundaries of his particular science, and moves forward in his investigations from that point. Statements of problems and the ideas of earlier times are outmoded and irrelevant for present-day science; they need not be known or considered. For the race scientist these two dogmas meant that anything said before Darwin or, at best, Jean Baptiste Lamarck, could safely be ignored. This of course left the philosophers out of bounds entirely, with the result that natural science categories were misapplied to the realm of human spirit.[22]

Race and the State is divided into two main parts, the first dealing with race theory and the second with the race idea. The distinction Voegelin draws is between the science of race as presented in biological and anthropological literature, which advances doctrines as scientifically true, and the idea of race as a "myth" or political symbol of the social community, especially as advanced from the mid-nineteenth century onward by Gustav Klemm and Comte Joseph Arthur de Gobineau down to Alfred Rosenberg and the contemporary surge of "dictatorial nationalism." After methodically demolishing the supposed science of the current race doctrinaires, Voegelin turns to the race idea. But before arriving at Klemm and Gobineau in the nineteenth century, he first carefully traces the origins of the race idea from Christianity in the universal idea of the *corpus mysticum* and its subsequent particularization as a decisive ingredient in the rise of modern nationalism, especially as displayed in the Ger-

22. *Ibid.*, 9–10, 64. Cf. Eric Voegelin, *Der Autoritaere Staat* (Vienna: Bermann-Fischer, 1938), 102–50; *Die politischen Religionen* (Vienna: Bermann-Fischer, 1939), 50–54; *The New Science of Politics*, 3–13; and "The Origins of Scientism," *Social Research*, XV, 4, pp. 462–94. Cf. Arendt's reaction in *The Origins of Totalitarianism*, 337–38.

man case by Fichte. The "rather banal conglomerate" of thought impulses found in Klemm's work intensified as Voegelin moved through the sources down to Rosenberg's banalities.[23]

A key ingredient of the race idea is millenarianism. The eschatological doctrine of Christianity, promising perfection in the eternal beyond of Last Judgment through the atonement of Christ, the fruit of faith for persons and the transcendental outcome of the historical process, had been thematic in Kant. Voegelin's careful analysis of *The Critique of Practical Reason* demonstrated that Kant had, on the one hand, rejected as "impossible" the notion of an immanent perfection of individual persons within history.[24] In this Kant and Saint Augustine were in agreement. Man's sensible nature is the symptom of his mortality, not its constituent. The essence of man is his rational nature, and it is in this that the mystery of the disintegration of being into time is represented, which is made whole and hale again in God's eternity. On the other hand, however, Kant had acknowledged the unending progress of the reason of the species in world history as pointing toward a perfection of man generically, even if such perfection lies beyond the reach of the generations of individual men down to the age of final fulfillment. The process dismays and astonishes Kant. Man's "double nature" is such that he generically (if not individually) evolves through time toward perfection, and this perfection of virtue and happiness is the goal of human striving throughout history. The individual life is too short to attain such perfection, for it necessarily presupposed an endless progress within an endless existence: only man generically can fulfill these conditions, and then only through the direction of his reason can he attain the perfection which is the plan of his being. Kant's astonish-

23. Voegelin, *Rasse und Staat*, 127–42, 142–56, 158, 182, 212, 220–25. Cf. Otto Ammon, *Die Gesellschaftsordnung und ihre natuerlichen Grundlagen. Entwurf einer Sozialanthropologie zum Gebrauch fuer alle Gebildeten, die sich mit sozialen Fragen befassen* (3. Aufl., 1900); Hans F. K. Guenther, *Rassenkunde des deutschen Volkes* (15. Aufl., 1930); *Der nordische Gedanke unter den Deutschen* (1925); *Platon als Hueter des Lebens. Platons Zucht- und Erziehungsgedanken und deren Bedeutung fuer die Gegenwart* (1928); Alfred Rosenberg, *Mythus des 20. Jahrhunderts. Eine Wertung der seelisch-geistigen Gestaltenkaempfe unserer Zeit* (2. Aufl., 1931); and other related literature cited by Voegelin in *Rasse und Staat*, esp. 181–225.

24. Voegelin, *Die Rassenidee in der Geistesgeschichte*, 130–32, citing Immanuel Kant, *Kritik der praktischen Vernunft*, from the Philosophichen Bibliothek edition, Meiner, paging as in the Akademienausgabe, 115–24.

ment lies in the recognition that earlier generations could never do more than prepare the way for the final harmony of the future; they are no more than the manure of the future harmony as Dostoevsky later said. Kant's system does not resolve the problem of the individual's prospective fulfillment in the eternal beyond but the race's perfection in a final historical age, despite the same rational structure in individual men and in man generically as the human essence.[25]

Both Klemm and Gobineau presented the spectacle of mankind historically unfolding as a cosmic revelation—the former to a happy destiny, the latter to an unhappy one. Fichte elaborated the Kantian idea of a final historical situation of perfectly rational mankind in the theory of the obliteration and death of the state, and the same idea was incorporated into the Communist notion of the withering away of the state. Deliverance from the state, as a mark of the blessed final age of history, also is brandished in the National Socialist proclamation of the Third Realm. In Kant, Klemm, and Gobineau the idea includes the whole of mankind, but in Fichte the agent of deliverance is the German nation, and in communism the proletariat is the anointed class. With national socialism the field of deliverance is contracted so that its agent is an elite society within the nation. "Parallel with this narrowing occurs the decomposition of the traditional social structure and increasingly 'power' ('Macht') makes itself felt" to provide "the visible bond of the new community" emergent from "a variety of particular societies." By this doctrine, the realization of power negatively signifies the disappearance from history of the traditional controlling ideas basic to the old social order.[26]

The Fichtean version of the final fight between the Kingdom of God and the kingdom of the devil becomes, in the Nazi case, the struggle between the Nordic idea and the Jewish idea as expressions of the ultimate contradiction to be resolved through power in the historical process. In Voegelin's view it was simply "astounding" that the Jews, who composed only one percent of the population of the German Reich, could be identified as the counteridea (Gegenidee). How could such a tiny minority arouse such hatred and fear as

25. Ibid., 135, (cf. 146–47), citing Immanuel Kant, Idee zu einer allgemeinen Geschichte in weltbuergerlicher Absicht at the end of the third sentence. For further implications see Voegelin, Die politischen Religionen, 51–56.

26. Voegelin, Rasse und Staat, 181.

was reflected in the anti-Semitic literature? What threat could so few be to the Germans (indeed, to the "Nordic race") whom they supposedly sought to rule and economically enslave through diabolical cleverness?[27]

The drift of Voegelin's analysis of the extensive literature in which hatred of the Jews was expressed leaves the question of why largely unanswered in substantive terms. He is forced to conclude that the naked fact of identifying the Jews *as* the contradictory idea to the "Nordic idea" is in itself the reason for Nazi anti-Semitism. To a considerable degree it was a "media happening," as we might say today, achieved by massive publicity in a thoroughly organized campaign of anti-Semitic propaganda so voluminous as to almost defy detailed examination. As to the merits of the portrayal of the Jews and Judaism, "little that is correct is said about the essence of Jewishness." But truth was not at all the purpose of the anti-Semitic writers. The Jewish idea was merely instrumental, the necessary contradictory diabolical idea of "the positive conception" of the Nordic idea and the future greatness of the new society that the Nazi ideologues were busy propagating. The Jews were a negation, an absolute "nothing" against which the positive aspiration of the German people must struggle to achieve its destiny and deliverance. They were by definition the antithesis of the Nordic ideal. The degradation of the Jews was, thus, the means of asserting the superiority of the Germans. But, Voegelin remarks, the implications of this convergence (*Zusammenfallen*) of the philosophy of the person and the philosophy of the political man for the nation states of the West could only be hinted.[28]

Finally, there was the "Nordic idea" itself. Its central purpose, he finds, was to strengthen the people's self-consciousness by building the image of the German in continuity with the mythic greatness of the ancient Teutonic heroes of the Icelandic sagas, the *Eddas*, and the *Nibelunglied* as representative of the best of mankind. This best of all human races is the Nordic race. The concept was drawn from multiple sources, among them: Linnaeus' *Homo europaeus;* Johann Blumenbach's Caucasian; Klemm's distinction within the active

27. *Ibid.*, 182, 184.
28. *Ibid.*, 185–99, 207, 208.

race between a lighter and a darker one; Gobineau's white race for which the prototype is the blond, long-headed, blue-eyed giant; Schlegel's Indo-Germanic race; Joseph Renan's Arian who stands in opposition to the Semite; Chamberlain's and Woltmann's German; Vacher de Lapouge's revival of Linnaeus' *Homo europaeus* as synonymous with Arian; and finally Joseph Deniker's coining of the term Nordic race. There is evident embarrassment, Voegelin enjoys noticing, as Lapouge observes: the blond dolichocephalic type of the "highest class" somehow stands on the same level with the "lowest class" Negro who also is long-headed. But such problems aside, the Nordic race is essentially contradistinguished from all other "ferocious, currish, and stupid natures" as the select type who alone can save civilization from the corrupt majority which has increasingly come to threaten it since the Middle Ages to the crisis point of the twentieth century.[29]

"The German Nordic Idea is revolutionary." It is also pure political propaganda, Voegelin manages circumspectly to say. To begin with, there is only a "very small percentage" of the "good" race in Germany. The Nordic idea is, therefore, an image with which to create the desirable mankind of the future. It does not arise as an expression of the self-image of a significant number or class of people actively living in Germany. It is not a national idea, for the German middle class (to whom its appeals are directed) has no such historically established consciousness of itself. Its function, then, is to serve as the evocative symbol for the creation of a new nation to rule in a new world. This can only be done if the masses of the society can be mobilized through the work of a mass party in its turn manipulated from above by the self-proclaimed ideological-racial "elite." As the vessel of the salvation of civilization, such an elite (which at the time is in dire danger of extinction, by its own scenario) must vigorously pursue power and purification of the elite Nordic race. The movement is an international one, for the Nordic race is the elite not just of the German world but of the whole of European culture. What Lenz called "blond internationalism" had already been translated in 1900 by Ammon as "Deutschland, Deutschland ueber

29. *Ibid.*, 208n, 215, 222, 215–16. The latter quotation is from Francis Galton, *Hereditary Genius* (2nd ed., 1892; repr. ed., New York: Horizon Press, 1952), 344.

Alles!" Yet militancy should only become outright warfare as a last resort, for the leading elements in all European countries—including those who become officers in time of war—are themselves members of the Nordic race. Warfare on the scale of a world war would only accelerate their annihilation, thereby leaving the world to the unblond, non-Nordic rabble and Jews. A concerted campaign of "propaganda of universal Nordic thought" must lie at the core of foreign policy so as to influence the other nations to embrace the Nordic idea and to subordinate their own inferior national ideas to it—as would be done in Germany.[30]

Voegelin's two books on the race question grew out of another project he had begun. Soon after publication of the American thought book, Voegelin had undertaken a system of political science and had actually written the theory of law and the theory of power. The third part was to have been on political ideas, but he discovered, to his chagrin, that he "knew nothing whatsoever about political ideas and had to give up the project of a *Staatslehre*" (AM, 38). Since the issues were of great moment at that time, the study of the race idea was his starting point for acquiring knowledge of specific ideas on the basis of concrete historical materials. In retrospect this may be seen as the beginning of the great "History of Political Ideas" which he worked on down through the 1940s, and which ultimately has been superseded by *Order and History*. The work on the race question convinced him that a knowledge of Classic and Christian philosophy was vital if ideologies were to be intelligently combatted and political existence understood through a sound political science. Thus Voegelin began his study of Greek around 1930 with a minor member of the Stefan George Circle, Hermann Bodek, as teacher. Within six months he was able to translate the poems of Parmenides, and the effect of his study already can be seen in the 1933 books in which the Greek New Testament is used (AM, 39).[31]

The German political events of 1933 stirred a ferment in Austria,

30. Voegelin, *Rasse und Staat*, 221, 217, 218, 224, 213, quoting Ammon, *Die Gesellschaftsordnung und ihre natuerlichen Grundlagan*, 284; and 225, quoting Guenther, *Rassenkunde des deutschen Volkes*, 472.
31. Cf. Voegelin, *Rasse und Staat*, 133–34.

leading to civil war in 1934, the murder of the politician Engelbert Dollfuss, and adoption of a new authoritarian constitution. After his return from abroad in 1927, Voegelin had turned in the direction of the Christian Democratic party, having first favored the Social Democrats. The Christian Democrats controlled the government in the 1930s and resisted the National Socialists. But the government was handicapped in these efforts by the opposition Social Democrats who interpreted the government's conciliatory policy toward Italy at the time as Fascist, rather than as a policy for survival as an independent country: "the Social Democratic party, due to its Marxist ideology, did not want to admit that a small country like the Austrian Republic had to accommodate itself to the political pressures of the time. The Austrian veering toward Mussolini as a protection against the worse evil of Hitler apparently was beyond the comprehension of ardent Marxists who could do nothing but yell fascism" (AM, 40).

There were, for Voegelin, several reasons for supporting the Christian Democrats during this critical period. First, the Christian Democrats represented the traditions of European culture, whereas the Marxists at least overtly did not—even though Austrian tradition was eminently democratic and habit-forming, even for ardent Marxists. Still, there were difficulties, for the party program explicitly stated that the Social Democratic party would abide by democratic procedures until it once gained power. Then, however, the Socialist revolution would start: "No return to the nefariousness of a capitalist democracy would be permitted; [such would] be resisted by force" (AM, 41). Second, there was what Voegelin could only call the "stupidity of ideologists" who were the leaders of the Social Democratic party. Although he agreed with their economic and social policies, "the silliness of their apocalyptic dream in the face of the impending Hitlerian apocalypse was simply too much to stomach." Voegelin's view was substantially that of Karl Kraus, and similar to that later expressed by United States Supreme Court Associate Justice Robert H. Jackson in the *Terminiello* case: the Bill of Rights is not a suicide pact—nor is democracy. In both instances, a rational response was blocked by the doctrinaire logic of dogmatic libertarians. "Ideological intellectuals who have survived the disaster have not forgiven Kraus for being too intelligent to sympathize with their foolishness. Of course they have not forgiven me either" (AM, 41).[32]

This attitude is reflected in Voegelin's fourth book, *The Authoritarian State*, which was published in 1936 against the backdrop of the Austrian events of the time. "It was my first major attempt to penetrate the role of ideologies, left and right, in the contemporary situation and to understand an authoritarian state that would keep radical ideologists in check as the best possible defense of democracy" (AM, 41). On the whole, he says, it was "a piece of forced labor" (AM, 52). Divided into three parts, the book first deals with the theoretical problems related to the words *total* and *authoritarian*. Since there was no literature in existence for dealing with such matters, Voegelin took this occasion to develop the distinction between political symbols and theoretical concepts, a subject he elaborated much later, in *The New Science of Politics*, into the distinction between *topoi* and concepts: *total* and *authoritarian* were definitely not theoretical concepts, but political symbols or *topoi*.

The distinction is basic for an adequate treatment of the language problems in politics. Conventionally whatever pops up as a language symbol in politics is simply accepted as such and enters the vague realm of political ideas. The first step in getting some rational order into this vague mass is to be clear about what constitutes theory (this question had already motivated my study of Classical political philosophy) and in what way the concepts of theory differ from other language symbols which do not express the order of existence but various disorders, only half understood by the illiterates on the vulgarian level. (AM, 52–53)[33]

Voegelin's accelerating study of the history of philosophy brought him to the recognition that the Fascist and Nazi totalitarian doctrines of total subordination of the population to the collective entity of the state or party or race paralleled the Averroist conception of the *intellectus unus*. By that conception the minds of human beings are only sparks of the one supreme mind. Although he may not have been quite sure of the full significance of this discovery at the

32. Cf. *Terminiello* v. *City of Chicago*, 337 U.S. 1 (1949) 25–26, Justice Jackson dissenting. The Court adopted Jackson's position shortly, in *Feiner* v. *New York*, 340 U.S. 315 (1951).
33. See Voegelin, *Der Autoritaere Staat*, 7–54, and *The New Science of Politics*, 27–34.

time, Voegelin did clearly see that the transfer of the transcendental conception to such world-immanent entities as the state or the race and its representatives was "lethal to a man's humanity. And I certainly was aware of the very serious split in the interpretation of Aristotle's psychology which took place in the Middle Ages between Averroës and Thomas, my preference being on the side of Thomas." He also concluded that both the National Socialist and Fascist ideologists were in "astounding agreement" in adopting the Averroist conception as the basis of their doctrine of the totalitarian idea and that the ideologies were, in fact, "religious" doctrines (as Mussolini explicitly said) which made the state into a "spiritual power"— themes he would further explore, modify, and refine in subsequent work. He related Rousseau's doctrine of the general will to the collectivist teaching of the ideologies in a brief passage which points toward the later important development of the relationship by J. L. Talmon.[34]

Voegelin's identification of the Averroist root of the totalitarian idea "had a funny side effect. Since Averroës happened to be an Arab, and Arabs are Semites, and Semites in the end are Jews, certain thinkers close to the National Socialist regime like Carl Schmitt seriously doubted that the National Socialist collectivism had anything to do with such dirty Semitic origins" (AM, 53–54). Sale of *The Authoritarian State* was, of course, stopped by the Nazis when they occupied Austria on March 11, 1938. And, during the Russian conquest of Vienna, a bomb fell on the Springer publishing house where the contraband copies were stored, destroying the entire edition.

Because of the force of Voegelin's attack on the Nazis, he was regarded not merely as politically unreliable, but actually as Jewish. His name appeared in print with *Jew!* in parentheses after it. One such volume was published shortly after Austria was occupied; its author was a colleague in the law faculty with Voegelin, Helfried Pfeifer.[35] When Voegelin asked him where the information about his

34. See Voegelin, "Siger de Brabant," *Philosophy and Phenomenological Research*, IV, 4, pp. 507–26; Voegelin, *Der Autoritaere Staat*, 23–24, 35–37, 177n. Cf. J. L. Talmon, *The Origins of Totalitarian Democracy* (New York & Washington: Frederick A. Praeger, 1960), 38–49, and *passim*; *Political Messianism: The Romantic Phase* (New York & Washington: Frederick A. Praeger, 1960).

35. See Helfried Pfeifer, *Die Staatsfuehrung nach deutschem, italienischem und*

being a Jew had come from, Pfeifer reluctantly named another colleague as the source, Ernst von Schwind, professor of Germanic law.
Voegelin paid a visit to Schwind. "After some evasive talk he said he
had no special source—but there was the general assumption that I
was a Jew. Reason? I am quoting: 'Our people are not as intelligent as
you are. (Unsere Leute sind nicht so intelligent wie Sie!)' After this
explanation I took a hurried leave, because I had difficulty restraining an outburst of hilarity."[36]

Since the conception of the Austrian corporate state was closely
tied to ideas of the papal encyclical *Quadragesimo Anno* (issued
May 15, 1931) as well as to earlier encyclicals on social questions by
Leo XIII and Pius XI, Voegelin's work during the period 1933 to 1935
brought him to the study of Saint Thomas Aquinas. He thus began
the serious study of medieval philosophy, reading among others the
works of A. D. Sertillanges, Jacques Maritain, Étienne Gilson, the
writing of the rather Augustinian Jesuits Hans Urs von Balthasar and
Henri de Lubac, and continuing work in this field over the years
thereafter (AM, 25).[37] A further result of these studies and the deterio-
ration of the European political situation to the catastrophe of 1938
may be seen in the book published as *Die politischen Religionen*
(*The Political Religions*) in April, 1938, and reissued by the Bermann-
Fischer Verlag the following year in Stockholm after the Gestapo
had confiscated the whole first edition in Vienna as it came off the
press.

"The intellectual apparatus for dealing with the highly complex
phenomena of intellectual deformation, perversion, crookedness,
vulgarization, etc., did not yet exist. Studies to create this apparatus
were required" (AM, 51). It is to this context that the small book on
political religions belongs. In adopting this terminology Voegelin
conformed to the usage of an expanding body of literature, such as
Louis Rougier's *Les Mystiques Politiques*, which treated the ideological movements as a variety of religion. From the standpoint of
his philosophy as it matured over subsequent decades, Voegelin
found the volume wanting, not because it was all wrong, but because

---

bisherigem oesterreichischem Recht (Vienna and Leipzig: Verlag Holzhausens Nach-
folger, 1938), 17 and 47.
36. Voegelin to the author, September 11, 1978.
37. Voegelin, *Der Autoritaere Staat*, esp. 206–14.

the term *religions* was too vague and deformed the real problem
(which lies in experiences) by confusing it with the further problems
of dogma and doctrine. Moreover, in this study he still pooled together such disparate phenomena as the cosmological spiritualism
of Ikhnaton (Egyptian King Amen-ho-tep IV, *ca.* 1375–1358 B.C.),
the medieval theological theories of spiritual and temporal power,
Jewish, Pauline, and Gnostic apocalypse, the *Leviathan* of Hobbes,
and the symbolisms of national socialism. From Voegelin's perspective in the 1970s, "a more adequate treatment would have required
far-reaching differentiations between these various phenomena"
(AM, 51–52).[38]

Given these technical reservations, however, it remains true that
The Political Religions is a gloves-off critical analysis of nazism and
fascism; and the book marks a new turn in the development of
Voegelin's thought. It is more than a summary statement and valedictory of the young Voegelin who will now turn his attention to
new things in a new environment (the Foreword to the 1939 edition
being written from Cambridge, Massachusetts). For Voegelin in this
brilliant essay sketches the problem of the ideologies in terms of the
disease of the spirit whose cure lies in rediscovery of the order of the
soul as a major task of his new science of politics. That central
ground of all his later work is clearly at the root of his argument in
The Political Religions. The disease of the spirit productive of such
monstrosities of evil as German national socialism and Italian fascism originates in the radical secularization of existence which finally swept the intellectual world during the Enlightenment and
whose mark is the "decapitation of God," the rejection of the transcendental *realissimum* as the source of order in history and the
Ground of being.[39] Therewith the demonic furies were released upon
the world in the form of the immanentist political religions whose
leaders proclaim themselves representatives of mankind, the mortal
gods (in Hobbes's sense) in whom the true and perfect man is real-

---

38. The genre continues into the present in such critically acclaimed works as
George L. Mosse, *The Crisis of German Ideology: Intellectual Origins of the Third
Reich* (New York: Grosset & Dunlap, 1964); *The Nationalizations of the Masses: Po-
litical Symbolism and Mass Movements in Germany from the Napoleonic Wars
Through the Third Reich* (New York: Howard Fertig, 1977); and J. P. Stern, *Hitler: The
Fuehrer and the People* (Berkeley: University of California Press, 1975).

39. Voegelin, *Die politischen Religionen*, 32, 56.

ized and through whom alone their followers can achieve their own true humanity. As in the first political religion that appeared with Ikhnaton, the people touch ultimate reality only through the mediation of the uniquely perfect one, the *Fuehrer*. He is both the dispenser of truth and the source of the salvation of mankind through the ascent of history to its climax in a final, "Third Realm,"[40] or age of perfection traceable to that announced by Saint Paul and given authoritative apocalyptical formulations for the modern age by Joachim of Flora and Dante in the twelfth and thirteenth centuries, by Hobbes in the seventeenth century, and by Kant at the end of the eighteenth century. While there was no mention here of Gnosticism, much else that aroused a furor fifteen years later when *The New Science of Politics* was published was already clearly stated in *The Political Religions*.[41]

This small book stresses the view that the ideologies, particularly national socialism and fascism, have their roots in "religiosity" and constitute secularistic, "anti-Christian religious movements." The radical critique of the ideologies, by Voegelin's assessment, had not so far been pursued with the requisite degree of thoroughness by humanist and social science researchers, partly because spiritual questions were taboo, prohibited by the prevalent dogmas of both Comte and Marx. Hence, any attempt to raise them even as critical matters in bringing to analytical focus the Nazi and Fascist movements was regarded not only as of dubious validity, but also as a symptom of "barbarism and a reversion to the Dark Ages."[42] Such dogmatism and theoretical obtuseness, argues Voegelin, makes modern intellectuals unwitting accomplices in their own destruction and in the destruction of the civilization under concerted attack by the likes of Hitler, Mussolini, and their henchmen. As the methods of the natural sciences became the sole acceptable forms of inquiry, the term *metaphysical* became a term of abuse, *religion* became the "opium of the people" and, more recently, an "illusion" portraying a questionable future state of mankind. Contradictory doctrines thereby arose to replace the old spiritual religion, ones au-

40. See pp. 107–111 herein for further discussion of the Third Realm.
41. *Ibid.*, 19–29, 39–42, 49–65. Cf. Voegelin, *The New Science of Politics*, Chaps. 4–6.
42. Voegelin, *Die politischen Religionen*, 8–9.

thenticated by the science of the world whose insights claim legitimacy as replacements of the old revelatory and mystical truths: scientific world views, scientific socialism, scientific race theory, and
the riddle of the world are substituted. Simultaneously, the sciences
of the fundamental questions of being and knowledge of the language of philosophical inquiry have vanished, so that the formation
of human existence in its tensional orientation toward the divine
Ground of Being has been supplanted by the characteristic attitudes
of indifferentism, laicism, and atheism implied by the socially binding new ideological pictures of secularized reality.[43]

But, Voegelin continues, if men can let the content of the world
expand so as to obscure the creation and the God Who stands behind
it, they still cannot overcome the structure of existence itself, for
this still lives in every single soul. When the transcendent God is
obscured, the content of the world supplies new gods. When the
symbols of transcendental religiosity are banished, new symbols appear in their stead, those developed out of the inner-worldly scientific language. Apocalypse and revelation are no less characteristic of
immanent than transcendental religiousness, as can be seen from a
succession of examples from Joachim to Gobineau. And every apoc-
alyptist also has his devil symbolisms as well: for Hobbes of the
Leviathan, it was the Catholic Church; for Fichte, the satanic Napo-
leon; for Comtean positivism, evil was concentrated in religion and
metaphysics; for the proletariat, the bourgeoisie; for the elected
race, the less valued races, particularly the Jews as the counter-race.

The general trait of these new symbolisms, says Voegelin, is their
"scientific" character. From the time of Marx onward, the new apocalyptical thought as "science" conducts an increasingly radical critique of prevailing "ideologies"—especially philosophy and Christianity. But this process of radical critique is not such that it serves
through science to expose the fallacies of the apocalyptists themselves. Rather something quite different and noteworthy occurs: the
grip of the immanent religiousness is so strong that, instead, the
concept of truth is itself transformed! In the first phase of this development, the nonscientific character of the inner-worldly apocalyptical symbolisms is recognized, but despite this they are not aban-

43. *Ibid.*, 49–50, 65.

doned because the apocalyptists prize their political-religious value in unifying the mass of the population into a community, even when the doctrines are known to be scientifically untenable. The naive apocalypytic outlook as a state of consciousness, expressed by systems of rational theory or political economy or sociology, is subsequently replaced by the myth, however. The myth is purposely manipulated to generate in the masses the affective conditions needed to arouse and sustain their united anticipation of deliverance from the dissatisfactions of present existence. A second phase develops because the myth is neither the expression of transcendental revelation nor capable of withstanding rational scientific critique. Therewith appears the new concept of truth, expressed by Alfred Rosenberg in the "so-called organic truth." This notion had already appeared in Hobbes's *Leviathan* (1651) when he insisted that any theory which disturbed the peace and concord of the commonwealth could not be true. The Nazi ideologue developed this doctrine by adding the postulate that *truth* is whatever the existence of the organically closed inner-worldly society requires. Knowledge and art, myth and custom are true whenever they serve the racially unified community. This is the decisive criterion. The result is that myth abolishes rational discussion so as to nurture the preeminent symbolism of the one Reich, constituted out of the sensible forms of the people. Consequently, all individual wills are submerged in the Reich. Men's worldly experience and transcendental expectations are blended and resolutely bound together in the unity of a projected world-immanent mystical body.[44]

IV

When one considers the content of Voegelin's four books on modern ideological politics published by 1938, it is small wonder that the Gestapo was hot on his trail after Hitler's annexation of Austria. We have seen that he barely escaped. He described the final day this way.

The emigration plan almost miscarried. Though I was politically an entirely unimportant figure, and the important ones had to be caught first, my turn came at last. Just when we had about finished our preparations, and my

44. *Ibid.*, 52–54.

passport was already with the police in order to get an exit visa, the Gestapo appeared in my apartment in order to confiscate the passport. Fortunately I was not at home, and my wife was delighted to tell them that the passport was with the police for the purpose of getting the exit visa, which satisfied the Gestapo. We were able, through friends, to get the passport, and the exit visa, from the police before the Gestapo got it—that all in one day. And the same day, in the evening, with two bags, I caught a train to Zurich, trembling on the way that the Gestapo would find out about me after all and arrest me at the border. But apparently even the Gestapo was not as efficient as my wife and I in these matters, and I got through unarrested. (AM, 43)

Still there had been moments of humor amidst the events lead-ing to the frantic final hours before escape to Switzerland.

For instance, in the general survey of university personnel, a Gestapo man came to our home and searched around—my desk, drawers, bookcases, etc., in order to see what I did. He was a young man in his mid-twenties, and when we got friendly he told me that he was originally a lawyer from Ham-burg. First he inspected my desk for incriminating material. At the time, since I had been fired and there was nothing to do but prepare my emigra-tion, I had complete leisure for the exploration of complicated problems. I was working at the time on questions of empire and my desk was piled high with treatises on Byzantium, several of them in French and English. So he thumbed through this Byzantine empire literature; after awhile he remarked that he was in charge of inspecting all of these professors in the law school and that my desk was the first he had seen that looked like the desk of a scholar. The atmosphere became more relaxed. He had to take with him some incriminating evidence concerning my political interests. I had of course standing on my shelves the principal sources of a political nature: Hitler's *Mein Kampf*; Kurt von Schuschnigg's *Dreimal Oesterreich, Doku-mente der deutschen Politik und Geschichte* (6 vols.), edited by Paul Meier-Bennekenstein; Mussolini's *Dottrina del Fascismo*; Marx's *Communist Manifesto*, etc. So he took away Schuschnigg and Marx. I protested that would give an unfair impression of my political interests which were strict-ly impartial and offered him to take along Hitler's *Mein Kampf*. But he re-fused, and that is how I have kept my copy of a very early edition. But by that time we had already become more friendly. As he also had to take with him some of my own books, *On the Form of the American Mind*, on the race question, etc., I suggested that it would not be nice to take the good hardcover copies; but he could take as well the volumes of the page proofs. He was agreeable and was satisfied with the page proofs. So I could keep the hardcover editions which I still have.

My wife who is a very orderly lady wanted to take his coat, which he had thrown over a chair, and hang it in a closet. Whereupon he yelled: "Don't touch it! My revolver is in there!"

But what had to be considered due process of law under the now valid statutes was on the whole observed, and while I was apparently a target of some interest my wife was not. Besides, when I left she could stay with her parents who were National Socialists and had a huge picture of Hitler in their living room. Of course, as soon as I had left on the evening of the day when the Gestapo wanted to confiscate my passport, the next morning he came back in order to ask where the passport and I were. Then a guard was put in front of the house where my wife stayed. But after I arrived in Zurich and had sent a telegram, first the guard disappeared, and twenty minutes later my telegram arrived. He had obviously known I had left for good. A week later my wife joined me in Zurich. Of course we had to leave everything behind, but it was possible to get some furniture out and, most importantly, the library. Certain items, however, had to be left. Again the details are more or less funny. For instance, I had to leave behind my stamp collection which I had accumulated as a boy, this being an object of value. Books apparently were not. I knew from other people that in spite of rather strict law enforcement one could get through a lot of things. I know for instance of a young lady who was an artist and had acquired a few original prints by Duerer. In order to export art objects one had to get a permit, and she put the Duerer prints in between her work. The official who examined the portfolio looked through one of these prints after another and when he came to this or that Duerer print he said "Well, well! You have made quite some progress as an artist," and left it at that. (AM, 55–57)

CHAPTER 3

Americanization:
A Scholar's Pilgrimage to 1981

Voegelin's first American home was in Cambridge, Massachusetts, where he held a one-year appointment as tutor and instructor at Harvard. The position had been secured through his friends there, William Y. Elliott, Gottfried von Haberler, Joseph Schumpeter, with the chairman of the department of government, Arthur Holcombe, consenting to the appointment. "I still remember my first conversation with Holcombe. When I presented myself to him at Harvard, he told me with dry precision that Harvard was pleased to give me this opportunity for a year and that with the end of the year the opportunity was ended" (AM, 58). Voegelin immediately began looking for a new job, writing some forty letters to universities over the country. The immediate result was appointment at Bennington College for the spring term of 1939. He was offered reappointment as assistant professor for the following year at the tempting salary of $5,000, but declined it in favor of a move to the University of Alabama in Tuscaloosa. His reasons were twofold. He found the faculty and students at Bennington to be strongly influenced by Marxism, and this was no more to his taste than national socialism had been. Secondly, he wanted to put some distance between himself and the flood of Central European refugees relocating in the eastern institutions. Voegelin determined that he did not want to be submerged in this refugee subculture but to make the break with Europe radical: he wanted to become an American and a political scientist not stigmatized as a member of a refugee group. This meant he had to familiarize himself with American politics and government by teaching them, an opportunity not likely to be his in the East Coast university environment.

Alabama was definitely free of the refugee culture, and through the political science chairman there, Roscoe Martin, Voegelin got his first chance to teach American government. The pay was a paltry $2,400 for the year, but he remained there until 1942 and gradually adjusted to the new setting through "the truly gracious reception by southerners who enjoyed protecting somewhat condescendingly an innocent from Europe," a process greatly facilitated by the rapport and friendship that developed between Martin's wife Mildred and Lissy Voegelin (AM, 59).

With customary energy Voegelin worked his way into the mysteries of American government, the Constitution, and even into a certain amount of public administration in addition to giving the course on the history of political theory. While at Harvard he had become acquainted with Fritz Morstein-Marx, then editor of a textbook series for McGraw-Hill, who encouraged Voegelin to do a concise introductory political theory textbook.

I

This may be regarded as the formal beginning of the "History of Political Ideas" publication project. He worked on the project before and after the move to Alabama, using at first George H. Sabine's standard work, *A History of Political Theory* (first edition, 1937), as a model. In digging through the materials, Voegelin soon concluded that the treatment hitherto accorded them was deficient, but that his own knowledge was insufficient to give a more adequate account. He began wading through the sources from the ancient Greeks onward. In Alabama he discovered he could not write about medieval theory without greater knowledge of Christianity, nor about Christian origins without going into the Judaic background. To accomplish the latter he had to learn Hebrew. He began the study of that language with a Tuscaloosa rabbi who taught Hebrew at the university. "The beginnings were hard but gradually I acquired a sufficient knowledge of grammar and vocabulary to be able to check translations and finally to make my own translations on the basis of the texts."

The size of the manuscript mounted, bursting the bounds of the textbook project, but Voegelin could not deliver the manuscript in time to meet the publisher's deadline anyway. The conception of a history of Western political theory commencing with the Greeks and progressively following a unilinear pattern of developing ideas "from a supposed constitutionalism of Plato and Aristotle, through the dubious constitutionalism of the Middle Ages, into the splendid constitutionalism of the modern period broke down" (AM, 63–64). Voegelin's study of the Israelite background of Christian thought had already exploded the notion that one had only to begin with the ancient Greeks. Worse than that, he went on to become acquainted with the explorations of the ancient Near Eastern civilizations conducted by the members of the University of Chicago's Oriental Institute. The background thereby further expanded, for the ancient Near Eastern empires were the background from which Israel emerged, the Israelites the background of the Christians, and the Christians the background of the ideas of the Middle Ages.

Work on the project continued after Voegelin left Alabama to accept appointment as an associate professor in the Department of Government at Louisiana State University in January, 1942. Having become active in the Southern Political Science Association, he attracted the attention of Robert J. Harris, then department chairman at Louisiana. Harris became a close friend and gratified Voegelin by permitting him to teach two sections of American government each term, an assignment that generally continued over the sixteen years of his tenure in Baton Rouge as part of a normal twelve-hour teaching load that often required four different preparations. A connoisseur of Supreme Court decisions, Harris deepened Voegelin's understanding of constitutional law, explaining among other things the key role of procedure in the Court's decisions. Voegelin also regularly taught comparative government, on occasion diplomatic history, as well as the law school's course in jurisprudence.[1] But his main course was always the history of political theory and the graduate seminars in theory which drew many of the university's best students. With the increasing prominence of China in the 1940s, Voegelin was elected, because of his linguistic facility, to teach a

1. Voegelin wrote an essay of one hundred pages entitled "The Nature of the Law" (1957) for use as a textbook in his jurisprudence course. Unpublished.

course on Chinese politics; and he learned enough Chinese to read the classical source materials in the process of developing this course, which he taught for a decade.

Upon his arrival in Baton Rouge Voegelin had just turned forty-one years old. He was something of a curiosity to a not-very-sophisticated undergraduate student population. One now-distinguished political scientist who was an eighteen-year-old sophomore at the time recalled his first impression of Voegelin in 1942:

My impression of his first appearance in class remains vivid in my memory, although it undoubtedly has been colored by imagination. He was, to say the least, a striking figure in my provincial eyes. He was dressed (in what I considered to be extremely formal fashion) in a tight-fitting black coat, striped trousers, and heavy black semi-brogue shoes that made his presence felt before his coming because they squeaked rather loudly when he came down the hall. Voegelin was, and is, a robust man, thick-chested and prominent-featured, with a florid complexion and sandy hair that could have been quite red in his youth. His hands, which he used with expressive grace in his lectures (and occasionally in conversation), form something of a complement by contrast to his features and frame because his fingers are long and tapered, with just a hint of delicacy about them. He carried himself most erectly and invariably walked at a brisk pace with his head thrown well back, as he still does [in 1971]. At the time he wore close-fitting, round, steel-rimmed spectacles; and then as now, he was rarely to be seen without a cigar.[2]

And how was the newcomer Voegelin as a teacher of introductory American government? Our sophomore of the time, William C. Havard, Jr., continued:

It was not long before I came to regard Professor Voegelin as being as striking in his capacity as a teacher as he then seemed to me to be in appearance. He brought to American Government a perspective that was totally unanticipated by those of us who had been brought up on orthodox institutional description. Although I am sure that most members of the class were as unsophisticated as I was, nearly all of us came very quickly to realize that Voegelin was a man of extraordinary intellectual power and possessed of that rare quality of being able to look at things with a special vision not open to others until they had been exposed to it by his guidance. Under his

2. William C. Havard, "The Changing Pattern of Voegelin's Conception of History and Consciousness," *Southern Review*, n.s., VII (January, 1971), 58. Professor Havard became chairman of the Department of Political Science at Vanderbilt University in 1977 and remained editor of the *Journal of Politics* until 1980.

tutelage one came to appreciate the enormous complexity of the interplay between ideas and institutions, and the subtle way in which historical experience manifested itself long after the original events which produced specific social responses in the form of ideas, patterns of habitual action, or a set of institutions had been lost to immediate consciousness. The Classical sources on which the founding fathers drew so heavily were clarified both in their original meanings and in the impact they had on the legal and institutional structure of the Constitution; a commonplace arrangement such as the separation of powers was placed in the perspective of its historical origin in the long drawn out struggles in the Middle Ages between the plenitude of power of the head of state and the emergence of consultative checks on these powers; and the tensions that remained in the religious sphere in America even after an apparent resolution of the problem had been achieved through church-state separation were elaborated within the context of the omnipresent search for religious truth in forms both theological and secular in all human settings.

As a teacher Voegelin never engages in pyrotechnics; his effect is based solely on the impressive breadth and depth of his learning and on the analytical powers of his mind. If one should stand just beyond the limits of the point at which his actual words could be understood, his lectures probably would sound monotonous because both the flow of the sentences and the lack of inflection make for an evenness that could be deadly in one whose ideas are less exciting than Voegelin's. Having sat through his classes and seminars as an undergraduate, graduate student, and later as a junior colleague, I was always surprised when I heard colleagues in the profession speak disparagingly of his "arrogance" or his "rigidity." I have always found him exceptionally considerate with students, patient with their problems of understanding, and in some ways a rather soft touch in the matter of grades. In supervising research he is an exacting critic, as one might expect; but he is also generous with both his time and his ideas. He has a pixyish sense of humor that comes through somewhat unexpectedly in the light of his German accent, until one remembers that the Austrians are as much Southern Europeans as they are Germanic in the more subtle aspects of their culture.[3]

Voegelin was promoted to full professor of government at Louisiana State University in 1946, and in 1952 he was appointed the first Boyd Professor of government, an endowed chair he held until his departure for Munich in 1958. When he arrived in 1942 the English faculty included the founders of the *Southern Review*, Cleanth Brooks and Robert Penn Warren, as well as Robert B. Heilman. Heilman assisted Voegelin in developing an idiomatic English style, and

3. *Ibid.,* 58–59.

both he and Brooks brought the problem of the social stratification of English usage to Voegelin's attention.

The nature of my problem can be gathered from a conversation with Cleanth Brooks. Once, when crossing the campus, I met him, deep in sorrow and thought, and asked him what worried him. He told me he had to prepare a chapter on typical mistakes for a textbook on English style which he had to reedit together with Robert Penn Warren, and that it was quite a chore to find typical mistakes. I was a bit surprised and innocently told him, "Well, that is very simple to find typical mistakes. Just take any education textbook and you will find half a dozen on every page." He then explained to me that he could not use this method because educationists were far below the level of average literacy; their mistakes could not be considered to be typical for an average English-speaking person. Instead he was using sociology textbooks and sometimes had to read twenty pages of that stuff before running into a really good example. But even so he had to worry because social scientists could not be considered to write typical English either but were far below the average, though not as far below as educationists.

This is the type of stratification of which I had gradually to become aware in order to achieve a moderately tolerable English style, free of ideological jargon and free of the idiosyncracies of the vulgarian levels in the academic community. (AM, 62)

Voegelin continued to write and publish in his new American environments, bringing out several important essays on national socialism such as "Extended Strategy: A New Technique of Dynamic Relations" and "The Growth of the Race Idea" in 1940, "Some Problems of German Hegemony" in 1941, and "Nietzsche, the Crisis and the War" in 1944. All were published in leading journals and, along with new material, communicated to the English reader something of the critique of nazism that he had published earlier in German. But his major efforts down to 1945 were devoted to the writing of "The History of Political Ideas," which he brought from antiquity to the end of the nineteenth century.

Voegelin's productivity as a scholar arises from a combination of remarkable facility and long hours: he gets up at 7:30 A.M. and seldom goes to bed before 2:00 A.M., only taking time out during the day for a nap after lunch. This eighteen-hour work day is a regimen he has followed for decades. In Baton Rouge he wrote hundreds upon hundreds of pages of detailed analyses for the *magnum opus*, the results of which are still to be seen on his study shelf in some fifteen manuscript binders containing over four thousand pages of type-script. A fragment of this work appeared in 1975 as the book entitled *From Enlightenment to Revolution*, edited by John H. Hallowell.

Why did Voegelin eventually abandon the huge project? What was wrong with it? Its general conception. The difficulties noticed already while he was in Alabama were compounded in time, and Voegelin's self-criticism became more and more exacting.

The pattern [of my work], then, cracked along other lines. I had written my "History of Political Ideas" well into the nineteenth century. Large chapters on Schelling, on Bakunin, on Marx, and on Nietzsche were finished. On occasion of the chapter on Schelling it dawned on me that the conception of a history of ideas was an ideological deformation of reality. There were no ideas unless there were [first] symbols of immediate experiences. Moreover, one could not handle under the title of ideas an Egyptian coronation ritual, or the Sumerian recitation of the *Enuma elish* on occasion of Sumerian New Year festivals. I was not yet in a position really to understand where the concept of ideas had come from and what it meant. Only very much later I discovered that the origin is to be found probably in the Stoic *koinai ennoiai*. These common, or self-evident, opinions were still the starting point of criticism in Chapter One of Locke's *An Essay Concerning Human Understanding*: he protested against them in order to return to the experiences which engendered ideas. (AM, 64)

II

The thought, study, and writing continued, but the period from 1945 to 1950 was a time of indecision, if not theoretical paralysis, in Voegelin's attempt to penetrate to his own satisfaction the mounting problems.

A breakthrough occurred on the occasion of the Walgreen Lectures I delivered in Chicago in 1951 [and which were published the following year as *The New Science of Politics*]. Here I was forced, in comparatively brief form, to formulate some of the ideas that had begun to crystallize. I concentrated on the problem of representation and the relation of representation to social and personal existence in truth. It was obvious that a Soviet government for instance was not in power by virtue of representative elections in the Western sense and nevertheless was the representative of the Russian people. By virtue of what? This question I called at the time the problem of existential representation. This existential representation I found to be always the core of effective government, independent of the formal procedures by which the existentially representative government achieved its position. In a comparatively primitive society where the mass of the people is incapable of rational debate and of forming political parties who select issues, a government will rest on traditional or revolutionary forces without benefit of elections. That the government is tolerated is the result of its fulfilling more or less adequately the fundamental purposes for which a government is established, *i.e.*, the securing of domestic peace, the defense of the realm, the administration of justice, and the welfare of the people. If these functions are fulfilled moderately well the procedure by which the government comes into power is of secondary importance. This existential representation, then, I found empirically supplemented in the historically existing societies by a claim to transcendental representation as I called it at the time. By transcendental representation I mean the symbolization of the governmental function as representative of divine order in the cosmos. That is the fundamental symbolism, back to the ancient Near Eastern empires where the king is the representative of the people before the god and of the god before the people. Nothing has changed in this fundamental structure of governmental order, not even in the modern ideological empires. The only difference is that the god whom the government represents has been replaced by an ideology of history which now the government represents in its revolutionary capacity.

The difference just mentioned had to be expressed in theoretical categories. For several years already I had been aware, through my studies in the history of Christianity and the Middle Ages, of various sectarian movements not too clearly described with regard to their attitudes and beliefs. During the 1940s and 1950s, I became gradually aware that besides Classic philosophy and revelatory Christianity, as represented by the main Church, there existed symbolizations of fundamental creeds which by the experts in the field were classified as Gnostic. As far as I remember, I became aware of the problem of Gnosticism and its application to modern ideological phenomena for the first time through the Introduction to Hans Urs von Balthasar's *Prometheus*, published in 1937. Ever since the 1930s a considerable literature on Gnosticism had been growing and incidental remarks concerning the modern parallelisms were to be found here and there. I discovered that the continuity of Gnosticism from antiquity into the modern period was still a matter of common knowledge among the scholars of the eighteenth and early nineteenth century. . . .

Since my first applications of Gnosticism to modern phenomena—in *The New Science of Politics* and in 1959 in my study on *Science, Politics, and Gnosticism*—I have had to revise my position. The application of the category of Gnosticism to modern ideologies, of course, still stands. In a more complete analysis, however, there are other factors to be considered in addition. One of these factors is the metastatic apocalypse deriving directly from the Israelite prophets, *via* Paul, and forming a permanent strand in Christian sectarian movements right up into the Renaissance. An excellent exposition of this continuity is now to be found in Norman Cohn's *The Pursuit of the Millennium* [second edition, 1961]. I found, furthermore, that neither the apocalyptic nor the Gnostic strand completely accounts for the process of immanentization. This factor has independent origins in the revival of neo-Platonism in the Florence of the late fifteenth century. The attempt to regain an understanding of cosmic order through a revival of neo-Platonism miscarried; a revival of the divine order in the cosmos in the ancient sense would have required a revival of the pagan gods; and that did not work. What was left of the intracosmic divine order which the neo-Platonists tried to revive was an immanent order of reality—an immanentism which had to become secularist when, following the pagan gods, the Christian God had been thrown out too.

Hence, the experiences that result in immanentist constructions had to be explored. As historical phenomena they are not unknown. Perhaps the most important one is the removal of the *amor Dei* from the Augustinian structure of the soul by Hobbes, and the reduction of its ordering force to the *amor sui*. This reduction to the *amor sui* then became dominant in the eighteenth century, through the psychology of the *amour-de-soi* developed by the French *moralistes*. While there is no doubt about the phenomenon as such, its interpretation is difficult because the conventional philosophical terminology has accepted the premises of the new reductionist position; that the position is reductionist does not come to analytical and critical attention. Only in recent years have I developed the concept of the "egophanic revolt," in order to designate the concentration on the epiphany of the ego as the fundamental experience which eclipses the epiphany of God in the structure of Classic and Christian consciousness. I had already used the term "apocalypse of man" to cover this problem in *The New Science of Politics*. On that occasion I wanted to stress the discovery of human possibilities that characterizes the modern period. Surely that discovery was made, but stressing the discovery alone does not take into account its reductionist context. The discovery of man had to be paid for by the death of God, as this phenomenon was called by Hegel and Nietzsche. The term *egophanic revolt*, distinguishing this experience of the exuberant ego from the experience of the theophanic constitution of humanity, is the best I can do terminologically at present. (AM, 65–69)

Voegelin explains in detail the deficiency of the "History of Political Ideas" and the transition to *Order and History* in this further important passage of the "Autobiographical Memoir."

The "History of Political Ideas" had started from the conventional assumptions that there are ideas, that they have a history, and that a "History of Political Ideas" would have to work its way from Classical politics up to the present. Under these assumptions, I had humbly worked through the materials, and a manuscript of several thousand pages was in existence.

Still, the various misgivings that had arisen in the course of the work now crystallized into the understanding that a "History of Political Ideas" was a senseless undertaking, incompatible with the present state of science. Ideas turned out to be a secondary conceptual development, beginning with the Stoics, intensified in the High Middle Ages, and radically unfolding into concepts which are assumed to refer to a reality other than the reality experienced. And this reality other than the reality experienced does not exist. Hence, ideas are liable to deform the truth of the experiences and their symbolization.

The points at which the misgivings had to arise are obvious. In the first place, there is no continuity between the so-called ideas of the Greek philosophers from the seventh to the fourth century B.C. and the contents of Israelite prophetic and New Testament revelatory writings. These two symbolizations touch different areas of experience and are not historically connected. Moreover, the farther one traces back the origin of ideas, the more it becomes clear that such symbolisms as myth and revelation can by no stretch of the imagination be classified as "ideas." One must acknowledge a plurality of symbolisms. An Hesiodic theogony, for instance, simply is not philosophy in the Aristotelian sense, even though the structure of reality expressed by myth and philosophy is the same—a sameness of structure already recognized by Aristotle. The problems were arising which I tried to express through such concepts as "compact" or "primary experience of the cosmos" and the "differentiations" that lead to the truth of existence in the Classic, the Israelite, and the early Christian sense. In order to characterize the decisive transition from compact to differentiated truth in the history of consciousness I used, at the time, the term *leap in being*, taking the term *leap* from Kierkegaard's *Sprung*.

The interest, thus, moved from ideas to the experiences of reality that engendered a variety of symbols for their articulation. That is not to say that the problem of ideas now simply disappeared. Of course it was very much present, but only gradually did I find out what it was. An important point, for instance, which grew in clarity over the years, was the understanding that the transformation of original experiences and symbolizations into doctrines entailed a deformation of existence, if the contact with the reality as experienced was lost and the use of the language symbols engendered by the original experiences degenerated into a more or less empty game. Some of the most obvious things about this deformation I discovered rather late, only in the 1950s and 1960s. I had not been aware clearly, for instance, that the term *metaphysics* is not a Greek term but an Arabic deformation of the Greek title of Aristotle's *meta ta physica*; that it had been taken over from the Arabs by Thomas and for the first time used in a Western language in the introduction to his commentary on Aristotle's *Metaphysics*; and that ever since there existed an odd science that was called metaphysics. Hence, the not-unjustified criticism of such doctrinal metaphysics by the thinkers of the Enlightenment and early positivism did not touch the problems of Classic philosophy at all. Classic philosophy was not too well known at the time; and it is still little known today, because the cliche "metaphysics" has become the magic word by which one can cast a shadow on all philosophical analysis in the Classic sense.

I had to give up the "ideas" as objects of a history and to establish the experiences as the reality to be explored historically. These experiences, however, one could explore only by exploring their articulation through symbols. The identification of the subject matter and, with the subject matter, of the method to be used in its exploration led to the principle that lies at the basis of all my later work: *i.e.*, the reality of experience is self-interpretive. The men who have the experiences express them through symbols; and the symbols are the key to the understanding of the experience expressed. There is no sense in pretending that the Egyptian priests, for instance, who wrote *The Theology of Memphis*, or the Mesopotamian priests who developed the *Sumerian King-List*, were not able to articulate the experiences clearly, because they had other problems than a Voltaire, or a Comte, or a Hegel. What is experienced and symbolized as reality, in an advancing process of differentiation, is the substance of history. The work on the "History of Political Ideas" had not been done in vain, because it had familiarized me with the historical sources. But reorganization of the materials under the aspect of experience and symbolization became necessary. Hence, I gave up the project of a "History of Political Ideas" and started my own work on *Order and History*.

At the time, *Order and History* had to begin with the Mesopotamian and Egyptian empires and their cosmological symbolization of personal and social order. Against this background of the cosmological, imperial symbolism occurred the breakthrough of Israelite revelation. Not in continuity with the pneumatic prophets but independently, there occurred the outburst of noetic thinking in the Greek philosophers. The study of the Near Eastern and Israelite experiences down to the period of Christ filled the first volume of *Order and History*. The evolution of the corresponding Greek experiences from the cosmological origins to the noetic differentiation filled volumes two and three. According to the original plan these volumes were to be followed by studies on empire, medieval imperialism and spiritualism, and on the modern developments.

That plan, however, proved unrealizable. Considerable parts of it were in fact written, but the work broke down on the question of volume. I always ran into the problem that, in order to arrive at theoretical formulations, I had first to present the materials on which the theoretical formulations were based as an analytic result. If I went through with the program, the sequel to the first three volumes would have been not another three volumes as planned but perhaps six or seven volumes more. Because the general public was unfamiliar with the materials that led to certain theoretical insights, the theoretical insights could not be presented without the materials.

I decided, therefore, to make a number of special studies on certain problems of early Christianity, of the mytho-speculative form of historiogenesis, on the transition from historiogenetic speculation to historiography, on the problem of the ecumene as developed by Herodotus, Polybius, and the Chinese historians, on certain modern theoretical problems such as the sorcery involved in Hegel's construction of his System, and so forth. It seemed to make better sense to publish two volumes with these special studies, arriving more shortly at the theoretical results, than to fill numerous volumes with materials, especially since over the years what I had seen as a problem in the 1940s and 1950s had also been seen by others and the historical exploration of such problems as Gnosticism, the Dead Sea Scrolls, the Nag Hammadi finds, the prehistory of pseudo-Dionysius, the revival of neo-Platonism in the Renaissance and its influence on subsequent intellectual Western developments up to Hegel, had made enormous progress, so that now I could refer to the studies on the materials conducted by a great number of scholars—materials that had not been accessible to the public in the 1940s and 1950s when I developed the conception of *Order and History*. I want to stress the development just mentioned, because it could not be foreseen at the time when I started on my work. We are living today in a period of progress in the historical and philosophical sciences that hardly has a parallel in the history of mankind.

As a matter of fact a number of theoretical assumptions from which I had started when I began to write *Order and History* have become obsolete through this rapid development of the historical sciences, especially in the fields of prehistory and archeology. When I wrote the first volume of *Order and History*, my horizon was still limited by the Near Eastern empires. I identified the cosmological symbolism which I found there with the imperial symbolism of Mesopotamia and Egypt. On the basis of the new expansion of our prehistoric and archeological knowledge I can now say that practically all of the symbols that appear in the ancient Near East had a prehistory reaching through the Neolithicum back into the Paleolithicum, for a period of some twenty thousand years before the Near Eastern empires. There has arisen the new problem of disengaging the general problem of cosmological symbolism from its specific, imperial variation. The cosmological symbolisms on the tribal level, back to the Stone Age, must be analyzed; and then the *differentia specifica*, introduced by the foundation of empires, as for instance in Egypt, must be distinguished. I have collected the materials for this purpose; and I hope to publish my findings sometime in the future.

Another great advance in science, which had been in the making for many decades, has more recently found its decisive support through the recalibration of the radiocarbon dates, beginning in 1966. The conception of a unilinear history, which had already been quite shaky in view of the chronologically parallel developments in the Near East, in China, and in Hellas, now definitely breaks down when the temple cultures in Malta, for instance, can be dated substantial periods of time before the Pyramid Age in Egypt. Independent Neolithic civilizations precede in time the imperial civilizations in the Mesopotamian and Egyptian areas. Findings of this nature are accumulating in such numbers that one can say definitely even now that the older conception of a unilinear history, which still dominates the vulgarian level in the form of epigonal constructions in the wake of Condorcet, Comte, Hegel, and Marx, is definitely obsolete. The history of mankind has become diversified. The differentiating developments are widely dispersed. The field can be characterized as pluralistic. The progress, or general advance, of an imaginary abstract "mankind" has dissolved into the manifold of differentiating acts, occurring at various points in time and independently in concrete human beings and societies.

Still, the possibility of civilizational advance through cultural diffusion has not been excluded by these new aspects of history, but the problem must be pushed back to a much earlier period, as Carl Hentze once said to me in a conversation. If the history of articulate expression of experiences goes back for fifty thousand years, anything can have happened in that time: what can be found by way of cultural parallels in the so-called historical period after 3000 B.C. must be seen against the vast background of human contacts in such time spans. To give an example: we have by now an excellent literature on Polynesian cultures, their art and their myth. What is sometimes not realized is the fact that the Polynesians did not spring from the earth on the Polynesian islands but migrated there from the Asiatic mainland. This migration from the Asiatic mainland hardly began before the eighth century B.C. Hence, before that time the tribal developments that today we call Polynesian and the other tribal developments that resulted in the rise of Chinese civilization still belonged to the same area of culture. It is not surprising, therefore, as again Hentze observes, when there are highly interesting parallels between ornaments of Polynesian origin and ornaments on vases in the Shang dynasty.

The splendid advance of science in our time should not, however, induce rash expectations regarding the death of ideologies and their social effectiveness. The discrepancies between science and ideology are of long standing. As a matter of fact, certain ideological tenets were developed in flat contradiction to ordinary historical facts well known at the time and especially to the ideological thinkers. When Marx and Engels, for instance, begin their *Communist Manifesto* with the proposition that all social history hitherto has been the history of class struggle, they are talking impertinent nonsense, because there were after all such struggles in history, well known to Marx and Engels from their high school days as the Persian Wars, or the conquest of Alexander, or the Peloponnesian War, or the Punic Wars, and the expansion of the Roman Empire, which definitely had nothing to do with class struggles. If ideologists can make such propagandistic nonsense statements, and get away with them for more than a century, one should not expect the expansion of our historical knowledge through science to make a dent in the corrupt existence of the ideological epigone in our own time. (AM, 79–86)

Voegelin's own analysis of his work, of the problems with the old history of ideas, of the new conception informing *Order and History*, and of the shifting of organization and character of that work serves to alert the reader to the fact that the philosopher has continually searched for keys to the subjects he addresses—discarding, recasting, and revising to get it right. He remains his own severest critic—heroically so, when one considers the decision not to publish the "History of Political Ideas." The foregoing summary of those developments may be taken as an introduction to subsequent chapters, which deal in some detail with salient aspects of *Order and History* and other principal writings published since 1952.

III

The first volume of *Order and History* appeared in 1956 to be followed the next year by publication of two more volumes. The projected six-volume work then did not further materialize. Voegelin moved from Baton Rouge in January, 1958, to accept appointment in Munich as professor and director of the new Institute for Political Science, and he remained at the University of Munich until 1969. Despite rumors and expectations, a decade and more passed without further publication of the *magnum opus*. To be sure, important work appeared, especially *Anamnesis* in 1966, and those eighteen-hour work days continued uninterrupted. But seventeen years were to elapse before the fourth volume of *Order and History* would appear in 1974 and a fifth and final volume to be promised. The decision to relocate in Munich was prompted by the opportunity it gave to organize a new program in political science, the increased financial benefits, and the opportunity to associate with such old friends as Alois Dempf, the historian and philosopher, in a congenial intellectual and spiritual environment. "Besides, I had some idea that perhaps a center of political science, carried on in the spirit of American democracy, would be a good thing to have in Germany" (AM, 93).

That the work went on during the eleven Munich years is attested by the publication of some twenty-five essays during the period, in addition to the *Anamnesis* volume. Voegelin energetically carried on the activities of the institute, recruiting assistants, developing a first-rate library and a variegated program of instruction. By the time he left in 1969 the institute's library was the best single collection at the university for the study of the contemporary sciences of man and society. He gave special attention, as might be expected, to the various areas essential for an understanding of Western civilization (Classic philosophy and Christianity); the modern history and modern political thought sources were given priority attention; and the most recent scholarly developments in prehistory, in the ancient civilizations of the Near East, China, India, and in the field of archeology were stressed. It was only for the comparatively brief period in Munich that Voegelin was in an academic position to supervise doctoral students, for Louisiana State University had no Ph.D. program in political science during his sixteen years there. No more than a handful of American students ever completed their doctorates with Voegelin. At Munich, however, the cumulative result was creation of a new force on the German intellectual scene, one little loved by ideologists of the left or the right.

In addition to his writing and his administrative duties, Voegelin regularly taught two lecture courses and a doctoral seminar each term during this period. And he found time to deliver guest lectures at universities and elsewhere on the Continent, in England, and the United States. He participated in a symposium on history with Toynbee at Grinnell College in 1963, taught for one semester as visiting professor at Harvard in 1965, at Notre Dame for a quarter every other year through a number of years, and delivered the Candler Lectures on the "Drama of Man" at Emory University in 1967. Many of his lectures subsequently appeared as articles. His inaugural lecture at Munich, published as *Science, Politics, and Gnosticism* (1959; English, 1968), caused a furor because of his uncompromising analysis of the Marxian "swindle." As he later remarked:

I flatly state that Marx was consciously an intellectual swindler for the purpose of maintaining an ideology that would permit him to support violent action against human beings with a show of moral indignation. I stated the problem explicitly in my inaugural lecture in Munich in 1958 and explored on that occasion the mental disturbance which lies back of such action. Marx, however, is conducting his arguments on a very high intellectual level and the surprise caused by my flat statement that he was engaged in intellectual swindle, with repercussions in the daily press, can easily be explained on the same line as the darkness that surrounds the premises of Hegel [*i.e.*, few people have philosophical knowledge equal to Marx's so as to identify his premises and detect their falsity; alternatively, the insistence of the Marxists (and others) that one can properly understand Marx only if one accepts his premises and does not subject them to criticism—thereby ignoring the fact that if the premises are wrong everything else is wrong, too.] The Marxian swindle concerns the flat refusal to enter into the etiological argument of Aristotle, *i.e.*, on the problem that man does not exist out of himself but out of the divine ground of all reality. Again as distinguished from the contemporaries who pontificate on Marx, Marx himself still had a very good philosophical education. He knew that the problem of etiology in human existence was the central problem of a philosophy of man, and if he wanted to destroy man's humanity by making him a "socialist man" he had to refuse to enter into the etiological problem. On this point he was, one must admit, considerably more honest than Hegel who never quoted the arguments into which he refused to enter. But the effect is the same as in the case of Hegel, because the contemporary critics, of course, know about Aristotle and the etiological argument just as much as about the neo-Platonic background of Hegel, *i.e.*, exactly nothing. The general deculturation of the academic and intellectual world in Western civilization furnishes the background for the social dominance of opinions which still would have been laughed out of court in the late Middle Ages or the Renaissance. (AM, 49)

Further sensation attended Voegelin's two-hour lecture course at Munich on "Hitler and the Germans," given in 1964 to a packed house for a semester. For example, when time came for the role of the churches to be discussed in Hitler's rise to power and subsequent events, the majority of the students (who were Roman Catholic Bavarians) reveled in Voegelin's savage delineation of the Evangelical church's supine complicity in events leading to the Nazi ascendancy and consequent atrocities. But he cautioned the audience from the rostrum to restrain their jubilation: the Catholics' turn would come next week. The Catholic church's turn came, and it fared no better at the professor's hands than had the protestants. The audience sat subdued and stunned as Voegelin drove home through factual account and analysis the nails of condemnation of moral and spiritual dereliction one by one. Although the lectures were taped and transcribed into an extensive manuscript, they have not been published. Voegelin found them too imprecise technically.

It is extremely difficult to engage in a critical discussion of National Socialist ideas, as I found out when I gave my semester course on "Hitler and the Germans" in 1964 in Munich, because in National Socialist . . . documents we are still farther below the level on which rational argument is possible than in the case of Hegel or Marx. In order to deal with language documents of this type one must first develop a philosophy of language, going into the problems of symbolization on the basis of the philosophers' experience of humanity and the perversion of such symbols on the vulgarian level by people who are utterly unable to read a philosopher's work. This level which I characterize as the vulgarian, and as far as it becomes socially relevant as the ochlocratic level, again, is not admissible to the position of a partner in discussion, but can only be an object of scientific research. The vulgarian and ochlocratic problems must not be taken lightly; one cannot simply not take notice of them. They are serious problems of life and death because the vulgarians create and dominate the intellectual climate in which the rise of figures like Hitler to power is possible. . . . They [and the National Socialist atrocities] are possible only when the social environment [especially language] has been so destroyed by the vulgarians that a person who is truly representative of this vulgarian spirit can rise to power. (AM, 50–51)

Upon reaching retirement age at Munich, Voegelin availed himself in 1969 of the opportunity afforded by the Hoover Institution on War, Revolution, and Peace at Stanford University to return to the United States as Henry Salvatori Distinguished Scholar, a title he held until 1974. The position provided leisure to continue his work, including writing, lecturing, and teaching at Stanford and as a visiting professor at Notre Dame, Harvard, the University of Dallas, the University of Texas at Austin, and elsewhere. *The Ecumenic Age* (the fourth volume of *Order and History*) appeared in 1974, as noticed previously, as did several important essays; particularly noteworthy among the essays were "Equivalences of Experience and Symbolization in History" (1970), "The Gospel and Culture" and "On Hegel: A Study in Sorcery" (1971), and "Reason: The Classic Experience" (1974).

Retirement is hardly the right word for Voegelin's status after he left Munich or, even, after formally departing the Hoover Institution. At eighty and residing in Stanford, in good health with undiminished powers, he remains constantly in demand as a lecturer in 1981. He has relaxed neither his work pace nor his long hours. Only the coffee and cigar consumption is down a little now, to perhaps a mere dozen cigars each day from the old rate of three boxes per week. Major work is in various stages of completion: the final, fifth volume of *Order and History*, the Aquinas Lecture of 1975 at Marquette University entitled *The Beginning and the Beyond*, a volume devoted to his study of the symbolisms of prehistory, such major essays as "Wisdom and the Magic of the Extreme: A Meditation" (1981), and the revision of the lecture on philosophical anthropology given in Chicago at the Conference for the Study of Political Thought's symposium on human nature in April, 1978. The work goes on, and it is regularly marked by acuity and fresh horizons.

Voegelin emerges from this biographical sketch a man of vast learning, great intellect, courage, energy, and stamina, one whose subtle humor and imaginative insight enliven the encyclopedic range of his work with the vitality of present truth and the excitement of new vision. Tough-minded, devastating in oral debate and written critique alike, unflinching in exposing fallacies, charlatanism, and murderous intent of ideologues of all stripes, Voegelin is yet both fiercely unsentimental and supremely sensitive to the movement of the spirit in all its guises, to the positive force of reality through whose beneficence man's existence is gently graced with hope, goodness, and a modicum of order. He has mastered life as the practice of dying, and old age finds him serene. This is simply to say that Voegelin is a philosopher and we remain his debtors because he has so loved the divine wisdom. Some of the themes of the loving search of wisdom informing Voegelin's thought will further come to view in the following chapters which address in systematic detail the major structures of his thought. Taken together, they constitute what we here call the Voegelinian revolution.

CHAPTER 4   The Science of History
and Politics: 1952

From around 1930 onward Voegelin showed his
intention to develop a new political science, and we have seen that
he actually began such a project at that early date only to abandon it
because his knowledge of political theory—"ideas"—was still too
imperfect. The development of his thought over the next twenty
years, then, brought him to the "breakthrough" of *The New Science
of Politics* (1952), which set the theme of much subsequent work in
these opening sentences.

The existence of man in political society is historical existence; and a theory
of politics, if it penetrates to principles, must at the same time be a theory of
history. . . . The analysis will . . . proceed to an exploration of the symbols
by which political societies [representatively form themselves as entities
organized for action in historical existence and, also,] interpret themselves
as representatives of a transcendent truth. . . . The manifold of such symbols . . . will not form a flat catalogue but prove amenable to theoretization
as an intelligible succession of phases in a historical process. An inquiry
concerning representation [so conceived], if its theoretical implications are
unfolded consistently, will in fact become a philosophy of history.

To pursue a theoretical problem to the point where the principles of politics meet with the principles of a philosophy of history is not customary
today. Nevertheless, the procedure cannot be considered an innovation in
political science; it will rather appear as a restoration, if it be remembered
that the two fields which today are cultivated separately were inseparably
united when political science was founded by Plato. (NSP, 1; bracketed passages at pp. 36, 47)

The grand design suggested by these lines was given its first incarnation in *The New Science of Politics* and in the first three vol-

umes of *Order and History* to which the former book serves as
something of a prolegomenon. The philosophy of history, thus, appeared at this point in Voegelin's development to be the controlling
level of his inquiry. And it will be the concern of this chapter to
show the main contours of his science of politics and history as first
formulated in 1952. The backdrop for Voegelin's undertaking is illuminated by these remarks from the 1970s.

Philosophy of history as a topic does not go farther back than the eighteenth
century. From its beginning in the eighteenth century, it became associated
with the constructions of an imaginary history made for the purpose of interpreting the constructor and his personal state of alienation as the climax
of all preceding history. Until quite recently philosophy of history has been
definitely associated with the misconstruction of history from a position of
alienation, whether it be in the case of Condorcet, or of Comte, or of Hegel,
or of Marx. This rigid construction of history, as a huge falsification of reality from the position of an alienated existence, is dissolving in the twentieth
century. Once the deformation of existence, which leads to the construction
of ideological systems, is recognized as such, the categories of undeformed
existence and systems must be judged. Hence, the ideological systems
themselves become historical phenomena in a process which reflects,
among other things, the human tension between order and disorder of existence. There are periods of order, followed by periods of disintegration, followed by the misconstruction of reality by disoriented human beings.
Against such disintegration, disorientation, and misconstruction there arise
the countermovements in which the fullness of reality is restored to consciousness. (AM, 106)

As both this passage and that quoted from the beginning of *The New
Science of Politics* suggest, the restoration of political science along
Classical lines lay at the center of Voegelin's effort. This was the
characteristic of his thought previously identified as its studied "unoriginality."[1] Some of the details of the endeavor as it first unfolded
will now be considered more fully.

I

The New Science of Politics is Voegelin's most widely read book. It
has remained on the publisher's list for three decades and through

---

1. "The test of truth, to put it pointedly, will be the lack of originality in the propositions." Voegelin, "Equivalences of Experience," 222.

nearly a dozen reprintings. Its "alarming title" may well be a reason for this success. And it is more surely a reason for various misgivings about Voegelin's political theory. As Sebba phrased the matter: "Calling a book of lectures on Truth and Representation 'The New Science of Politics' was a challenge to the academic bull who promptly and unnecessarily lowered his horns. For The *New* Science is the old science of Aristotle, the sire of all the new sciences. It is not just a science of politics, but science per se: theory dealing with reality."[2]

While these statements are quite accurate, it is also true that the academic bull knew a foe when it saw one. For the old science of Aristotle is not the new science of the new social scientists of this or the past generation. Neither the theory developed by Voegelin in emphatic continuity with the Classical philosophers nor the reality dealt with are commensurate with the conventional understanding of those terms and their referents in current parlance. And to make matters worse, for all of the stress on studied unoriginality, and the conduct of the analysis in accordance with "the Aristotelian procedure" (NSP, 28–31, 34, 52, 80), Voegelin's political science is not vintage fourth century B.C. Hellenic but twentieth century A.D. eclectic. Indeed, for it to be otherwise would make his work an elegant contribution to Classical scholarship (which it is), but not the reconstituted modern science of human affairs that he means it to be. These matters, however, may best be set aside for the moment and reserved for later discussion (pp. 188–216, herein).

The New Science of Politics is divided into three parts: an introduction which waves the red flag before Sebba's academic bull through a noteworthy demolition exercise of explicitly rejecting Positivist social science and affirming the foundations of Classical science; three chapters that develop the theory of representation proper on a broad basis of ancient and medieval source materials; and three final chapters that relate the theory of representation to patterns of modern politics from the Reformation down to the present, with particular attention to Gnosticism's variants and "the antitheoretical derailments" which eventuate in such *mis*representations as the rise of totalitarianism abroad and of sundry activist movements at home (NSP, 79–80, 132, 163–76, and *passim*).

2. Gregor Sebba, "Prelude and Variations on the Theme of Eric Voegelin," *Southern Review*, n.s., XIII (Autumn, 1977), 656.

By his own description of it, Voegelin's purpose is to introduce readers to the "restoration of political science" that began at the turn of the century and has proceeded apace since then. To do so, he devotes the analysis to the "problem of representation" whose exploration affords him the opportunity of synthesizing major facets of the restorative movement and, also, of showing the promise it holds for a revitalized political science. The ultimate task faced, once the ground has been cleared and the pertinent empirical materials assessed, was to find "a theoretically intelligible order of history into which [the] variegated phenomena could be organized" (NSP, 24–26). That intelligible order is here viewed through the prism of representation considered as a complex symbolism.

What is to be studied and *how* is it to be addressed? The answer to the first question is "social reality." But that answer requires clarification. For social reality is not an object in nature to be studied by the theorist merely externally. Rather one finds that social reality is organized into a great multiplicity of concrete human societies in a variety of historical contexts dispersed geographically over the whole globe. Each society, Voegelin suggests, possesses not only externality but also an internal dimension of meaningfulness through which the human beings who inhabit it interpret existence to themselves. Each society is an illuminated "cosmion" or little world to itself; and the self-interpretation of existence through the elaborate symbolisms arising therein comprises the substance of the cosmion as social reality. Moreover, this integral structure of social reality is not experienced merely as an accident or a convenience by the members of the society, but is expressive of "their human essence. And, inversely, the symbols express the experience that man is fully man by virtue of his participation in a whole which transcends his particular existence" (NSP, 27). These symbolisms taken together, Voegelin continues, represent the truth of existence commonly held by the members of the society—the Heraclitean *xynon*, or Aristotelian-Pauline *homonoia* (the common, the likemindedness) that forms the basis of human association. Finally, since man's historical existence exhibits numerous such cosmions, the theorist (as one seeking universal truth) is confronted with the problem of exploring not only these in their monadic isolation from one another, but also of sifting the relationships among the sometimes rival "truths" claimed by each in his search for a truth representative of mankind itself (NSP, 59–60).

The "what" of the study as just described implies the "how" of it as well. For the desire to know the truth of man's existence confronts the theorist with a field of inquiry which, so far from being a *tabula rasa* waiting to be sumptuously served the splendid fare of philosopher's culinary art, is already preempted by the elaborate symbolisms of rite, myth, religion, and even theory itself. The aggregate tends to form a solid amalgam of self-interpretive meaning, the society's orthodoxy of belief touching on the major issues of existence, including ultimate ones. Men have not waited for philosophers and scientists to explain their existences for them! The sensible thing to do in these circumstances, then, may be to do as Aristotle did. Begin from the commonly received opinions about each topic of political inquiry and, through a process of "critical clarification," try to ascertain the truth of the matter. This is the course Voegelin recommends and follows. Thus he writes:

When Aristotle wrote his *Ethics* and *Politics*, when he constructed his concepts of the polis, of the constitution, the citizen, the various forms of government, of justice, of happiness, etc., he did not invent these terms and endow them with arbitrary meanings; he took rather the symbols which he found in his social environment, surveyed with care the variety of meanings which they had in common parlance, and ordered and clarified these meanings by the criteria of his theory. (NSP, 28)[3]

II

The realm of social reality explored, then, is the self-interpretations of societies as these are expressed in common parlance. The method of investigation generally will be the Aristotelian procedure of critically clarifying the meaning of the various topics of interest, beginning from the opinions commonly held or argued with some cogency, whether popular or philosophical. Although the societies' self-interpretations of man's existence are not the last word, they do compose the *empirical* basis of the critical science of human affairs, Voegelin argues. The insights into reality they contain are of highest

3. Citing Aristotle, *Politics* 1280A7ff. For the *methodos* in Aristotle, see also the excellent illustration in *Nicomachean Ethics* 1145B3–1146B8.

importance. As Aristotle, for example, wrote near the beginning of the *Ethics* with respect to the meaning of the key symbol *happiness*:

Some people think that happiness is a virtue, others that it is practical wisdom, others that it is some kind of theoretical wisdom; others again believe it to be all or some of these accompanied by, or not devoid of, pleasure; and some people also include external prosperity in the definition. Some of these views are expressed by many people and have come down from antiquity, some by a few men of high prestige, and it is not reasonable to assume that both groups are altogether wrong; the presumption is rather that they are right in at least one or even in most respects.[4]

For Voegelin's purposes (and ours here), the attitude reflected in this passage is of significance for more than one reason. Foremost, it shows deference to the historical materials as the empirical basis of the philosophical scientist's endeavors. Secondly, it suggests the movement of critical clarification to run from the uncertainty of opinions (*doxai*) held by a variety of people toward the greater certainty of the scientific knowledge (*episteme*) arrived at by the philosopher who critically weighs truth and falsity according to the standards of the philosopher's own right reason. Thirdly, this attitude implies an openness to the whole horizon of experience-symbolization, whatever the sources: all of the pertinent evidence deserves consideration in arriving at an impartial judgment. Fourthly, it suggests a complication, for the clean dichotomy of "two sets of symbols" faced by the theorist, "the language symbols that are produced as an integral part of the social cosmion in the process of its self-illumination and the language symbols of political science" (NSP, 28), turns out to be not so clean after all. In addition to the traditional and popular opinions alluded to in the passage from the *Ethics*, for example, Aristotle also has identified the viewpoints of a number of philosopher-scientists, among them Antisthenes, the Cynics (and, later on, the Stoics), Socrates, Anaxagoras, Plato (*Philebus* 27D, 60D–E, 63E), and Plato's pupil Xenocrates.[5]

The complication noted does not negate the distinction Voegelin draws between the two sets of symbols, but it does ultimately require him to qualify it: "theorists and saints," too, contribute to so-

4. Aristotle, *Nicomachean Ethics* 1098B23–29, trans. Martin Ostwald (Indianapolis & New York: Bobbs-Merrill, Library of Liberal Arts, 1962), 19–20.
5. Cf. *ibid.*, 20n.

ciety's self-interpretation (NSP, 80). At the same time the blurred distinction underlines and clarifies something fundamental to the character of the new science itself. For the social reality explored by the theorist is the *participatory reality* of Everyman. Hence, the "objectivity" or cognitive validity of the science of man does *not* arise from some mysterious ability of the investigator to abstract himself from reality, to view it impartially from "an Archimedean point" beyond it or outside of it as a dispassionate subject of cognition. Rather, it arises through the work of critical clarification of the kind previously illustrated by Aristotle's *methodos*: in a movement from opinion to knowledge, one conducted from the perspective of a participant who self-reflectively explores the order and disorder of the common reality of which he and all men are consciously parts. If the method is adequate, it follows a path that brings "to essential clarity the dimly seen" to yield objective knowledge (NSP, 5).

As Voegelin even more forcefully stresses in later phases of his work, man's existence is emphatically participatory; and his knowledge of human reality is ineluctably bound to that perspective. The self-interpretation of reality is a principle basic to science as he pursues it, as previously noticed. This is not merely because societies provide such symbolisms as the stuff of their reality and, hence, as the raw material investigated by the scientist. It is also because the prophets' and saints' and philosophers' own self-interpretations of reality experienced-symbolized themselves supply the only available criteria whereby truth and falsity, science and opinion, can be discriminated.

Thus, we find the two sets of symbols, distinguishable yet intermingling, not only in the *Ethics* but also in *The New Science of Politics*. On the one hand, for example, "imperial truth" can be challenged by "theoretical truth" (NSP, 60) when a philosophizing man pits his own interpretation of the truth of reality against the conventional truth of an empire. The results of this are momentous, for as Voegelin notes, "with our questioning *we* have set up *ourselves* as the representatives of the truth in whose name we are questioning" (NSP, 59–60, emphasis added). An adversarial relationship tends to lie between the society and the philosopher as its critic. This tensional relationship is productive of the two sets of symbolisms Voegelin identifies. These are, in principle, familiar to readers of Plato

[handwritten margin note:] 2 sets of symbols: theory vs. empire

and Aristotle from the debate over truth in terms of *physis* and *nomos*, nature and convention,[6] and in terms of the rival claims to authority of the sophists' socially dominant opinion and the philosophers' truth with its assertion of superior authority as science.[7] The basis of the philosophers' claim, of crucial importance, must concern us in later pages. For the moment it is enough to stress the adversarial relationship which, especially in times of social disintegration, compels the philosopher "to pit his authority against the authority of society" (NSP, 66).

On the other hand, however, the philosophers' truth, even in the instances of Plato and Aristotle, is so indebted to the common experience of their society that they "could hardly have accomplished their theoretical generalization without the preceding concrete practice of Athenian politics" (NSP, 70–71). Their work marked the end of a long history, not merely in the development of Greek speculation, but of those decisive political and social events of a more pragmatic kind climaxing in the golden hour in history marked by the victory at Marathon (490 B.C.) and the establishment of Aeschylean tragedy. Why were these events of such importance? Because then actually occurred "the miracle of a generation which individually experienced the responsibility of representing the truth of the soul and expressed this experience through the tragedy as a public cult" (NSP, 71). In other words, the philosophers' truth was then compactly prefigured in society's truth. The Hellenic culmination of philosophy in the work of Socrates, Plato, and Aristotle is thereby seen to be: (1) the theoretical elaboration of the truth of reality concretely approximated and exemplified in praxis in the first half of the fifth century B.C. by the Athenians; and (2) an effort pragmatically calculated as a cogent appeal to restore the order subsequently lost from the public sphere and its institutional life. The palpably reformist intent of Socrates and Plato had its persuasive as well as its em-

---

6. For example, see Plato, *Republic*, Bk. II; Aristotle, *Nicomachean Ethics*, Bk. I, Chap. 3. A useful discussion of the issues is given in the introduction to *Aristotle's Constitution of Athens and Related Texts*, trans. and intro. by Kurt von Fritz and Ernst Kapp (New York: Hafner Publishing Co., 1950), 32–54. "It is true that [Aristotle] uses 'nature' in *almost* exactly the same way as Plato used the idea [*idea, eidos*] of the just and the good," Fritz and Kapp, *Aristotle's Constitution*, 40. Emphasis as in the original.

7. *E.g.*, Plato, *Republic* 476A–480A.

pirical basis in an appeal to the historical memory of their fellow Athenians. Even after their pragmatic efforts were spent, and philosophy retreated to the later Academy and to Aristotle's Lyceum, then to become a concern of the schools, the insights of philosophers and saints penetrated the self-interpretive symbolisms of empires from Alexander onward and ultimately of the nations, with varying degrees of effectiveness. Hence, the socially effective carriers of the truth of reality are not to be exclusively numbered among the philosophers and their followers. They also include political vessels and institutional configurations ranging from the medieval Church and empire to the contemporary "American and English democracies which most solidly in their institutions represent the truth of the soul [and which] are, at the same time, existentially the strongest powers" (NSP, 189).

III

Several features of the theory of representation developed by Voegelin have been glimpsed in the foregoing pages. For present purposes the theory may be summarized as follows. It is mainly concerned with identifying and analyzing the modes of ordering truth which have emerged in history clad in the mantle of authority, whether of a society or of a paradigmatic figure such as a prophet or philosopher. We have seen that such ordering truth arises willy-nilly in a society as the self-interpretation of reality. It finds expression in elaborate symbolisms, communicating the fundamental consensus of the society and shaping the fabric of its institutional life and the personal and public lives of its people. It forms the belief structure which is the distinctive foundation of association in society; and it also shapes the essential humanity of the individual members of the society by supplying meaning in their existence as participants in a reality which they experience as transcending merely private existence. Such ordering truth, then, has the status of *existential* representation, in that it articulates in an authoritative way the meaning of human existence in society and history. We have also seen that the appearance of such commanding personalities as the prophets of Israel and the philosophers of Hellas carries important consequences. The differentiated insight into the order of reality therewith gained creates a critical tension of new truth at odds with the societies' self-interpretations. Such theoretically superior truth may, in varying degrees, be assimilated into the societies' self-interpretations as dimensions of them, or it may be rejected and the bearers destroyed. In either case, the now-familiar two sets of symbolisms through which human existence is represented result. These coexist and overlap because of the common participatory existences of prophets and philosophers as human beings who also happen to share membership with other men who populate their respective societies. The coexistence of rival truths within society tends to produce a critical dialogue—one that is sometimes amicable, sometimes hostile to the point of becoming murderous—between differentiated and conventional truths. A result of this perennial tension as it uniquely forms in the horizon of Ancient Greece is the emergence of philosophy, with political science as a division.

Voegelin himself, of course, does not arrive at the station of the analysis just summarized by quite the same route we have followed. Rather, he pursues the topic of representation from its use in common parlance to its technical meanings. He begins with the ordinary meaning of representation in public discourse, in the sense of Western representative systems as an appurtenance of modern democratic governments with their electoral machinery and all the rest. This he terms _conventional_ representation. He then considers the more generic meaning of representation, so as to account for the fact that the Soviet government, for example, though not democratic does after all act for or represent the Russian people. This is a more inclusive category, which Voegelin calls _elemental_ representation. In other words, regardless of _how_ legitimate rule is established and maintained in history, those who as "the political and intellectual ruling minorities of a society" externally act for the society and its population as its ruling elites serve as their representatives in the "theoretically _elemental_" sense (NSP, 31, 32, 50, emphasis added).[8] Elemental representation as a descriptive term is wide enough to include (whatever their differences) the _externals_ of both Western democracies and their representative systems and the Soviet Union whose government "represents the Soviet society as a political so-

[handwritten margin note: types of representation in ordinary discourse]

8. Cf. the discussion in Hanna F. Pitkin, _The Concept of Representation_ (Berkeley: University of California Press, 1967), 44–59.

ciety in form for action in history." It brings into view "the clearly distinguishable power units in history" (NSP, 36). And since its meaning includes the ability of governors to organize the society for action in history, elemental representation also covers the requirement that political societies possess an *internal* structure that permits some of its members to serve as rulers. Such sovereigns and magistrates qualify as representative by finding ready obedience to their acts of command, to the end of securing the safety of the society from external dangers and of maintaining peace and justice for the citizenry. The criterion of such representation, then, is "effective imputation" (NSP, 37).

A more searching exploration of representation is demanded at this juncture, one that leads to the theoretical insights previously noticed in the discussion of *existential* representation. Behind the equipage of elemental representation lies the understanding that existence itself is at stake in terms of the society's safety, the preservation of peace, and the administration of justice. Not only procedures, but the substance of representation are at issue. The matter of substance raises the existential question of just *what* is represented? The people? The permanent revolution of the proletariat? Such brief responses point up the fact that societies organized for action as power units do not exist as fixed phenomena of nature, but emerge in history through a complex process of social and political *articulation*, the rudimentary result of which is constitution of the ruling power of the society. In Anglo-American history, for example, the process of articulation occurs over the three centuries following the *Magna Carta* (1215 A.D.) through a succession of phases beginning from the representation of the people in "the common council of our realm" with the realm itself possessively represented by the king; to a second phase of composite representation when the shires, boroughs, cities, and principal nobility organized as the *baronagium* form communes for representing themselves for action; to the rise of Parliament where the lesser communes organize into a higher one as the two houses representative of the realm as a whole, in competition with the king as representative of the realm; to the sixteenth century "melting of this representative hierarchy into one single representative, the king in Parliament." One "body politic" now emerges in the Tudor period, symbolized as having its head in the king, its members in Parliament, "the royal estate being enhanced by its participation in parliamentary representation, the Parliament by its participation in the majesty of royal representation" (NSP, 38–40).

The direction of the process of articulation just summarized and illustrated points toward its dialectical limit. This is reached when the membership of the society (and people) becomes politically articulate down to the last individual as the representable unit. It is the optimal symbolization of this insight, Voegelin suggests, that is the secret of the marvelous effectiveness of Lincoln's famous formula "government of the people, by the people, for the people." What is to be represented in the fully articulated institutional order of Anglo-American society is the substance of human existence itself that is politically vested in every man. To put it more generally: the public order of a society as institutionalized, if it is to be optimally satisfactory as a habitat for men, must truly represent the order of human existence as participated in by every human being. And it is Voegelin's argument that this is the concrete historical tendency displayed in the Greco-Roman and Western civilizations,— and only there—as just illustrated from the evolution of English and American symbolisms toward that theoretical limit (NSP, 50).

IV

To so identify the embodiment of the reality of the truth of the soul in political existence as the substance of historical process clearly echoes Plato and Aristotle. The understanding that existential representation as found in the concrete historical development of Greek, Roman, and Western civilizations in some degree achieves such an embodiment composes the central thread of Voegelin's philosophy of history and politics as here unfolded. A number of issues now arise which require brief clarification, if the cogency of the argument is to be appreciated.

To begin with, we may be reminded that the truth of existence represented in political reality assimilates, in varying ways and however imperfectly, the truth of existence attained by prophets, saints,

and philosophers. The society's truth, therefore, is not narrowly parochial, but represents a core of universally valid truth. This universal dimension of society's truth is itself, however, not a Western pe-
culiarity, as was poignantly attested, for example, by the collision of
the Western empire's Christian truth as asserted by Pope Innocent
IV with the expansive Mongol empire's truth of the Order of God as
asserted by the Kuyuk Khan in the thirteenth century (NSP, 56–59).
Moreover, by the claim made to universal validity, it is clear that in
its self-interpretation the "society itself becomes the representative
of something beyond itself, of a transcendent reality" (NSP, 54). So,
in addition to the previously identified types of representation (conventional, elemental, and existential), there must now be added a
further dimension of representation, namely, "a concept of _transcen-
dental_ representation" (NSP, 76, emphasis added). Voegelin explains
the point as follows: "As a matter of fact, this relation is to be found
as far back as the recorded history of major political societies beyond
the tribal level goes. All the early empires, Near Eastern as well as
Far Eastern, understood themselves as representatives of a transcendent order, of the order of the cosmos; and some of them even understood this order as a 'truth'" (NSP, 54).

The discovery of transcendental truth is the achievement of the
spiritually gifted men who throughout history have linked human
existence with the ultimate ground of reality. As priests, prophets,
philosophers, and saints, their insights have pluralistically formed
the substance of human existence as it unfolded historically. These
individual achievements influence the orthodoxies of societies by
endowing social reality with meaning that is representative for all
members of a concrete society. The transcendental dimension of
meaning, then, relates a society's truth to the truth of universal
mankind. Insights into reality of this class arise out of a particular
range of experiences as symbolized in the forms of myth, philosophy, and history. The experiences and symbolizations develop historically so that different types of truth can be identified; and the
truths themselves show a directional movement from the more
compact truth of the early empires toward the differentiated truth
preeminently attained in Christian revelation and medieval philosophy. Voegelin summarizes by sketching a typology of truth as
follows:

Terminologically, it will be necessary to distinguish between three types of truth. The first of these types is the truth represented by the early empires; it shall be designated as "cosmological truth." The second type of truth appears in the political culture of Athens and specifically in tragedy; it shall be called "anthropological truth"—with the understanding that the term covers the whole range of problems connected with the psyche as the sensorium of transcendence. The third type of truth that appears with Christianity shall be called "soteriological truth." (NSP, 76)

In the cosmological phase, human order, in imperial societies such as Egypt or Persia, is interpreted as an analogue of the overarching cosmic order it represents and reflects; rulership is preeminently the task of securing the social order in harmony with the cosmic order. "The term 'cosmion,' thus, gains a new component of meaning as the representative of the cosmos" (NSP, 54). The break with the cosmological style of truth constitutes an epoch in human history, as dramatically suggested by Karl Jaspers' term "Axis-time of human history" and by Henri Bergson's contrast of "closed" and "open" societies. For in the period between 800 and 200 B.C., to follow Jaspers, there simultaneously occurs, as a worldwide phenomenon, the "outbreak of truth of mystic philosophers and prophets," especially concentrated around 500 B.C. "when Heraclitus, the Buddha, and Confucius were contemporaries" (NSP, 60).

cosmological truth [margin annotation]

By concentrating on the philosophers, Voegelin shows how the rise of Classical philosophy out of the noetic experience of Hellenic thinkers created the new interpretation of reality in terms of the well-ordered soul. The creed of the new epoch is Plato's "anthropological principle," summarily stated in the *Republic* (368C–D) in the phrase that "a polis is man written large." Political society is no longer merely a microcosm, although it remains that; it is reinterpreted as also a macroanthropos. By this interpretation, the true order of society depends upon the true order of man; the true order of man, in turn, depends upon the constitution of the soul; and the constitution of the soul, its order and disorder, comes to view through the experiences symbolized in the course of a sensitive man's loving search of reality for the divine Wisdom—through philosophy in the literal sense.[9] Since, then, what is decisive is that "God is the Measure" (in opposition to Protagoras' "Man is the Mea-

anthropological truth [margin annotation]

9. E.g., *Symposium* 204A.

sure"), the anthropological principle was supplemented by Plato with the "theological principle." He coined the term *theology* so as to classify the "types of theology" as a prophylaxis against misconceiving truth, or being ignorant, about highest reality—a disease of the soul he called *alethes pseudos*, the "arch-lie" (NSP, 66–70).[10]

Soteriological truth, finally, emerges through the enlargement of the Platonic-Aristotelian range of experiences in a central aspect. That enlargement is illustrated by the contrast between Aristotle's *philia* and Thomas' *amicitia*. The former is possible only between equals, and this bars friendship between men and God, so that the philosopher's love of the divine is a reaching out that is not reciprocated; and this lack of mutuality is characteristic of the whole of anthropological truth.

[handwritten margin note: Soteriological truth]

> The Christian bending of God in grace toward the soul does not come within the range of these experiences—though, to be sure, in reading Plato one has the feeling of moving continuously on the verge of a breakthrough into this new dimension. The experience of mutuality in the relation with God, of *amicitia* in the Thomistic sense, of the grace which imposes a supernatural form on the nature of man, is the specific difference of Christian truth. The revelation of this grace in history, through the incarnation of the *Logos* in Christ, intelligibly fulfilled the adventitious movement of the spirit in the mystic philosophers. The critical authority over the older truth of society which the soul had gained through its opening and its orientation toward the unseen measure [*i.e.*, in Plato] was now confirmed through the revelation of the measure itself. (NSP, 78).[11]

V

The foregoing discussion leads to a clarification of the fundamental assumption about history and the consequences for the theory of human existence. Fulfillment of the Hellenic philosophers' experi-

10. Plato, *Laws* 716C; Plato, *Republic* 379A–382B.
11. Aristotle, *Nicomachean Ethics* 1158–1178; Thomas Aquinas, *Contra Gentiles*, iii, 91. This contrast between the Classical and Christian truth and the attendant terminology were subsequently dropped by Voegelin, it should be noted. Cf. *Order and History*, III, 254–55; see also his "The Gospel and Culture," in D. Miller and D. G. Hadidian (eds.), *Jesus and Man's Hope* (2 vols., Pittsburgh: Pittsburgh Theological Seminary Press, 1971), esp. II, 71–75: "Plato was just as conscious of the revelatory component in the truth of his *logos* as prophets of Israel or the authors of the New Testament writings. The differences between prophecy, Classic philosophy, and the Gospel must be sought in the degrees of differentiation of existential truth" (p. 75).

ences of reality in Christianity implies that the "substance of history consists in the experiences in which man gains the understanding of his humanity and together with it the understanding of its limits." Man the rational contemplator and master of a nature now purged of its demonic terrors, grand as he is, has a limit placed on his grandeur. That limit is concentrated by Christianity in the danger of a fall from the spirit, bestowed by divine grace, into the demonic nothingness of man's mere humanity and the autonomy of the self—symbolized by Augustine as the lapse from the *amor Dei* into the *amor sui*. The principle basic to the theory of human existence in society that follows from this assumption, is this: "A theory . . . must operate within the medium of experiences which have differentiated historically." This means there is a strict correlation between theory and the self-understanding gained through the historical differentiation of experiences. The theorist can neither ignore a part of the historical experiences nor place himself at some imaginary point outside of them. In this sense, theory is "bound" by history considered as essentially composed of the differentiating experiences.

Since the maximum of differentiation was achieved through Greek philosophy and Christianity, this means concretely that theory is bound to move within the historical horizon of Classic and Christian experiences. To recede from the maximum of differentiation is theoretical retrogression; it will result in the various types of derailment which Plato has characterized as *doxa*. Whenever in modern intellectual history a revolt against the maximum of differentiation was undertaken systematically, the result was the fall into anti-Christian nihilism, into the idea of the superman in one or the other of its variants—be it the progressive superman of Condorcet, the positivistic superman of Comte, the materialistic superman of Marx, or the Dionysiac superman of Nietzsche. (NSP, 78–80)

These pivotal formulations provide the foundation for everything that follows in Voegelin's science of politics. On the one hand, they permit the analytical application of Plato's symbolism of types of theology, as augmented by Varro's concept of civil theology, to the struggle for truth in the Roman Empire and to the renewal of that struggle in the medieval empire down to the triumph of the Augustinian solution. On the other hand, they open the way for the analysis of the break with Christian truth and the rise of modern Gnosticism which first crystallized in the twelfth-century trinitarian speculation on history by Joachim of Flora and reaches into the present politics of contending ideologies. The details of this elaborate study of two millennia of Western history cannot be recounted here. It is the main thrust of the argument to which we must be attentive. And that thrust is to show that a major consequence of the triumph of Christian truth in the West was to effect a revolution. In the present context, the revolutionary substance of Christianity consisted in "its uncompromising, radical de-divinization of the world." This not only spelled the end of paganism, it meant that the spiritual destiny of man could no longer be represented on earth by the power sphere of political society at all (as it had been in the philosophers' paradigmatic polis) but could only be represented by the Church. Life in the world became temporal, the sphere of power de-divinized, and the dual representation of empire and Church as formulated in Gelasius' doctrine of Two Swords endured to the end of the Middle Ages (NSP, 100, 159).

In a world free of the gods, the destiny of man emphatically lay in the transcendental beyond of time and the world. Augustine's authoritative exposition of the faith portrayed the rise and fall of earthly powers as essentially meaningless, the final age of the world being a waiting for the end of an age that grows old, a *saeculum senescens*. The eschatological symbolisms conferring meaning on human existence applied to spiritual destiny and to it alone, so that the life of man was interpreted as a pilgrimage whose fulfillment came only in the eternal beyond of salvation through Christ. Literal belief in the millennium was dismissed as a ridiculous fable: the thousand-year realm in the sense of Revelation 20:2 was understood to be the present earthly reign of Christ in his Church, which would endure to the "Last Judgment and the advent of the eternal realm in the beyond" (NSP, 109, 118). In this waiting for the end, Western society was existentially and transcendentally represented by the temporal and spiritual orders, by emperor and pope, empire and Church.

The specifically modern problems of representation arose in this horizon and did so through a resurgence of the eschatological and apocalyptical speculation that had remained subdued, if not entirely dormant, so long as the institutionalization of the medieval *Christianitas* held and the Augustinian interpretation prevailed. And just here it is important to stress the intricacy of the theory of politics and history developed by Voegelin through the analysis of "modernity." The breakup of the medieval *Christianitas*, as manifested in the rise of a multiplicity of nations out of the ruins of the Western empire and of a multiplicity of churches in the period of the Reformation, resulted from institutional and experiential changes that signaled a wholesale rearticulation of Western political existence. The self-interpretive thrust of these changes was to heighten the meaning of mundane existence by endowing it with a sense of ultimacy that contradicted the meaninglessness and triviality accorded temporal affairs in Augustine's interpretation. The experiential tenor of the shift was a reversal of the de-divinization of existence by a re-divinization of the realm of power as the preeminent mode of human action. The disintegration of the medieval synthesis of spirit and power was, at the same time, a surge of civilizational expansiveness and vigor in all departments of secular life. And the life of faith itself was afflicted by the lacerating contentions of the faithful in waves of relentless persecution and religious wars when faith turned pawn in a maelstrom of ubiquitous power politics (NSP, 107–89).

Modernity

The symbolisms for the modern interpretation of Western existence under these stresses had appeared already in the twelfth century in the work of a leading churchman, the abbot Joachim of Flora (d. 1202). In a speculative reinterpretation of history that broke with the Augustinian pattern, Joachim divided mankind's existence on earth into the three ages of Father, Son, and Holy Spirit, each expressing a progress in spiritual development and climaxing in the third age which would see final perfection through a free outpouring of divine grace on all men with the descent of the Holy Spirit. The trinitarian speculation arose from Joachim's meditation on Revelation and the meaning of John's apocalypse of the end of history. History itself, by this account, became the arena of human fulfillment; each of the three ages was articulated by the appearance of a trinity of two forerunners or prophets followed by a leader. Abraham and Christ as leaders of the first two ages were now to be superseded in the year 1260 (cf. Revelation 11:3) by the appearance of the *Dux e Babylone* of the final age, of whom Joachim himself was the prophet, the brotherhood of autonomous persons climaxing history. The perfect final age as originally conceived was concretely an order of monks;

but "the idea of a community of the spiritually perfect who can live together without institutional authority was formulated on principle" (NSP, 113). The aggregate of four symbolisms—History itself as a sequence of three ages moving toward intelligible fulfillment; the Leader who introduces each age; the Prophet (in later secular versions, the Intellectual); and the Third Realm of perfection—governs "the self-interpretation of modern political society to this day" (NSP, 111).

revival of Gnosticism in modernity

From the perspective of the theorist's critical clarification of the Joachitic symbolisms and their mutations in ideologies of subsequent centuries, the self-interpretation is analyzed as a revival of Gnosticism in the peculiarly modern form of a speculation on history. Gnosis as a largely "underground" movement accompanied Christianity from its beginnings, and the Joachitic speculation's long prehistory reaches back to the ninth-century thinker Scotus Eriugena who translated the writings of Dionysius Areopagita, and to the trinitarian speculation of Montanus in the second century (NSP, 118–28, 139–40).[12] By regarding the Holy Trinity of the Christian faith as a kind of cryptogram secretly disclosing the structure and meaning of history, Joachim proclaims the knowledge of the coming millennium immanent to the historical process. The speculative Gnosis, then, has the decisive result of re-divinizing the world of man by drawing the divine essence into its fully unfolded meaning. The transcendental destiny of man of traditional eschatology is eclipsed through an immanentization of Christian faith symbolisms which had viewed man's worldly existence as a pilgrimage toward beatitude, union with God in the beyond of eternity. In this immanentization of the Christian eschaton, three principal variants are possible. If the accent falls on the teleological component of the pilgrimage as a movement toward some indefinite future state of perfection, then progressivism results—as in Denis Diderot and Jean Le Rond d'Alembert. If the accent falls on the axiological component of perfection itself, without clarity about the means of achieving that highest state, then utopianism results—as in Thomas More and recent social idealisms. If both the movement toward

12. Cf. Ellis Sandoz, *Political Apocalypse: A Study of Dostoevsky's Grand Inquisitor* (Baton Rouge: Louisiana State University Press, 1971), 141–43.

fulfillment and the goal itself are clearly known or envisaged, then revolutionary activism results—as in Marx and communism. In any case Gnosticism's proclamation of the meaning of history is purchased at the price of a twofold theoretical fallacy. On the one hand, it commits the mistake of immanentizing the Christian eschaton, *i.e.*, of treating faith symbols as though they represented immanent reality rather than the transcendental reality of man's supernatural destiny. On the other hand, it assumes that history possesses a knowable essence and proclaims its meaning; but this is an impossibility, since the course of history extends not only from the past into the present but also into an unknown future. Hence, it cannot be experienced as a whole and is essentially unknowable. Since these are elementary considerations, how is the diagnosis cogent that "the essence of modernity [is] the growth of Gnosticism" (NSP, 119–21, 126)? A part of the answer is that with the fall from faith, which broadly characterizes the modern era, an experiential alternative was demanded that lay close enough to faith to substitute for it. Modern Gnosticism as just sketched filled that need. It promised what Christianity did not: assured deliverance from the misery of the world through perfection of existence in time, *i.e.*, by the transfiguration of the world and man through the apocalypse of the superman.

Gnostic speculation overcame the uncertainty of faith by receding from transcendence and endowing man and his intramundane range of action with the meaning of eschatological fulfillment. In the measure in which this immanentization progressed experientially, civilizational activity became a mystical work of self-salvation. The spiritual strength of the soul which in Christianity was devoted to the sanctification of life could now be diverted into the more appealing, more tangible, and, above all, so much easier creation of the terrestrial paradise. (NSP, 124, 129)

VI

The Gnostic eschatology of the Third Realm and the transfiguration of man into superman decisively affects modern politics both pragmatically and theoretically—in the struggle for power and in the struggle for existential representation against Gnostic misrepresentation. Immanentization of the Classic and Christian symbolisms by Joachim and his successors gives way in the nineteenth century

to Feuerbach's, Marx's, Comte's, and Nietzsche's radical secularization of truth. The specifically "modern" strand of contemporary politics is identified with the Gnostic varieties of dogmatic belief that
form a spectrum of dynamically interrelated doctrines ranging from
progressivism and idealism on the right to revolutionary activism
on the left. Expressive of the dominant civil theology of modern society, the Gnostic end form is the twentieth-century totalitarian
state as exemplified in the patent banality and brutality of National
Socialist Germany and Communist Russia (NSP, 132, 163, 175, 178).
Moreover, the pragmatic confrontation of the Western liberal powers
and the totalitarian states since the 1930s should not obscure the
ideological kinship between the rival systems. Voegelin stresses the
point, for instance, in discussing Harold Laski's position, which he
derides as "expert surf-riding on the wave of the future."

[But] one should not deny the immanent consistency and honesty of [Laski's
sympathetic perception of the] transition from liberalism to communism; if
liberalism is understood as the immanent salvation of man and society,
communism certainly is its most radical expression; it is an evolution that
was already anticipated by John Stuart Mill's faith in the ultimate advent of
communism for mankind. (NSP, 175)

The celebrated theory that Gnosticism is the essence of modernity is a cardinal feature of Voegelin's philosophy of politics and history. But it is not the whole of it. This is clear, as we have seen, from
the context of the analysis, which is a general theory of representation. Nor is Gnosticism the whole of modernity. As Voegelin forcefully writes, "it must never be forgotten that Western Society is not
all modern but that modernity is a growth within it, in opposition to
the Classic and Christian tradition" (NSP, 176, 165, 187–88). Indeed, if this were not so, then the swing to the left, implicit in the
logic of immanentization, would long ago have led to the triumph of
radical revolution and the establishment of Gnostic dream worlds
by Western totalitarian states. But this has not happened. And apart
from the ephemeral success of national socialism in establishing for
twelve years the thousand year *Dritte Reich*, radical revolution has
succeeded primarily in non-Western societies that do not enjoy the
restraining influence of a Classic and Christian tradition, the consequence of Westernization. On the other hand, while Gnosticism re-

mains a central component in the theory of modernity, and Voegelin has repeatedly returned to its elucidation, other relevant factors have been stressed in subsequent studies as his research continued. Thus in 1958 his inaugural lecture at the University of Munich was devoted to the Gnosticism of Hegel, Marx, Nietzsche, and Heidegger in an extension of the argument presented in *The New Science of Politics*. In 1968 he could "find nothing to retract or correct [in that account], though a good deal would have to be added after the lapse of a decade, especially with regard to the problem of alienation."[13] In reflecting on the issues in 1975, with particular reference to Hegel's pivotal role in the deformation of modern consciousness, Voegelin provided this summary listing of relevant factors: "The contemporary disorder will appear in a rather new light when we leave the 'climate of opinion' and, adopting the perspective of the historical sciences, acknowledge the problems of 'modernity' to be caused by the predominance of Gnostic, Hermetic, and Alchemistic conceits, as well as by the Magic of violence as the means of transforming reality."[14]

VII

In conclusion, then, what of Voegelin's philosophy of history, the "theoretically intelligible order of history into which [the] variegated phenomena [can] be organized"? To begin with, although meaning *in* history can be discerned in finite lines of development,

13. The Munich lecture appeared as Voegelin, *Wissenschaft, Politik, und Gnosis* (Munich: Koesel-Verlag, 1959); the quotation is from the preface to the American edition, *Science, Politics, and Gnosticism* (Chicago: Henry Regnery, 1968), vii.

14. Eric Voegelin, "Response to Professor Altizer's 'A New History and a New but Ancient God?'" (1975), 769. Of value for further study of modernity in Voegelin are, especially, "On Hegel: A Study in Sorcery" (1971); *Order and History*, IV, 18–27 and *passim*; "Wisdom and the Magic of the Extreme: A Meditation," *Southern Review*, n.s., XVII, 2, pp. 235–87. See also the discussion of magic in *The New Science of Politics*, 169–73. The chapters devoted to Marx in Eric Voegelin, *From Enlightenment to Revolution*, edited by John H. Hallowell (Durham, N.C.: Duke University Press, 1975), 240–302, may usefully be consulted; this volume is cited textually herein as ER. Finally, an extensive exploration of the problems of modernity along lines posed in Voegelin's work is conducted by David J. Walsh, "The Esoteric Origins of Ideological Thought: Boehme and Hegel" (Ph.D. dissertation, University of Virginia, 1978).

the meaning *of* history in its entirety remains shrouded in mystery. To hold otherwise would be to commit the twofold fallacy of the Gnostic speculators' declarations of the end of history. Or, alternatively, it would be to repeat the mistake exemplified in Thomas Hobbes's valiant but defective resistance to Gnosticism by attempting to secure existence by "freezing history" (NSP, 161). In a closed order like Leviathan's, the Augustinian psychology of orientation is replaced by a new mechanistic psychology of motivations. The *libido dominandi*, then, is posited as the root of normal human action, community is achieved through the fear of violent death, the pneumopathology of Gnostic enthusiasm is curbed through a ruthless repression of the life of the spirit in principle, including its pursuit in philosophy and Christianity (NSP, 169, 179–82). But neither the Gnostic dogma of immanent transfiguration nor the Hobbesian counterposition to it is theoretically tenable, if the insight is taken to heart that the theory of human existence "is bound by history in the sense of the differentiating experiences" (NSP, 79). According to this principle, as we have seen, the substance of history is understood as a movement from the compact truth of the cosmological type to the differentiated truth of the anthropological and soteriological types. And we have also seen that the aim of Gnostic activism is the transfiguration of man into superman. But the differentiated awareness of man's humanity and his communion with God in loving reciprocity carries with it, also, a heightened sense of human limits. Under the terms of the mystery of participatory existence in the In-Between of time and eternity, man is forever man, God is God. The driving force of Gnostic revolution to break this ontological limit upon the human condition by effecting a change in human nature faces an impossibility: "human nature does not change"— neither into Joachim's autonomous person, nor the Puritans' Godded man, nor Nietzsche's *Uebermensch*, nor the Nazis' master race (NSP, 152, 165).

With the evolution of Gnosticism into the radically secularist ideologies of the nineteenth and twentieth centuries in the wake of Hegel's proclamation that "God is dead," Hobbes's counterposition to Puritan zealots of his time through Leviathan and the freezing of history merged into the eschatology of the Third Realm, to blend with Joachism. From the first, of course, Hobbes's solution palpably broke with the Classic and Christian interpretation of reality to partake of the very Gnosis it was designed to combat by declaring an end of history. In certain key aspects, then, Leviathan was an adaptable prefiguration of the end form of Gnosticism, the totalitarian state. The Hobbesian symbolisms expressed the radical immanence of existence and were woven into the civil theology of modern politics: the new psychology of the pneumopathological state for which the *amor Dei* is madness; the new man whose diseased orientation by *amor sui* is taken as normal motivation; and Leviathan as the omnipotent state whose sovereign is the mortal god that rules by terror and suppression of existential debate (NSP, 179–87). Ultimately, the Gnostic dream of perfection turns out to be systematized brutality, the banality of evil.

From this perspective, then, Voegelin finds that history displays the configuration of a "giant cycle," open to an uncertain future. At its acme lies the epochal differentiation of the soul or spirit as the sensorium of transcendence that reached optimal expression in the Incarnation of the *Logos* in Christ. Transcending the cycles of single civilizations, this civilizational cycle of world-historic proportions is structured by the pre-Christian high civilizations as the ascending branch adventitiously moving toward the acme of the Advent in a dynamic from compact to differentiated experiences of being. The modern, Gnostic civilization, following a recessive dynamic that reverses the process of differentiation, forms the descending branch of the cycle into the crisis of the present. "While Western society has its own cycle of growth, flowering, and decline, it must be considered—because of the growth of Gnosticism in its course—as the declining branch of the larger advent-recession cycle" (NSP, 164).

What of the future? Voegelin's answer is cautious, but hopeful. Writing in the midst of Cold War anxieties, he is at pains to reject the proposition "that Western society is ripe to fall for communism" as "an impertinent piece of Gnostic propaganda at both its silliest and most vicious [that] certainly has nothing to do with the critical study of politics" (NSP, 176; cf. 177–79, 187–89). Hope for the future paradoxically arises because of the character of the two major dangers posed by Gnosticism as the civil theology of modern society: (1) it supplants rather than supplements the truth of the soul; and (2) it misrepresents reality rather than truly representing it. By the first danger, the differentiation of the soul and its order in philosophy and Christianity are ruined and systematically repressed in favor of the Gnostic dogmas. But however energetic a totalitarian or other Gnostic regime may be in its repression of individual human beings, it cannot remove the soul and its transcendence from the ontological structure of reality itself. An "explosion" of resistance to repression in due course is, thereby, assured. By the second danger, Gnosticism's systematic misrepresentation of reality is not merely a theoretical fallacy; it also carries a self-defeating factor by forcing thought and action along perversely mistaken lines with disastrous consequences for rational politics and policy. It operates with a "false picture of reality," specifically one that perverts into their opposite the two great principles governing existence: "What comes into being will have an end, and the mystery of this stream of being is impenetrable." Gnosticism replaces truth with "a counterexistential dream world" (NSP, 164–67). This systematic misrepresentation insists that the society of the Third Realm will have no end, and that the mystery of the stream of being is solved because its goal is known to the Gnostic elite. Dream and reality are identified as a matter of principle, and anyone who challenges official truth in the name of reason and truth meets vituperation or worse. Rational debate is impossible. Practical dangers are not met with appropriate measures rationally calculated to resolve them.

They will rather be met by magic operations in the dream world, such as disapproval, moral condemnation, declarations of intention, resolutions, appeals to the opinion of mankind, branding of enemies as aggressors, outlawing of war, propaganda for world peace and world government, etc. The intellectual and moral corruption which expresses itself in the aggregate of such magic operations may pervade a society with the weird, ghostly atmosphere of a lunatic asylum, as we experience it in our time in the Western crisis. (NSP, 170)

The result is the oddity of continuous chain warfare, hot and cold, in which all parties resolutely claim to be devoted to peace. The structure of reality cannot be rationally taken into account. "There can be no peace, because the dream cannot be translated into reality and reality has not yet broken the dream" (NSP, 173). How it will all end, one cannot be sure; but reality in one way or another will assuredly assert itself—either in a horrible conflagration or, through the course of changing generations, in the abandonment of Gnostic dreaming "before the worst has happened." A glimmer of hope for the latter outcome arises because, as was noticed earlier, Voegelin finds the English and American democracies to be both the strongest powers and the nations with the most effectively preserved representative truth in their institutional orders. "But it will require all our efforts to kindle this glimmer into a flame by repressing Gnostic corruption and restoring the forces of civilization. At present the fate is in the balance" (NSP, 189).

The themes sounded in *The New Science of Politics* run through all of Voegelin's work as published in subsequent decades, and their development is the concern of the following chapters. We turn now to the thread of the argument in the first three volumes of *Order and History*.

CHAPTER 5

History and Its Order: 1957

In aiming his work in *The New Science of Politics* toward the philosopher's resistance to social disorder as fomented by the Gnostic systematizers' political dreamworlds, Voegelin chose as epigraph the words of Richard Hooker: "Posterity may know we have not loosely through silence permitted things to pass away as in a dream." For the broader canvas of *Order and History*, he drew from Saint Augustine: "In the study of creature one should not exercise a vain and perishing curiosity, but ascend toward what is immortal and everlasting." The architectonic majesty of the ascending line of inquiry into history and its order, then, is sounded in recollection of Plato's late work. For Voegelin's first word, too, is *God*, but the differentiation of the horizon of reality from that of the father of all the philosophers is signaled in the last word of *Israel and Revelation* which is *Jesus* (OH, I, 1, 515).[1]

Revelatory, no less than philosophical, experiences and their symbolizations form the empirical base of Voegelin's exploration. The perspective is consonant with that of Aristotle when he wrote: "The student of politics must study the soul, but he must do so with his own aim in view, and only to the extent that the objects of his inquiry demand." Hence, in train with announced intentions of *The New Science of Politics*, Voegelin's subject in subsequent work is the comprehensive reality pertaining to man's humanity, which critically restores the study *peri ta anthropina*, or philosophy of human affairs, in full grandeur. By finding its focal point in the study of the

1. Cf. Richard Hooker, Preface, ad init., *Of the Laws of Ecclesiastical Polity*; Saint Augustine, *De Vera Religione* XXIX, 52; Plato, *Laws* 625A.

order and disorder of existence, the work explores the vertical dimensions of human reality symbolized by Aristotle in terms of the synthetic, specific, and political nature of man. In doing so, the expanded empirical horizon of the present compels expansion of the Classical categories so as to address the whole range of human existence, from the personal to the social to the historical and ontological.[2]

In the present chapter I shall follow the central speculative thread running through the initial three volumes of *Order and History*—that is, Voegelin's attempt to trace the emergence of human consciousness through analysis of the experiences of the order of being and their attendant symbolic forms. The crucial event in this historical continuum of experience and articulation is represented in what Voegelin calls the *leap in being* (or discovery of transcendent reality) by prophets in Israel and philosophers in Hellas, events which create the historical form of human existence. For the present, I shall concentrate on this nexus as the one that dominates Voegelin's philosophy of order and history in its first full formulation. The symbolic form of the myth, of basic importance to Voegelin's analysis (OH, III, 183–99), and the form of philosophy will be more fully discussed in the following chapters.

leap in being *(handwritten marginal note)*

I

The experience giving rise to history as a symbolic form of existence for mankind is so momentous as to demand the dramatic term *leap in being*: "The leap in being, the experience of divine being as world-transcendent, is inseparable from the understanding of man as human" (OH, I, 235).[3] In its stark clarity, the Israel of the prophets is the primary and commanding instance of the event, for there the leap in being occurs in the revelation of God to Moses on Mount

2. Aristotle, *Nicomachean Ethics* 1.13 at 1102a23–25 and 10.9 at 1181b15, trans. Martin Ostwald (Indianapolis & New York: Bobbs-Merrill, 1962), 29 and 302. Cf. Voegelin, "Reason: The Classic Experience," *Southern Review*, n.s., X, pp. 260–64, quoted in full herein at pp. 215–16.

3. The term *leap in being*, though not invented by Voegelin, is given new amplitude. It is taken from Kierkegaard, and he was indebted to Hegel for the expression: *Der Begriff Angst*, trans. E. Hirsch (Duesseldorf: Eugen Diederichs Verlag, 1958), 27, 114, 246, citing Hegel, *Vorrede zur Phaenomologie des Geistes*, *Werke* (Jubilee Edition) 2:18–19; *Logik*, *Werke* (Jubilee Edition) 4:457–62.

Sinai (OH, I, 402). In the parallel Hellenic leap in being, the experience develops the form of philosophy and achieves depth and grasp from the time of Xenophanes' experience that "'The One is the God'" (OH, II, 181) to the Aeschylean Dionysiac descent into the depth of the soul to reach a decision for *Dike*, Justice, (OH, II, 262) and the Platonic vision of the *Agathon*, Good (OH, I, 496, III, 113). These parallel leaps in being were absorbed into Christianity (OH, II, 8) after the climax of revelation in Jesus, the "entrance of God into history through the sacrificial assumption of human form" (OH, II, 11). The specific character of the Hellenic experience of transcendence, as contrasted with the Israelite-Christian leap in being, requires further clarification, and we shall return to it. Other "multiple and parallel" leaps in being occurred "contemporaneously in the India of the Buddha and the China of Confucius and Laotse," but their character and content are so diverse that a preliminary negative distinction is best emphasized: in each case they broke with the myth (OH, II, 1).[4]

The problem of ranking and classifying these multiple and parallel experiences emerges as a main undertaking of *Order and History*; but the generic character of the experience and its ontological consequences most concern us here. If we are to understand Voegelin's meaning, we must keep firmly in mind a point that is well illustrated by the Platonic vision of the *Agathon*. "Concerning the content of the Agathon nothing can be said at all. That is the fundamental insight of Platonic ethics. The transcendence of the Agathon makes immanent propositions concerning its content impossible. The vision of the Agathon does not render a material rule of conduct, but forms the soul through an experience of transcendence" (OH, III, 112). Or, put more simply, the experience of transcendence, or leap in being, does not yield a truth that one can possess like a thing. It is the "flash of eternity into time" (OH, III, 363). It revolutionizes human existence, but, far from relieving man of his essential ignorance, the experience only deepens that ignorance by permitting him a glimpse of the abysmal mystery of transcendent Being.

---

4. The first three volumes of *Order and History* make only passing mention of the Chinese and Indian experiences. See Volume IV, 272–99. All four published volumes of *Order and History* are cited textually, with volume and page numbers as OH.

The leap in being, while it gains a new truth about order, neither gains all of the truth, nor establishes an ultimate order of mankind. The struggle for the truth of order continues on the new historical level. Repetitions of the leap in being will correct the initial insight and supplement it with new discoveries; and the order of human existence, however profoundly affected by the new truth, remains the order of a plurality of concrete societies. With the discovery of its past, mankind has not come to the end of its history, but has become conscious of the open horizon of its future. (OH, II, 3)

[handwritten margin note: about the leap in being]

To elucidate the problem, we must return to the very first words of *Order and History*. "God and man, world and society form a primordial community of being" (OH, I, 1). Man's role in being is that of a participant. He is thrown into and out of existence without knowing either the why or the how of it. He only knows himself as a participant in the lasting and passing of existence, in the durability and transiency that characterize his own existence and that of others around him. "Participation is the essence of existence" (OH, I, 1). In this position of essential ignorance concerning both himself and being, man fastens on the knowledge his experience gives him in seeking to understand the essentially unknowable order of being and his place in it.

These efforts at comprehending the essentially unknowable find expression in symbols, and the first great category of symbols is that of the cosmological form. The first faint illumination of existence, which prefigures the comparative flood of light generated by the leap in being, comes with man's recognition that true participation in existence means spiritual attunement to what is most lasting in the scale of lasting and passing existents. The spiritual development of mankind follows from a man's discovery that existence demands attunement to the truth of being.[5] Attunement in this pregnant sense is "the state of existence [that] hearkens to that which is lasting in being . . . maintains a tension of awareness for its partial revelations in the order of society and the world . . . listens attentively to the silent voices of conscience and grace in human existence itself"

5. This sentence should not be permitted to slide into the conventional meaning that a climate of opinion fashioned under the influence of evolutionism and progressivism might tend to give it. The language depends on Voegelin's notions of *compactness* and *differentiation* as discussed here and in the earlier chapters. See *Order and History*, I, ix, 60.

(OH, I, 4–5). This attunement, variously symbolized in myth and ritual of the cosmological form, builds upon the fundamental experience of the divine nature of the cosmos, of the endless expanse of earth and heaven as the embracing order into which man must fit himself if he is to survive; and, so, this "overwhelmingly powerful and visible partner in the community of being inevitably suggests its order as the model of all order, including that of man and society" (OH, I, 5). The strength of this "compact" form lies in its foundation in the readily experienced reality of visible and palpable vegetative rhythms and celestial revolutions that pervade the nature world and the cosmos—and, seemingly, man and society with them. The sense factor in the primordial experience of the truth of being as cosmic-divine is the root of a persistent problem of which Voegelin remarks: "The many need gods with 'shapes.' When the 'shapes' of the gods are destroyed with social effectiveness, the many will not become mystics but agnostics" (OH, II, 239).

It is precisely the problem of "gods without shapes," of the unseen God, that emerges with the leap in being and the experience of transcendent Being as the source of the ultimate truth of order and being. The cosmological form is broken, and existence in the historical form begins. The experience of *participation* sharpens and deepens to become emphatic partnership with God. A radical new relationship between man and the source of the order of being is discovered, and this discovery necessitates an equally radical reorientation of individual existence. By Plato, this radical reorientation is symbolized as the *periagoge*, the turning about of the whole soul (OH, III, 68); in Christianity, it is the conversion.

[handwritten margin note: leap in being = experience of transcendent Being = beginning of participation in history]

Existence is partnership in the community of being; and the discovery [through the leap in being] of imperfect participation, of a mismanagement of existence through lack of proper attunement to the order of being, of the danger of a fall from being, is a horror indeed, compelling a radical reorientation of existence. Not only will the [old cosmological] symbols lose the magic of their transparency for the unseen order and become opaque, but a pallor will fall over the partial order of mundane existence that hitherto furnished the analogies for the comprehensive order of being. Not only will the unseemly symbols be rejected, but man will turn away from world and society as the sources of misleading analogy. He will experience a turning around . . . an inversion or conversion toward the true source of order. And this turning around, this conversion, results in more than an increase of knowledge concerning the order of being; it is a change in the order itself. For the participation in being changes its structure when it becomes emphatically a partnership with God, while the participation in mundane being recedes to second rank. The more perfect attunement to being through conversion is not an increase on the same scale but a qualitative leap. And when this conversion befalls a society, the converted community will experience itself as qualitatively different from all other societies that have not taken the leap. Moreover, the conversion is experienced, not as the result of human action, but as a passion, as a response to revelation of divine being, to an act of grace, to a selection for emphatic partnership with God. . . . The emphatic partnership with God removes a society from the rank of profane existence and constitutes it as the representative of the *civitas Dei* in historical existence. Thus, a change in being actually has occurred, with consequences for the order of existence. (OH, I, 10–11)[6]

The leap in being was representatively taken by Moses for Israel and by Israel, as God's Chosen People, for all mankind (OH, I, 115).[7] The complicated consequences of this event will occupy us throughout this exposition.

Through divine choice Israel was enabled to take the leap toward more perfect attunement with transcendent being. The historical consequence was a

6. In the noteworthy statement that "a change in being actually has occurred," Voegelin appears to be following his analysis of the historiographic materials even in the face of a most serious difficulty in what one takes to be his metaphysical position, one for which no solution is indicated in the initial three volumes of *Order and History*. Bergson, too, followed his analysis of an experience substantially identical with the one Voegelin terms the "leap in being" and perceived radical change in the structure of being: from static to dynamic man, from closed to open society, as a result of the opening of the soul through the mystical experience. (Cf. Henri Bergson, *The Two Sources of Morality and Religion*, trans. by R. A. Audra and C. Brereton [New York: Henry Holt, 1935], 209, 246ff.) But for Bergson, being was not being but an endless becoming through the agency of the *élan vital*. (Cf. Bergson's *Creative Evolution*, trans. Arthur Mitchell [New York: Henry Holt, 1924], 205; also Bergson, *The Creative Mind*, trans. by Mabelle L. Andison [New York: Philosophical Library, 1946], 17, 21, 37.) Despite this, Bergson's troubles are acute, though they proceed from a different source than Voegelin's. At the first stage in the publication of *Order and History*, two points seemed clear: *first*, despite the "change in being," Voegelin seriously maintains that being is being: the nature of being does not change; *second*, his bold statement of the problem makes it evident that he is acutely aware of its existence as well as its ramifications. For Voegelin's resolution of this problem in OH, IV, see Chapter 8, esp. pp. 231–51, herein.

7. The universalist implications of the leap in being are not necessarily understood at once, and in Israelite history the development of the universalist components of Yahwism was the achievement of the prophets. See *Order and History*, I, 144, for this and 164 for the related problem of "the mortgage of the world-immanent . . . on the transcendent truth."

break in the pattern of civilizational courses. With Israel there appears a new agent of history that is neither a civilization nor a people within a civilization like others. Hence, we can speak of an Egyptian or a Mesopotamian but not of an Israelite civilization. . . .

Israel alone constituted itself by recording its own genesis as a people as an event with a special meaning in history, while the other Near Eastern societies constituted themselves as analogues of cosmic order. Israel alone had history as an inner form, while the other societies existed in the form of cosmological myth. History, we therefore conclude, is a symbolic form of existence, of the same class as the cosmological form; and the paradigmatic narrative[8] is, in the historical form, the equivalent of the myth in the cosmological form. Hence it will be necessary to distinguish between political societies according to their form of existence: the Egyptian society existed in cosmological, the Israelite in historical form. (OH, I, 116, 124)[9]

II

Voegelin is to be understood quite literally when he writes: "Without Israel there would be no history, but only the eternal recurrence of societies in cosmological form" (OH, I, 126). There is a crucial distinction to be drawn between existence in cosmological civilizations and historical existence. Does that mean, for example, that Egypt had no history? The answer to this question leans upon the principle of compactness and differentiation (OH, I, 60).[10] Because human nature is a constant and because the range of human experience is always present in its full dimensions, cosmological civilizations are not devoid of history. The soul, which is ontologically the "sensorium of transcendence" (OH, I, 235), is everywhere and at all times capable of experiencing the order of being. The mysterious welling-up of transcendental experiences into consciousness oc-

8. That is, in the instance of Israel, the Old Testament.
9. In the course of his discussion of the Old Testament as pragmatic and paradigmatic history, Voegelin wryly remarks that, although the story from Genesis to II Kings is constructed as an account of Israel's relation of God rather than as a critical history of pragmatic events, this "does not mean that the account has no pragmatic core; for we have no more reason to doubt the existence of some sort of pragmatic Moses behind the story of Exodus than of some sort of world behind the story of its creation in Genesis," *Order and History*, I, 21.
10. Voegelin formulates this key interpretive principle in the following propositions: "(1) The nature of man is constant. (2) The range of human experience is always present in the fullness of its dimensions. (3) The structure of the range varies from compactness to differentiation."

curred also in the cosmological civilizations. But this could be known clearly only in retrospect, only after the experience had broken through and been differentiated fully in the "clarity of revelation" (OH, I, 407), only after it had created an "historical present." As Voegelin has put it, "When the order of the soul and society is oriented toward the will of God, and consequently the actions of the society and its members are experienced as fulfillment or defection, a historical present is created, radiating its form over a past that was not consciously historical in its own present" (OH, I, 128).

The truth of being is a reality that presses in upon men even if it is not experienced with sufficient intensity to become fully articulate. From the luminous center of the historical present, the past will then be seen in retrospect: *negatively*, as the *Sheol* (Death) of the soul and as existence in substantive untruth; and *positively*, as the *praeparatio evangelica* in which increasing attentiveness to the stirring in the ground of the soul loosens up the authoritative hold of myth and makes possible a more profound plumb of being.

History is the revelation of God's way with man. As a form in which society exists, it has the tendency to include all mankind—as it did on the first occasion in the Old Testament, and as it inevitably must if the movement of history is the tracing of the finger of divine Providence. The tendency of historical form to expand its realm of meaning beyond its present into the past raises three problems.

FIRST, there is the problem of the ontological reality of *mankind*. "History creates mankind as the community of men who, through the ages, approach the true order of being that has its origin in God; but, at the same time, mankind creates this history through its real approach to existence under God" (OH, I, 128). The beginnings of this reciprocal process lie deep in the strata of the cosmological civilizations, and even deeper in the remotest human past. The struggle of mankind for attunement to the true order of being assumes, at the most compact level (in primitive societies and cosmological civilizations), the form of play (OH, III, 257ff), ritual, and myth. At the opposite end of the spectrum of experience, it assumes the form of the leap in being. The process of history is real, although an ambiguity attaches to it as a meaningful process since it is created by men who do not know what they are creating.

The meaning of history now becomes topical. Voegelin uses this phrase, but one must be cautious not to misunderstand him. On the one hand, history is no finite unit of observation susceptible to treatment by the methods of the natural sciences (OH, I, 2; III, 335). On the other hand, there can be no question of constructing a "system" after the fashion of Hegel, Marx, or Comte. Both of these approaches are eliminated when Voegelin writes "History has no knowable meaning (eidos, or essence)" (OH, II, 2).[11] History must be understood from the perspective of participation, upon the basis of man's experiences as a partner in being, because this is man's place in the structure of being; there is no alternate vantage point, no other role to play: "Man's partnership in being is the essence of his existence" (OH, I, 2). The meaning of history, then, discovered by the leap in being, "reveals a mankind striving for its order of existence within the world while attuning itself with the truth of being beyond the world, and gaining in the process not a substantially better order within the world but an increased understanding of the gulf that lies between immanent existence and the transcendent truth of being" (OH, I, 129). The pungent awareness of this gulf increases the dramatic tension of the historical present. Voegelin finds in this awesome tension an effective cure for the spiritual pride so characteristic of modern mankind. "Anybody who has ever sensed this increase of dramatic tension in the historical present will be cured of complacency, for the light that falls over the past deepens the darkness that surrounds the future. He will shudder before the abysmal mystery of history as the instrument of divine revelation for ultimate purposes that are unknown equally to the men of all ages" (OH, I, 129).

SECOND, there is the problem of a multiplicity of historical presents, since history originates in an historically moving present. The discerning of historical presents involves the incidental showing that the experience of transcendence is an objective event in reality not to be discounted as illusory or subjective. Voegelin bases his argument upon the critical acceptance of historiographic documents. Historical form, understood as the experience of the present under God, will be construed as subjective only if *faith* is "misinterpreted as a 'subjective' experience. If, however, it is understood as the leap in being, as the entering of the soul into divine reality through the

11. Cf. Voegelin, *The New Science of Politics*, 110–17, and *Order and History*, II, 18–19.

entering of divine reality into the soul, the historical form, far from
being a subjective point of view, is an ontologically real event in history" (OH, I, 130).

Indeed, this is the very source of whatever objectivity history
may be said to have. Insofar as history has objective truth, it has it as
a result of experience of transcendence and the explanation of these
experiences in rational discourse by the men to whom they happen.
These explanations "cast an ordering ray of objective truth over the
field of history in which the event objectively" occurs. The symbols
created for explicative use on these occasions conform to a general
type. The specific content of each such event supplies a principle for
classifying men and societies of the past, present, and future by relating human existence to its degree of·approach to the historical
form (OH, I, 130).[12] The "model" for treating the past from an historical present was set by Saint Paul in the Letter to the Romans (OH, I,
131; II, 10ff). In every instance of a new historical present, the great
discovery divides the stream of life into the Either-Or of life and
death, divides time into the Before-and-After, and divides mankind
into the New men and the Old men, according to acceptance or rejection of the "infusion of divine Being" (OH, II, 5).

But no matter what the response may be, the acceptance or the
rejection of the representative authority of the carriers "of the truth
for mankind" (OH, I, 144) is to be respected as a mystery of history.
Just as from the perspective of Plato this mystery and the obligation
of tolerance could be formulated as "every myth has its truth" (OH,
I, 11), so a more highly differentiated historical present does not
abolish the truth of an historical present of a more compact level.
There is one mankind and one being. Truths differentiated may historically become untruths; but they remain essentially true nonetheless (OH, I, 198ff).[13] Judaism illustrates the point.

Judaism has its own theology of sin and salvation which runs parallel, on
the level of ethnical compactness, with the universalist theology of Christianity. This recognition of the parallelism, to be sure, does not deny the
differences in the levels of truth between Judaism and Christianity. Nevertheless, every order has its own present under God, as we formulated the

12. Compare with *Order and History*, III, 95f.
13. Cf. *Order and History*, III, 198, for the theory of myth, and III, 362ff, for the
problem of the "Historicity of Truth."

principle; and this present is not abolished when it becomes a past in retrospect from a differentiated experience or order. Hence, the resistance to representative advances of truth about order, and the continued existence of more compactly ordered societies by the side of more differentiated orders, is intimately a part of the mystery of mankind that unfolds in history. This mystery must not be destroyed by progressivist slogans about "backward" peoples, or by inflicting on the survival of Judaism the pseudoscientific epithet of "fossilizations." It must be treated with the utmost caution and respect in a critical philosophy of history.[14]

Since history originates in an historically moving present and since symbolic formulations are of necessity restricted by the empirical horizons of those who make them, the Pauline historical present, after being eminently true for nearly two thousand years, has grown insufficient. Modern philosophy must relate the even more comprehensive past of mankind to a Western historical horizon that has become worldwide.[15] This can be done only by articulating a new historical present in "our own historical form of maximal clarity, which is the Christian" (OH, I, 132).[16] One glimpses here the grandeur of the philosophical goal Voegelin set for himself.

THIRD, there is the problem of loss of historical substance. Here, confusion about *history* shows its gravity. "A society in existence under God is in historical form. From its present falls a ray of meaning over the past of mankind from which it has emerged; and the *history* written in this spirit is part of the symbolism by which the society constitutes itself" (OH, I, 132).

The reasoning then runs as follows: history is a symbol; symbols can lose their substance; the emptied symbol can still be used for purposes widely differing from its original and essential function as the indispensable means of constituting existence in historical form. The Spengler-Toynbee giant historiographic enterprises are the prime illustration. Here is an expression of a tension between

14. See Arnold J. Toynbee, *A Study of History* (12 vols.; London: Oxford University Press, 1935–61), I, 90ff, II, 54ff, 234ff, 12f.

15. Toynbee makes much of this expansion of Western society. He points out as the "unique fact of Western history" that, in the five centuries from 1450 to 1950, the expanding Western society and culture had penetrated "all other extant civilizations and all extant primitive societies" to such a degree that they had become parts of the Western "Great Society's" province. *Ibid.*, IX, 14.

16. Compare the similar view already in the preface to Voegelin's *Die politischen Religionen*, 8.

the Judeo-Christian historical form (in which Western civilization still exists) and the loss of substance it has suffered. Voegelin considers the motivation for the Spengler-Toynbee undertakings a blunted perception of the West's real danger of a fall from attunement to the truth of being. Their fervid attention to history reflects the anxiety that "historical form, as it was gained might also be lost when man and society reverse the leap in being and reject existence under God" (OH, I, 133). This is, indeed, the real cause of a contemporary "crisis" that is more sensed than understood. The concrete results of Spengler and Toynbee should not be taken entirely at their face value. They should, rather, be regarded as symptomatic manifestations. The degree of their confusion supplies an index of the seriousness of a situation that reveals history about to be reswallowed by the civilizations.

The shift in accents [i.e., the preoccupation with the sheer mechanics of civilizational process as opposed to any concern with an originating historical present] is so radical that it practically makes nonsense of history, for history is the exodus from civilizations. And the great historical forms created by Israel, the Hellenic philosophers and Christianity did not constitute societies of the civilizational type—even though the communities thus established, which still are carriers of history, must wind their way through the rise and fall of civilizations. (OH, I, 133)

III

The tension between the civilizations and history is of more than passing importance, since history "is the exodus from civilizations." A return to the civilizations is a reversal of the leap in being. In reducing history to civilizations, contemporary "historians" are playing a game of spiritual brinkmanship, only a step away from the fathomless abyss of dead souls. Again speaking of Spengler and Toynbee, Voegelin says:

Neither of the two thinkers has accepted the principle that experiences of order, as well as their symbolic expressions, are not products of a civilization but its constitutive forms. They still live in the intellectual climate in which "religious founders" were busy with founding "religions," while in fact they were concerned with the order of human souls and, if successful, founded communities of men who lived under the order discovered as true.

If, however, the Israelite discovery of history as a form of existence is disregarded, then the form is rejected in which a society exists under God. The
conception of history as a sequence of civilizational cycles suffers from the
Eclipse of God, as a Jewish thinker has recently called this spiritual defect.[17]
Spengler and Toynbee return, indeed, to the Sheol of civilizations, from
which Moses had led his people into the freedom of history. (OH,
I, 126)

Before considering the consequences of this deleterious reduction of history to cycles of civilizations, it remains to clarify the relationship between historical form and civilizational form. As the
result of the "interpenetration of institutions and experiences of
order," a society's *form* is a unique and authoritative articulation
of the truth of being (OH, I, 60). This articulation into constellations
of related symbols literally constitutes a society and orders it in a
distinctive way. A symbolic form of existence creates a society. In
the course of being preserved and reaffirmed through ritual obser-
vance[18] and repeated experiences in the tradition of the founding experience,[19] the symbolic form sustains the society by harmoniously
securing the attunement of the society and its members to the truth
of being. This is the means by which a society attains and retains its
identity in existence. A society's civilizational form is, therefore, its
mode and allotted measure of participation in the world-historic
process of experience and symbolization of order that extends indefi-
nitely into the future (OH, I, 61).[20] Seen thus, a civilization's form
has historical singularity that can never be absorbed by phenomenal
regularities, because the form itself is an act in the drama of mankind striving toward the truth of being. It is this very striving, de-

17. Martin Buber, *Gottesfinsternis* (Zurich, 1953).
18. See, for examples, "New Year Festival" in the indexes to *Order and History*.
19. For the "continuum of revelation" and the "continuum of the people's response" from Moses through the prophets, see *Order and History*, I, 428f. The Sinai-
tic revelation is analyzed at I, 406ff, 417. The fundamental experiences founding the
Hellenic form of philosophy present a similar problem, as is suggested in the following formulation: "What philosophy is, need not be ascertained by talking *about* philosophy discursively; it can, and must, be determined by entering *into* the speculative
process in which the thinker explicates his experience of order" (OH, II, 170). This
quoted sentence, it should be observed, also articulates the cardinal principle of
Voegelin's method; the procedure it indicates is rigorously followed throughout
Order and History. The Hellenic experience is perhaps most acutely analyzed in connection with Socrates' *zetema* in the *Republic* at III, 82ff; see also, III, 112ff.
20. Compare the handling of this same problem in terms of existential and transcendental representation in Voegelin's *The New Science of Politics*, pp. 52–75.

scriptive as the "dynamics of human nature," that *is* history (OH, I, 63).

Why, then, a tension between history and civilization? Specifically, how can the historical form be the constitutive form of Western civilization and, simultaneously, be said not to have constituted a society of the civilizational type?

The tension arises, in part, because of a failure to distinguish between (1) a civilization as a mechanical concatenation of institutional phases, divisible into periods of genesis, growth, and decay, which succeed one another *ad infinitum*,[21] and (2) a civilization as a mode of participation in the world-historic process of attunement to the truth of being. The phenomenological civilizational theory tends to preempt the field of history with the effect that human existence is reduced to perennially recurring civilizational cycles. The essential meaning of history as God's way through time with man is thereby lost. Societies constituted by the historical form are not "civilizational" in type because history, as an inner form of existence, is the source of spiritual order for universal mankind. A civilization is bound to the lasting and passing of existence. It must maintain its attunement to the mundane order of existence as well as to the transcendent order of Being, and it must be cautious not to mistake one for the other or to lose the essential balance between the rival orders.

Western civilization has articulated its mode of participation in the world-historic process in the form of history—that is, in a universalist, noncivilizational form. This is a fact of far-reaching consequences. The Western historical form, established by the Judeo-Christian and Hellenic experiences of order, is the constitutive form of worldwide or *ecumenical* society. The truth of existence articulated in the Western historical form is not merely the parochial truth of a civilization, nor the equally parochial truth of one "higher-religion"[22] among others. It communicates, rather, the profoundest

21. Toynbee calculates a possible 1,743 million civilizations on the basis of the life expectancy of the earth. See Toynbee, *A Study of History,* I, 463f (cited by Voegelin, *Order and History,* I, 125) and IV, 9f.

22. Cf. Toynbee, *A Study of History,* IV, 222ff; V, 58–194 and *passim.* For the Toynbee *credo in nuce* see "A Study of History: What I Am Trying To Do," *International Affairs,* XXXI (1955), reprinted in *Toynbee and History,* ed. M. F. Ashley Montagu (Boston: Porter Sargent, 1956), esp. pp. 6–7.

experiences of the truth of being achieved by mankind and its implications are universal in scope. "Revelation comes to one man for
all men" (OH, II, 6). And it is the representative character of the carriers of the truth of being for mankind (OH, I, 144) that is the essential point, not the ostensible parochialism of their location on this or
that particular ethnic, geographic, or civilizational horizon. "The
revelation of God to man in history comes where God wills" (OH, II,
264), and it is the obligation of all men to be attentive to the truth of
existence as it is revealed and discovered in the response of sensitive
souls who act through the ages as the link between universal mankind and the transcendent God.

The creation of history by the Mosaic leap in being unalterably
changed the structure of being itself (OH, I, 11, 464f). Mankind was
representatively freed from existence in the form of cosmological
myth.[23] History, differentiating through faith as a pneumatic structure of experience and symbolization in the soul, added new and essentially human dimensions to the field of reality. The experiential
source of this expansion of the human sphere was the revelation of
divine transcendent Being.

Existence in historical form presupposes the existence of the world-transcendent God, as well as the historical fact of his revelation. . . . History,
once it has become ontologically real through revelation, carries with it the
irreversible direction from compact existence in cosmological form toward
the Kingdom of God. Israel is not the empirical human beings who may or

23. As indicated, such formulations as the present one must be understood as
qualified by the fact that the leap in being radically reorders existence centering
around the area of the experience, but leaves other aspects of existence, already ordered through less-differentiated experiences, relatively untouched. The point is discussed by Voegelin in *Order and History*, I, 298ff: "Once the adequate expression for
an experience of order has been developed within the cosmological form, it does not
disappear from history when divine revelation becomes the organizing center of symbolic form." The new symbols pertain primarily to the relationship between God and
man and to that between man and man; the old symbols validly order existence for
the world. A problem that "is unsolvable on principle" (OH, I, 183) emerges at this
point: that of achieving a balance between "the life of the spirit and life in the world."
Complete attunement either to immanent order or to transcendent order would involve either spiritual or physical suicide. The strenuously difficult accommodation of
the rival orders of existence is possible at all only because they are "linked by the
identity of the order of being and existence which man experiences" (OH, I, 299). Cf.,
for the problem of *balance* in the wake of the Hellenic experiences of transcendence,
II, 255. For the problem in Christianity, see the discussion of the Sermon on the
Mount at III, 225f. For the "postulate of balance" see IV, 228.

may not keep the covenant, but the expansion of divine creation into the order of man and society. (OH, I, 464)

It is this movement from "compact existence in cosmological form toward the Kingdom of God" describing the historical form's implicit line of spiritual expansion that, on the pragmatic plane, is reflected in the empirically observable contemporary expansion of Western civilization to become worldwide.[24] This tacitly raises the question of the "destiny" of the West, in the sense of "the meaning which the order of an existent has in relation to its own lasting and passing, as well as in relation to the order of mankind in historical existence" (OH, I, 315). Voegelin expresses himself on this subject as follows:

The program of universal history valid for all men, when it is thought through, can mean only one of two things: the destruction of Western historical form, and the reduction of Western societies to a compact form of order in which the differentiations of truth through philosophy and revelation are forgotten; or, an assimilation of the societies, in which the leap in being has not broken the cosmological order as thoroughly as in the West, to existence in Western historical form. (OH, II, 22)

IV

The reduction of history to existence in civilizations constitutes spiritual rebellion. The attendant deformation of the historical form entails a fall from being, the supreme existential catastrophe and summation of spiritual ills. Insofar as there is order at all during rebellion, it is the vestigial order of the compact cosmological form.[25] Pertinent in this connection is Voegelin's analysis of modern political movements (NSP, 107–89), which shows how precarious is the contemporary foothold in being.[26] The fall from being, as the cardinal consequence of reducing history to civilizations, is best elucidated by showing the relationship of modern Gnosticism (the essen-

24. See OH, I, 1. Cf. Toynbee, *A Study of History*, IX, 406–644.
25. For the phenomenon of spiritual rebellion, see, for example: "The Wrath of Achilles" (OH, II, 83); for the discussion of Hesiod (OH, II, 133); the "'great' problems of theodicy" (OH, II, 255); Hobbes's solution and Plato's analysis (OH, III, 76–80).
26. On Gnosticism, in addition to Voegelin's writings, see Hans Jonas, *The Gnostic Religion: The Message of the Alien God and the Beginnings of Christianity* (2nd ed.; Boston: Beacon Press, 1963), esp. Chaps. 2 and 12.

tial component of modern political ideologies) to the cosmological myth. This connection emerges in a brief critique of Hegel's philosophy of history (OH, II, 16–19; IV, 66–78 and *passim*).

After remarking on the ambiguity of Hegel and the controversy surrounding whether or not he meant that history and mankind came to fulfillment in his work in Berlin in 1830, Voegelin goes on to discount the importance of the controversy for his purposes beyond its testimony that the ambiguity does in fact exist. He notes that what gave rise to the ambiguity was Hegel's "experience of consciousness, of the subject, as the substance of being." This is critical.

For under the aspect of this experience, the Hegelian Gnosis is closely related to the speculation of the Upanishads on the identity of the *atman*, the self (consciousness, subject) with the *brahma*, the supra-personal and supramundane reality. The operations with the *Geist* [in the Hegelian Identities], who is ontologically God and man as well as the identity of both, belong to a type of speculation within the medium of the cosmological myth that can appear pre-philosophically in the Indian and post-philosophically in the Hegelian Gnosis. . . . Moreover, the similar experiences, with their corresponding speculative articulation, have curiously similar historical sequels: from the late Upanishads the way leads to the atheistic salvation of the Buddha; from Hegel it leads, via Bruno Bauer and Feuerbach, to the atheistic salvation of Marx. . . . These atheistic sequels bring more clearly into view the ahistoric character of Gnostic speculation. . . . Gnosis is a speculative movement within the form of the myth; and modern Gnosis, as the Hegelian identifications show, is a throwback from differentiation into the prehistoric compactness of the myth. . . . Neither Hegel's own protests, nor those of the Hegelians, against the charges of atheism, can abolish the fact that in a consistent unfolding of Hegel's work its ambiguity has given way to the unambiguous attack on philosophy and Christianity by Marx. When finite speculation possesses itself of the meaning of history, philosophy and Christianity are destroyed and existence in historical form has ceased. (OH, II, 18–19)

The roots of Gnosticism are many and they run as deep in time as those of Christianity itself. The predominant modern form of Gnosticism is that of a speculation that claims knowledge of the meaning of history. The Gnostic variant presumes to reorder human existence on the basis of a program formulated in light of "scientific knowledge" that will bring history to perfection (NSP, 107–32). The irony is that this proclaiming of the end of history, while, indeed, capable[27] of effectively destroying history as a form of existence if it gains social acceptance, has the effect of throwing human existence back three millennia to a deformed version of the compact form of immanentized prehistoric existence first broken by the Mosaic leap in being. A staggering relapse into primitive existence is the spiritual fruit of modern ideologies for all their talk of science and progress. "Ideology," Voegelin writes, "is existence in rebellion against God and man . . . the violation of the First and Tenth Commandments, if we want to use the language of Israelite order . . . the *nosos*, the disease of the spirit, if we want to use the language of Aeschylus and Plato" (OH, I, xiv).

At the ontological level, this is precisely *disorder*. Order and disorder are preeminently conditions of the *soul*. It is the order or disorder of the soul that engenders and reflects, in the dialectics of existence, the order and disorder of society.[28] It is the order or disorder of the soul that reflects man's attunement to or defection from the truth of being in the rhythm of the historical process. It was Plato, in the act of resisting the social disorder of his time, who discovered that the "substance of society is psyche" and that "society can destroy a man's soul because the disorder of society is a disease in the psyche of its members" (OH, III, 69). The "disease" or *nosos* of the soul is designated by Plato as the "ignorance of the soul" of the truth of being. The remedy prescribed is "setting aright the relation between man and God" through conversion, or, in Plato's language, through the *periagoge*—"a turning about of 'the whole soul' from ignorance to the truth of God, from opinion [*doxa*] about uncertainly wavering things to knowledge [*episteme*] of being" (OH, III, 68).[29]

27. *Capable* is to be emphasized. Voegelin would, perhaps, subscribe to Mr. Justice Brandeis' *bon mot* that "the irresistible is often only that which is not resisted" (Quoted by Isaiah Berlin in: *Historical Inevitability* [London: Oxford University Press, 1954], 78, *fn.2.*). Voegelin himself writes: "The spiritual disorder of our time, the civilizational crisis of which everyone so readily speaks, does not by any means have to be borne as an inevitable fate. . . . On the contrary, everyone possesses the means of overcoming it in his own life. . . . . No one is obliged to take part in the spiritual crisis of a society; on the contrary, everyone is obliged to avoid this folly and live his life in order," in *Science, Politics, and Gnosticism*, 22–23.

28. This is a central principle in Voegelin's theory of politics. See OH, II, 227; see also the discussion of the problem of theodicy at II, 255.

29. Cf. OH, III, 264f. See also, "Plato's masterpiece in his attempt to penetrate the nature of social corruption," at III, 78ff.

A further aspect of the problem is what Voegelin calls "metastatic faith." This phenomenon first appears with Isaiah. *Metastasis* is the distention of faith to accommodate the expectation of a change in the constitution of immanent being. It is this element in contemporary ideologies that drives them to program the perfection of man and society. American progressivism, no less than Soviet communism, partakes of this heady optimism—for the good reason that despite overt antagonism at the level of power politics, they are spiritually "brothers under the skin." "Metastatic faith is one of the great sources of disorder, if not the principal one, in the contemporary world; and it is a matter of life and death for all of us to understand the phenomenon and to find remedies against it before it destroys us" (OH, I, xiii). Voegelin subsequently clarified his terminology in these words.

The term *metastatic apocalypse* [or *faith*] will require a little explanation. I had to develop the term on occasion of the Israelite prophets. In the prophecy of Isaiah we run into the oddity that Isaiah counseled the King of Judah not to rely on the fortifications of Jerusalem and the strength of his army but on his faith in Yahweh. If the king would have the true faith, the God would do the rest by producing an epidemic or a panic among the enemies, and the danger to the city would dissolve. The king had common sense enough not to follow the advice of the prophet, but rather to rely on fortifications and military equipment. Still, there was the prophet's assumption that through an act of faith the structure of reality could be effectively changed. In studying this problem and trying to understand it my first idea, of course, was that the prophet indulged in magic. Or, at least, believed in magic. That would not have been surprising, because in the history of Israel it had been the function of prophets to guide the hand of the king in shooting a bow against the enemy as a magic operation that would result in victory. What happened in the case of Isaiah would have been what in modern psychology, by Nietzsche or Freud, would be called a sublimation of the more primitive physical magic. Still, I felt uneasy about it, and I consulted about the matter especially with Gerhard von Rad in Heidelberg who was horrified at the idea that a grandiose spiritual prophet like Isaiah should be a magician. I was so impressed by his attitude that I made a concession. I did not use the term magic for the practice advised by Isaiah but coined a new term characterizing the peculiar sublimated magic belief in a transfiguration of reality through an act of faith. And this kind of faith I called *metastatic faith*, that is, the belief in metastasis of reality through an act of faith. I am not so sure that today [in 1973] I would make this concession, because this kind of faith is indeed magic, though one has to distinguish this sublimated variety from more primitive magical operations. If one would really draw a hard line of difference between magic and metastatic faith, I am afraid, the factor they have in common, that is, the attempt to produce a desired result by means outside of the cause-effect relations in nature, would be smudged. (AM, 69–70)

The line of analysis in the present and preceding sections should not, of course, be construed to mean that Voegelin questions the legitimacy of the scientific study of civilizational courses as such. On the contrary, his critique of Spengler and Toynbee is constructive to the extent that, though praising their extensive researches into the phenomena, he blames their theoretical inconclusiveness on their single-minded reliance on mere classification. A more promising method, he suggests (and one originally suggested by Plato and followed by Giambattista Vico), would be "a theoretical analysis of institutions and experiences of order, as well as the form that results from their interpenetration" (OH, I, 62). Of central importance is the problem of the "substance that undergoes the evolutionary changes in the course of a cycle." Voegelin points out that "a growth and decay must be a growth and decay of something." And ascertaining what this *something* is must be faced as the first theoretical problem of those intent on finding "finite lines of meaning in the stream of history" (OH, III, 317). At another point, after a brief critique, the problem is cautiously reformulated in the following language:

The historical process of civilization seems, indeed, to have for its nucleus a process of psychic decomposition. . . . The process of decomposition, if and so far as it exists, presupposes an initial order of the soul. The empirical investigation of a civilization and its political phases must, therefore, clarify this initial order of the soul, its growth and ramifications, and then study the phases of its decomposition. The approach to the problem will rest on the assumption that a political society, insofar as its course in history is intelligible, has for its substance the growth and decline of an order of the soul. The problem of the political cycle we conclude, cannot be solved through generalization of institutional phenomena, but requires for its solution a theory of the ordering myth of a society. (OH, III, 129)

V

The Hellenic experiences of transcendence occur over a span of centuries. They climax in the public cult of Aeschylean tragedy (OH, II,

241ff) and in the Platonic vision of the *Agathon* (OH, I, 496; III, 112ff). Decisive in deepening the consciousness of history to its fullness in Plato was the experience of social crisis. This crisis followed the "Great Awakening" (OH, II, 241) of the Athens of Marathon and Aeschylus. It is given fair expression in Thucydides' *Syngraphe* (OH, II, 349ff), and it reaches its nadir in the judicial murder of Socrates (OH, III, 7ff). The specific historical awareness generated by Plato was the theory of the cycle of history (OH, II, 50ff).[30] Unlike the historical form created by Israelite revelation, the Hellenic historical form was created only gradually. It achieved its greatest clarity only through the experience and understanding of disorder marking the *end* of a phase of the Hellenic civilization. The past of mankind discovered by the philosopher's leap in being was the past of the untruth of the "people's myth"; the Before-and-After of the experience divided time into the untruth of polytheistic myth and the truth of the philosopher's well-ordered soul.

The difficulties that Voegelin's analysis encounters in attempting to penetrate the movement of Hellenic experience from Homer to Aristotle, and its relationship to the historical form, result from the fact that philosophy, in contrast to revelation, creates history only obliquely. The central thrust of the experiences symbolized in philosophy produces the self-conscious, reflective soul in personal existence under God. This is in contrast to the consciousness of the collective historical existence of the Chosen People which is generated immediately by revelation in Israel. The symbolic form of philosophy is not the narrative of paradigmatic history as in the Old Testament from Genesis to Second Kings, but the Platonic dialogue with its unique perfection of the *myth* as the articulating symbol of the philosopher's leap in being.[31] The intricate movement of experience through poets, mystic-philosophers, and historians, which is traced in detail by Voegelin,[32] to direct, specific achievement of historical existence through tragedy by the Athenian warriors at Marathon and by Aeschylus in his dramas, and then the further deepening of this experience by Plato, poses subtler problems of interpretation than are encountered in the bold contours of revelation. In defining the

30. Cf. *Order and History*, III, 156f and 286ff.
31. The varieties of the myth are distinguished *ibid.*, 185.
32. In Volumes II and III of *Order and History*.

essential difference between the historical forms constituted by revelation and by philosophy, Voegelin uses the following language.

> The word, the *dabar*, immediately and fully reveals the spiritual order of
> existence, as well as its origin in transcendent-divine being, but leaves it to
> the prophet to discover the immutability and recalcitrance of the world-im-
> manent structure of being; the philosopher's love of wisdom slowly dis-
> solves the compactness of cosmic order until it has become the order of
> world-immanent being beyond which is sensed, though never revealed, the
> unseen transcendent measure. (OH, II, 52)

The process, the content of the experience, and the symbolization
are quite other than in the revelation. The discovery of history in
Hellas comes into full view only in the Classic period; and, even
then, the Hellenic historical form does not attain the full luminosity
of revelation but remains bound by the symbolic limitations of a
nature myth of cosmic cycles (OH, III, 156) and by the dimensions
of the Dionysian soul (OH, II, 264; III, 61, 70, 141). In contrasting the *Logoi* of philosophy and revelation, Voegelin remarks that
when "man is in search of God, as in Hellas, the wisdom gained remains generically human" (OH, I, 496). Only the Israelite experience
achieved an immediate and radical break with the myth. The Hellenic experience is ranked as "intermediate" between that of Israel
and that of the China of Confucius and Laotse (OH, II, 262f).[33]

The development of the historical form in Hellas took the following course. The decisive step toward the creation of history was
already taken by Homer, who transformed the fall of the Achaeans
into the past of the Hellenic society (OH, II, 127).[34] By the time of
Hesiod (in the late eighth century B.C.), Hellenic society is constituted as existing in the *present*, if not under God, under the
Olympian gods of Homer. Then began a tension between the polis
and the poets and philosophers, a tension that was the fundamental
influence shaping the symbolic form of philosophy. The self-conscious awareness of the individual soul emerged from it and, along
with that, the recognition of the order of the soul as the authoritative

33. Voegelin's criteria for ranking and classifying the multiple and parallel leaps
in being are developed in *Order and History*, II, 7. The passage is quoted herein,
pp. 206–207.

34. Homer's "central problem [was] the breakdown of Mycenaean civilization"
(OH, II, 109).

source of transcendent order for man and society. Poets and philosophers alike existed in opposition to the corrupt order of the polis. The persistence of this tension is such that it developed into the "very form of Hellenic civilization" (OH, II, 169). The symbolic form created through the efforts of individuals who discovered the order of the human psyche beyond the order of the polis was *philosophy* itself.

The origin of philosophy in the conscious opposition of the well-ordered soul to the disorder in the society around it is emphasized by Voegelin. He holds it fundamental to an adequate understanding of Greek philosophy (OH, III, 62–69).[35] Philosophy as the symbolic form of Hellenic civilization is elusive compared with the symbolic forms of existence of the Near Eastern civilizations because of the nature of the experiences symbolized. The personal order of the philosopher's soul, gained through orienting movements toward transcendent truth in the ground of the soul, cannot be institutionalized but must depend upon autonomous formation in individuals. Moreover, "since this [very] elusiveness of the form is the cause of the error that philosophy is an 'intellectual' or 'cultural' activity conducted in a vacuum, without relation to the problems of human existence in society, it becomes all the more important to stress the roots of philosophy in the polis" (OH, II, 168).

Philosophy is similar to revelation in that both are separated from the cosmological form and myth by the leap in being, "that is, by the break with the compact experience of cosmic-divine order through the discovery of the transcendent-divine source of order" (OH, II, 126). The achievement of the early Greek mystic-philosophers consists of (1) their break both with the myth and the corrupt gentilitian social order (OH, II, 116, 170);[36] and (2) their advancing symbolization from the stage of theomorphic myth to the consciousness of movements in the ground of the soul itself and in the discovery of the "radical transcendence of the divine realissimum" (OH, II, 239). This epochal "transcendental irruption," experienced and expressed by the generation of mystic-philosophers, ushers in a new problem of authority which thereafter has remained a perennial

35. See above Chapter 1.
36. For the "old myth" and the "new myth," see OH, III, 188f.

source of friction and conflict: "the old collective order on the less differentiated level of consciousness is under permanent judgment by the new authority, while the new order of the spirit is socially an aristocratic achievement of charismatic individuals" (OH, II, 240).

The Hellenic differentiation of experiences of order reached the point of clarity sufficient to create existence in historical form in the fifth century Athens of Marathon and Aeschylus. In Hellas, but no-where else, "history was born from tragedy" (OH, II, 263). It was the concrete existence of an Athenian society possessing the spiritual substance capable of tragic action which brought the Hellenic civilization into history. The leap in being, achieved by the warriors at Marathon and by Aeschylus in his dramas, takes the form of a Dionysian descent into the depths of the soul to reach a decision for divine *Dike*, Justice (OH, II, 251). The experience itself is the consciousness of the reflective movement of the soul descending into its own depth, there to arrive at a just decision which then becomes the basis of mature, existentially responsible, action. When the meaning of the tragic action penetrated society sufficiently to make possible Marathon and the public cult of Aeschylean tragedy, it illuminated the order of society. Social order was seen as the triumph of man; it was experienced as a precarious incarnation of *Dike*, as order wrested by tragic action from demonic forces of disorder. Its preservation was understood to be dependent upon the socially effective presence of tragic action. In the differentiation of human consciousness, a "course of human affairs becomes a course of history when the order of the soul becomes the ordering force of society," because *only* "then can the rise and fall of a polity be experienced in terms of a growing or disintegrating psyche" (OH, II, 263). The Hellenes, through the Athenians, approach existence in freedom under God (achieved at once by the Israelites through revelation) through the tragic efforts of the people "to descend into the divine depth of *Dike*" (OH, II, 263).[37]

Beyond this, little is said which directly elucidates the relationship between the Hellenic experiences of order and the historical form. The struggle for attunement, which begins with the early

37. For the critique of Aristotle's theory of tragedy and its rejection, see OH, II, 246.

poets' asserting their spiritual authority against the polis and the myth in a contrapuntal configuration beginning with Hesiod, briefly climaxes in the miracle of fifth century Athens. For one splendid moment, the truth of the soul becomes the dominant source of public order, and the contending sources of authority—spiritual and temporal, transcendental and existential—blend. The tension of philosophy dissolves into tragic action. But, after that the dissociation begins anew. The tension between order and disorder grows to deadly intensity in the trial and judicial murder of Socrates by Athens and the trial and judgment of Athens by Socrates.[38] The gap widens hopelessly.[39] After Plato, the tension that became philosophy is broken.

The corruption and disintegration of Hellenic society is not, however, unmitigated misfortune. The breakdown of society, though foreshadowing political doom, is the stimulus which provokes Plato's mighty response: his perfection of philosophy as "*the* symbolic form in which a Dionysiac soul expresses its ascent to God" (OH, III, 70). The ontological perspective of the problem is to be remembered. Just as it could be said of Heraclitus that in "a corrupt society there may be only one man in whose soul burns the cosmic fire, who lives in love to the divine nomos" (OH, II, 239), so the *Gorgias* (513C, 521D) proclaims the transfer of authority "from the people of Athens and its leaders to the one man Plato" (OH, III, 39). The truth of being does not cease to be the truth of existence simply because a corrupt society and its leaders choose to ignore it or even because they resolutely deny its very existence. The truth of existence is part of being itself. As the principle is formulated by Voegelin in the Israelite context: "No amount of empirical defections can touch the constitution of being as it unfolds in the light of revelation. Man can close the eye of his soul to its light; and he can engage in the futility of rebellion; but he cannot abolish the order by which his conduct will be judged"

38. Reported in Plato, *Apology*. Cf. *Order and History*, III, 7. For the parallel development in Israel's history and its analysis, see the discussion of Jeremiah in OH, I, 436–38.
39. Voegelin discusses "*The Consciousness of Epoch*," including Aristotle's recognition that the Athens of his day was beyond reform, in OH, III, 284–92. The last act in the Hellenic drama of philosophy is Pyrrho of Elis' "withdrawal from philosophy" (OH, III, 368–72).

(OH, I, 464–65).[40] And this is substantially the answer of Plato to the anomalous spectacle of his contemporary Athens which, like the Israel of the Suffering Servant, had fallen from the truth of existence leaving it a living force in the soul of only one man.[41]

However profound the experiences of the Hellenic philosophers, even the full development of Platonic and Aristotelian philosophy leaves history without any meaning that can bear comparison with that gained through Israelite revelation. "The philosopher's leap in being has set free the paradigmatic *physis* of man and society, but it has not disengaged, as has the Mosaic and prophetic leap in being, the order of history from the myth of the cosmos" (OH, III, 336). History cannot be understood as the revelation of God's way through time with man without revelation itself, a matter resumed in Chapter 6.

VI

It is philosophy as a form of existence that is evoked in *Order and History*. In his introduction to the first volume, Voegelin speaks of philosophy as "the love of being through love of divine Being as the source of its order" (OH, I, xiv). As becomes clear from his study of Greek philosophy, philosophy has its origin in the resistance of the soul to its destruction by society. As an "act of resistance illuminated by conceptual understanding," it has two functions: *first*, it is an act of spiritual salvation for the philosopher and for others around him, because the philosopher's evocation of true order and his reconstitution of it in his own soul creates "the substantive center of a new community which, by its existence, relieves the pressure of the surrounding corrupt society. Under this aspect, Plato is the founder of the community of philosophers that lives through the ages"; *sec-*

40. The entire passage at this point deserves careful consideration. It concludes with this statement: "Man exists *within* the order of being; and there is no history *outside* the historical form under revelation. . . . There are times when the divinely willed order is humanly realized nowhere but in the faith of the solitary sufferers."

41. One of the loftiest sections of *Order and History* is the spiritual biography of the Suffering Servant of Deutero-Isaiah, I, 488–515. For the *Gorgias'* "Myth of the Judgment of the Dead" and Plato's *logique du coeur*, see OH, III, 30, 39–45. See also OH, I, 429.

ond, philosophy is an act of judgment, for in the arduous struggle of the soul to resist the evil forces that seek its destruction, pairs of concepts are developed which cast light on both good and evil, and these illuminating pairs of concepts become criteria of social order and disorder. "Under this second aspect, Plato is the founder of political science" (OH, III, 68–69).

The philosopher is the man who literally loves wisdom because it puts substance into his freedom and enables his soul to travel the road toward salvation through wisdom rather than out of blind habituation through dogma. He is the representative of mankind and, therefore, rightfully claims spiritual authority: "The philosopher is *man* in the anxiety of his fall from being; and philosophy is the ascent toward salvation for *Everyman*" (OH, III, 70, emphasis added). Plato, as the founder of philosophy, distinguishes between philosophers and philodoxers, between science and opinion; hence, one must not suppose that Plato himself was merely one philosopher among others or that what he has to say is mere opining (OH, III, 69–75). On the contrary, to once again use Voegelin's own energetic language: "Plato's philosophy, therefore, is not *a* philosophy but *the* symbolic form in which a Dionysiac soul expresses its ascent to God. If Plato's evocation of a paradigm of right order is interpreted as a philosopher's opinion about politics, the result will be hopeless nonsense, not worth a word of debate" (OH, III, 70).[42]

The initial volumes of *Order and History* convincingly reestablish ontology on the secure footing of experience and, thereby, radically expand the scope of the philosophical sciences. Moreover, they emphatically reassert the authority of the philosopher's soul as a source of order in the midst of existential disorder. The implications of these statements will be of concern in the next chapters, as will be the development and modification of the key issues identified in Voegelin's work in his 1957 horizon as we have just analyzed them.

---

42. For the challenging view that "the history of philosophy is in the largest part the history of its derailment," see OH, III, 271–79. The assertion is discussed herein, at pp. 155–63.

CHAPTER 6 Myth, Philosophy,
and Consciousness:
1966

In the first sentence of *The New Science of Politics*
(1952), Voegelin had stated that "The existence of man in political
society is historical existence; and a theory of politics, if it penetrates to principles, must at the same time be a theory of history"
(NSP, 1). That theory of history was to be unfolded in *Order and
History*; and when the first volume of the work appeared in 1956,
the first sentence of the Preface announced the course to be followed
toward the present from ancient Mesopotamia and Egypt in these
now-familiar words: "The order of history emerges from the history
of order." A few lines further on the enterprise is clarified:

While there is no simple pattern of progress or cycles running through history, its process is intelligible as a struggle for true order. This intelligible
structure of history, however, is . . . a reality to be discerned retrospectively
in a flow of events that extends, through the present of the observer, indefi-
nitely into the future. Philosophers of history have spoken of this reality as
providence . . . [and in doing so] they referred to a reality beyond the plans
of concrete human beings—a reality of which the origin and end is unknown and which for that reason cannot be brought within the grasp of
finite action. (OH, I, ix)

By this restatement, the theory of politics that had been expanded
into the theory of history in 1952 was further metamorphosed into
the philosophy of order to be attained through recollection and analysis of the trail of experiences and their symbols manifested in the
field of history. The next major reformulation came a decade later.

The first sentence of *Anamnesis* (1966) stated the central thesis of Voegelin's political philosophy thus: "The problems of human order in society and history arise from the order of the consciousness. The philosophy of consciousness is for that reason the centerpiece of a philosophy of politics" (A,7). With this 1966 formulation, the philosophy of politics was, then, further augmented by the experiences and symbols through which the process of consciousness articulates itself in time.

I

This succession of first-sentence formulations is not conflicting or contradictory, but complementary. Voegelin states that the materials published in the first part of *Anamnesis* (and written in 1943) express the theory of consciousness "presupposed" by both *The New Science of Politics* and *Order and History* and already of concern to him in the late 1920s when William James's theory of consciousness was explored in *On the Form of the American Mind*. That theory is exemplified in *Anamnesis*, most particularly in "What Is Political Reality?"

"The philosophy of order," Voegelin says, "is the process in which we as men find the order of existence in the order of consciousness" (A, 11). Plato expressed his own philosophy of consciousness in terms of the symbolism of Recollection. Since Voegelin builds his theory on the foundation supplied by Plato, the meaning of that symbolism is crucial. Plato appears to have coined the word *anamnesis* from *mnemosyne* (memory or remembrance; mythically, the Mother of the Muses); its meaning is remembering-again, recollection, or reminiscence (cf. *Philebus* 34A–C; 60A–E). The Well of Memory is known from the Orphic tablets, amulets buried with the dead and indispensable sources of knowledge for Orphic eschatology. The inscription of the *Petelia Tablet* reads as follows:

> Thou shalt find on the left of the House of Hades
> a Well-spring,
> And by the side thereof standing a white cypress.
> To this Well-spring approach not near.
> But thou shalt find another by the Lake of Memory
> (*Mnemosynes*),

Cold water flowing forth, and there are Guardians
                              before it.
Say: "I am a child of Earth and Starry Heaven;
But my race is of Heaven (alone). This ye know yourselves.
And lo, I am parched with thirst and I perish. Give
                              me quickly
The cold water flowing forth from the Lake of Memory."
And of themselves they will give thee to drink from the
                              holy Well-spring,
And thereafter among the other Heroes thou shalt have
                              lordship. . . . [1]

The divine origin of man is affirmed; it is nurtured, and his heav-
enly destiny saved, through the blessed water of Remembrance. The
nameless and forbidden well of the tablet is connected with the person of *Lethe* (Forgetfulness) in Hesiod (*Theogony*, 227); and Lethe
appears for the first time as a water, a river, at the end of Plato's *Republic* (621), where she is also called *Ameles* (Unmindful). No less
to Plato than to the Orphics and to Hesiod, Lethe is from the first
thoroughly bad, identified with the unconsciousness of death and
with the living death which is forgetfulness of that which ought to
be remembered—the amnesia of the soul and society of which Voegelin speaks at the beginning of *Order and History*. It is the ignorance in the soul (*agnoia*) which nullifies wisdom in the *Republic*;
and it combines with vice to obscure truth, thereby binding the soul
to earth, in the great myth of the *Phaedrus* (248D).

Truth in Greek (*aletheia*) connotes an uncovering, unconcealing,
or unforgetting; Plato etymologically designates it as "an agglomera-
tion of *Theia ale* (divine wandering), implying the divine motion of
existence" (*Cratylus*, 421B; cf. 411A–413C). The experience of *déjà
vu* or *anamnesis* is offered as evidence not only of the immortality
of the soul and of metempsychosis by Plato, but also as the sign of
essential humanity itself and as the equivalent of intuitive or noetic
reason (*Nous*): that mysterious divine something in man, the highest rational faculty or capacity of intellect whereby the transcendental Ideas and undemonstrable First Principles of scientific knowledge are, through participation, grasped and known.[2] Plato writes:

1. Quoted from Jane Harrison, *Prolegomena to the Study of Greek Religion* (repr.
ed.; New York: Meridian Books, Inc., 1955), 573–83, 659–60.
2. Plato, *Phaedo*, 73–76; *Symposium*, 208; *Meno*, 81–87; *Republic*, 617; *Tim-*

The soul which has never seen the truth will not pass into human form. For a man must have intelligence of universals, and be able to proceed from the many particulars of sense to one conception of reason; —this is the recollection of those things which our soul saw while following God—when regardless of that which we now call being she raised her head up toward the true being. And therefore the mind of the philosopher alone has wings; and this is just, for he is always, according to the measure of his abilities, clinging in recollection to those things in which God abides, and in beholding which He is what He is. And he who employs aright these memories is ever being initiated into perfect mysteries and alone becomes truly perfect. But, as he forgets earthly interests and is rapt in the divine, the vulgar deem him mad, and rebuke him; they do not see that he is inspired.[3]

This same identification—or at least close alliance—of *anamnesis* with *nous* is to be seen in the dilemma posed to Socrates in the *Meno* that through inquiry one "either . . . will learn nothing or what he already knows" (to accept Aristotle's formulation) which is resolved through the famous experiment with the slave boy that shows "all inquiry and all learning is but recollection," understanding learning to mean knowledge (*episteme*) of truth in terms of unchanging principles or essence.[4]

II

Because the process of consciousness informs and adumbrates the field of history, the best point of access for a critical understanding of Voegelin's political philosophy remains the historical symbolisms. The approach permits discussion of *Anamnesis* in the context of both earlier and later writings. The impressive continuity of his thought over a period of five decades also invites this approach, for Voegelin's attention to these problems did not cease with the pub-

---

aeus, 42, 91; cf. Aristotle, *Nicomachean Ethics*, 1140b31–1141a9; 1177a12–1178a8; *Posterior Analytics*, 100b5–14. Cf. Martin Heidegger, *Was ist Metaphysik?* (Frankfort: V. Klostermann, 1951), 10ff, trans. as "The Way Back Into the Ground of Metaphysics," in Walter Kaufmann, ed., *Existentialism from Dostoevsky to Sartre* (New York: New American Library, 1975), cf. pp. 210ff for remarks on *aletheia*.

3. Plato, *Phaedrus*, 249C–E.

4. Aristotle, *Posterior Analytics*, 71a29; *Meno*, 80E, 81E; cf. *Euthydemus*, 293Eff. Cf. the discussion of "Wissende Fragen und fragende Wissen," in *Anamnesis*, 150–52, 290, and at p. 159 herein. References to *Anamnesis* are to the German edition unless otherwise noted.

lication of this book. The two complexes of experiences and symbol-isms—those of history and those of consciousness—are held to-gether by the only "constant" Voegelin finds in either field. This link and constant is man himself; more specifically, it is man "in search of his humanity and its order." We must again recollect the first sen-tence of the Introduction to *Order and History*: "God and man, world and society form a primordial community of being."[5] In this starting point of Voegelin's philosophy, reality is symbolized as a community of being articulated into a four-fold relationship.

The field of being is not, however, simply postulated. Rather it arises in the symbol-forming consciousness as an expression of experience, in its most comprehensive reach. The mode of this com-prehensive and fundamental experience is implicit in the term *com-munity*. Being is no mere abstraction, but the concretely apprehended divine Ground; nor is being a thing. Neither abstraction nor thing, the term *community of being* expresses the content of man's inner experience of conscious participation in a whole greater than him-self, both like and unlike himself. This embracing whole finds its resting point in the divine Ground, which encompasses all that is. The experienced whole is symbolized as "being" (*ousia*) in philo-sophical language. The core of the experience forms as the sense of mutual interpenetration, sameness, and oneness of all that falls within the purview of consciousness.

This essential oneness, or consubstantiality, is not, however, per-fect homogeneity. It is articulated by tensions within the field of consciousness that are identified as distinct polarities. These ten-sional poles are designated by the symbols that define the structural boundaries of experienced reality. Hence, experienced consubstan-tiality of being differentiates itself as a community in which man participates as a polarity and member. It is precisely the tension of this partnership that man—and this means the concrete conscious-ness of each man—experiences and knows as the essence of his being. In Voegelin's words, "Man's partnership in being is the es-sence of his existence." Or, alternatively, "The 'specific nature of

5. The exploration of the question of "constants" ("intelligible structure") in his-tory and consciousness is explicit on the first page of the Preface of *Order and His-tory*; it is profoundly developed in Voegelin, "Equivalences of Experiences," 215–34.

man' is his 'consciousness of the existential tension to the Ground'"
(OH, I, 2; A, 340). The second formulation can be taken as the equivalent of the first only if *participation* is given full weight. *Partnership* is synonymous with *participation*; and man's consciousness
forms precisely as this same participation. Hence the essence of man
is this luminous inward dimension (or consciousness) which forms
as participation in the divine Ground of being. Participation is,
therefore, the pivotal conception for an understanding of Voegelin's
theories of consciousness, experience, symbolization, and reality
and, so, of his whole philosophy.[6]

It must be emphasized that the experience now under discussion
is the "inner" experience, which forms as participation—not the
outward experience of sensory perception of things. The Kantian critique raised persuasive doubts as to the very possibility of fully objective perceptual experience of "things in themselves"; it suggested
that the experience of things depends upon a complex interpretive
operation of the human mind in which what is apparently objectively observed partakes heavily of the observing subject. This process is described in Kantian language as the injection of *thingness*
into perception by the "synthetic function of pure intuition and the
synthetic unities of pure understanding."[7] Even such objectivization
as this is a late development in the differentiation of human consciousness and is merely a further mode of symbolization—one of
distinctive merit in bringing to hand the mode of material reality of
things existing in time and space. In the current climate of positivistic and behavioralistic obsession in the humane disciplines, it will
perhaps be salutary to recall Goethe's observation that "all fact is in
itself theory."[8] And it is, in any event, evident that the material and
quantifiable do not exhaust the whole of experienced reality. No account that takes only these factors into consideration can form a sufficient basis for understanding man in his humanity or for understanding the science of politics.

Beginning, then, from the experience of participation, and from

6. For a further discussion of participation, see Voegelin, "Immortality: Experience and Symbol," (1967), 235–79.
7. Ernst Cassirer, *The Philosophy of Symbolic Forms*, trans. Ralph Manheim
(3 vols.; New Haven: Yale University Press, 1953–57), III, 60.
8. *Ibid.*, III, 25.

the understanding that participation is the form of consciousness itself, it can be said that whatever man knows he knows from the
manifold of experience gained from his inevitable perspective as *participant* in the community of being. The oneness or unity of being is
juxtaposed to the oneness of the nature of man, according to Voegelin's key interpretive principle. The range of experience, moreover,
is always present in the fullness of its dimensions. Finally, the structure of the range, insofar as it attains articulation in consciousness,
varies from compact to differentiated (OH, I, 60). The differentiation
of experience and symbolization is the manifestation of the intellectual and spiritual—of the specifically human—in the history of
mankind. Indeed, it is the very action which constitutes societies
and creates history itself.

From the matrix of experience a man gains partial understanding
of the order of being and of the obligations of existence. Yet the
paradoxical quality of the perspective of participation must be emphasized.

He is an actor playing a part in the drama of being and, through the brute
fact of his existence, committed to play it without knowing what it is. . . .
Both the play and the role are unknown. But even worse, the actor does not
know with certainty who he is himself. . . . Man's partnership in being is
the essence of his existence, and this essence depends on the whole, of
which existence is a part. Knowledge of the whole, however, is precluded by
the identity of the knower with the partner, and ignorance of the whole precludes essential knowledge of the part. This situation of ignorance with regard to the decisive core of existence is more than disconcerting: it is profoundly disturbing, for from the depth of this ultimate ignorance wells up
the anxiety of existence. (OH, I, 1–2)

The anxiety of existence, the mystery of being and the horror of a
fall from existence into the nothingness of nonexistence, motivates
the creation of "symbols purporting to render intelligible the relations and tensions between the distinguishable terms in the field"
(OH, I, 3). Man's essential ignorance of himself and being, though a
permanent attribute of existence, one given paradigmatic expression
in the irony of Socratic ignorance, is not complete ignorance. It is
not in the spirit of a detached search for scientific truth that man
seeks to render existence intelligible; rather, it is out of the anxiety

of a fall from being that he searches the texture of the experiential content of consciousness to render existence itself meaningful.

The "primary experience" centers in the apprehension of the cosmos as divine and generates the first great symbolic form, the *myth*. In a beautiful passage, Voegelin describes it this way:

The cosmos of the primary experience is neither the external world of objects encountered by man when he has become a subject of cognition, nor is it the world created by a world-transcendent God. Rather, it is the whole, *to pan*, of an earth below and a heaven above—of celestial bodies and their movements; of seasonal changes; of fertility rhythms in plant and animal life; of human life, birth and death; and above all, as Thales still knew, it is a cosmos full of gods. . . . In the Memphite Theology, imperial order is established by a drama of the gods that, by virtue of the consubstantiality of all being, is performed on the human plane as the drama of Egypt's conquest and unification. In the Sumerian King List, kingship is created in heaven and then lowered to earth; and two thousand years later, in Jewish apocalypse, there is still a Jerusalem in heaven, to be lowered to earth when the time for God's kingdom has come. Yahweh speaks from Mount Sinai, out of a fiery cloud; the Homeric Olympians dwell on earth, on a mountain reaching into the clouds, and they have quarrels and agreements affecting the destinies of peoples in Asia and Europe. The Hesiodic gods Uranus and Gaea are indistinguishably heaven and earth themselves; they enter into a union and generate the gods, and the generation of gods in their turn generate the races of man. This togetherness and one-in-anotherness is the primary experience that must be called cosmic in the pregnant sense. (OH, IV, 68–69)

Wherever the great cosmic mythologies appear—and they appear in all the ancient empires, from Egypt to China—they reflect the experience characterized in the foregoing passage. The creation of myth is the work of men motivated by the anxiety of existence. Myth is an expression of this anxiety and its conquest by a compact search of the Ground articulated in concrete imagery. Neither for Voegelin nor for Ernst Cassirer is myth simply irrational thought; rather, it is compact or undifferentiated, prephilosophical and prescientific thought which comprehends within itself compact equivalents of more differentiated thinking, including the mythic equivalent of *Noesis*—of rational, etiological thought.[9]

The process of symbolization at the level of the cosmic myth dis-

9. *Ibid.*, I, 88ff, 111–14, 285–316; II, xivff, 4ff, 16ff, 35ff, 43ff, 60–61, 69–70, 71ff, 171ff, 194ff, 252ff, 258n; III, xi–xii, xiii, 13, 22ff, 48ff, 62–63, 68, 73, 83, 99–100, 102,

plays certain typical features of interest in the present context. Five of these can be enumerated.[10]

1) The experience of participation is predominant, *i.e.*, the experience of the oneness or consubstantiality of the whole of being of which man himself is a part.

2) There is reflected a preoccupation with the lasting and passing of the partners in the community of being, their durability and transiency, and this looks to the construction of images that portray an apprehended hierarchy of existence—from man to society to the cosmos and the everlasting gods themselves.

3) Participation is heightened into *attunement* to the order of being, to the lasting and enduring as this is distinguished through the experience of a hierarchy of unequally enduring existences. The soul thereby remains "open" (in Bergson's sense) to the divine Ground; and this openness is the substance of human rationality (A, 289).[11]

4) The attempt is made to make the essentially unknowable order of being intelligible as far as possible through the creation of symbols that interpret the unknown by analogy with the really, or supposedly known. It is under this aspect of the process of symbolization that the life of man and society are represented as reflecting the visible order of the cosmos, as a microcosm or a cosmion. Human existence is integrated through ritual and myth into the perceptible rhythms of the cosmic order. The differentiation of the primary experience, perhaps spurred by some social crisis, develops the tendency to further penetrate the field of experience, thereby inverting the symbolisms when the order of reality (including society and the world) is experienced as essentially consciousness and symbolized by Plato on the pattern of the well-ordered soul attuned to the unseen God beyond the visible cosmos—that is, as a macroanthropos, as a MAN.[12]

5) The analogical character of symbols is understood early in the

---

107. In Voegelin, see especially "Historiogenesis," in *Anamnesis*, 79ff, and the expanded version in *Order and History*, IV, Chap. 1.

10. The following enumeration is drawn from *Order and History*, I, 3–11.

11. Cf. Henri Bergson, *Two Sources of Morality and Religion*, trans. R. A. Audra and Cloudesley Brereton (New York: Henry Holt, 1935), esp. 168, 228ff, 240ff, 252, 265, 280–306. See also Voegelin, *The New Science of Politics*, 79.

12. Plato, *Republic*, 368D–E; see Voegelin, *Order and History*, III, 69–70.

process of symbolization, perhaps from the very beginning. On the one hand, symbol and referent tend to blend and assume an identity; yet, on the other hand, the very abundance and apparent contradictoriness of symbolic representations of divine order reflect a tolerance of symbolization rooted in the knowledge that reality outruns representations, which are inevitably partial and inadequate. Symbolization is no more than a serious play. This early tolerance reflects the insight that the order of being can only be represented imperfectly—but in a multiplicity of mutually complementary and valuable ways. "Every concrete symbol is true insofar as it envisages the truth, but none is completely true insofar as the truth about being is essentially beyond human reach" (OH, I, 7). Yet the limits of tolerance can be and are reached whenever symbolization itself becomes a source of error about the order of being. Then the issue of the unseemliness of symbolisms is raised (as in Xenophanes and Plato), which provokes with new intensity the anxiety and horror of a fall from being through imperfect attunement fostered by a false theology perpetuated through outworn symbols. Lastly, the differentiation of the fundamental experience by the "leap in being," which reveals the unseen God of transcendence historically, carries with it a revulsion against any symbolization. The Holy of Holies stands empty; no images are carved to honor this God; and what the *Agathon* is Plato cannot say.[13]

The mystery of the transcendent divine partner in being, who reveals himself as the I AM THAT I AM and finds his most suitable name in the unpronounceable Tetragrammaton YHWH,[14] emerges out of the differentiation of the primary experience in the pneumatic mode. Israel creates the symbolism of the Chosen People, in the present, under God, and articulates itself in the historical form of existence. The form of the myth is decisively broken and its authority dissolves. History thereby becomes the new form of existence for universal mankind and is first constituted by the experience of the world-transcendent God. The representative act taken by Moses for

13. Plato, *Republic*, 517B. See Voegelin, *Order and History*, III, 112ff, and *Anamnesis*, 338ff.

14. Exodus 3:14; Thomas Aquinas, *Summa Theologica*, I, 13, 11; Voegelin, *Order and History*, I, 402–14, and *Anamnesis*, 338.

Israel is taken by Israel as God's Chosen People for all mankind (OH, I, 115).[15]

Less radically but no less certainly, the primary experience also differentiates in the noetic mode in the horizon of ancient Greece. This is the achievement of the mystic-philosophers climaxing in Socrates, Plato, and Aristotle. Here the symbolic form of existence is not paradigmatic history (such as that recounted in the Old Testament from Genesis to Second Kings) but philosophy, which finds optimal symbolic expression in the Platonic dialogue. In contrasting the *Logoi* of philosophy and revelation, Voegelin remarks that when "man is in search of God, as in Hellas, the wisdom gained remains generically human" (OH, I, 496). Differentiation of the primary experience in Israel occurs as a passion, "as a response to a revelation of divine being, to an act of grace, to a selection for emphatic partnership with God"—not as the result of human action but as an encounter with a divine initiative the human response to which is symbolized as *conversion* in the religious sense (OH, I, 10). In Israel, God is in search of man, in Hellas man in search of God.

Still, the contrast between the pneumatic and noetic modes of differentiation is far from absolute, as is clear from both Hellenic philosophy and from the New Testament. The insight of the mystic philosophers is gained not only by means of the noetic mode of philosophical inquiry (*zetema*) which ascends the arduous way (*methodos*) through the realms of being to the point where the divine Ground is sensed in a transcendental beyond (Plato's *epekeina*). But this reflective, rational, self-conscious search of the Ground also is accompanied by and intertwined with the pneumatic mode in its Dionysian variety. The pneumatic element is displayed in the eroticism of the Socratic soul as it strives toward the divine *Sophon* as the fulfillment of its limitless desire. So, also, the philosopher's symbolization of the existential impact of the Vision of the Good is *conversion*—the Platonic *periagoge* or turning about of the whole soul: away from world and society as the sources of misleading analogy and untruth, toward the true source of order and of the only knowledge that can claim to be scientific.

What at first approach seems an intricate yet clear contrast in

15. See Chapter 5, above.

modes of experiential differentiation between Israel and Hellas displays still greater complexity on closer examination, as Voegelin argues in *Anamnesis*.[16] Both pneumatic and noetic components of the primary experience differentiate in the Hellenic horizon and find decisive symbolization in the form of philosophy itself. Nor is this simply, it may be emphasized, a mythic hangover or a vestige of the old compactness—although this element is present as a third factor as well, since the insights gained through myth into the order of being are of abiding validity. In certain respects, there is no getting beyond the myth.

The differentiated noetic and pneumatic experiences can be seen together in the Hellenic horizon, for example, in the *Phaedo* (69C) where the very goal of philosophy is identified as equivalent to mystical participation in the divine. Thus Socrates expressed the matter this way: "For 'many,' as they say in the mysteries, 'are the thyrsus-bearers but few are the mystics'—meaning as I interpret the words, 'the true philosophers.' In the number of whom, during my whole life, I have been seeking according to my ability, to find a place." Viewed from the perspective of the differentiated noetic science of Classical philosophy, the meaning of this statement is that the optimal clarity of the Logos of consciousness is such that the philosopher's grasp of the Logos of the realms of being is equivalent to that attained by initiation into the Bacchic mysteries. The Greek term rendered as *mystics* in Jowett's translation is *Bakchos*, which is equally the God and God-related man (A, 292). In arising out of mythic compactness, itself an undifferentiated compound of pneumatic, noetic, and other experiential modes, Classical philosophy differentiated its specific form of participation in unbroken continuity with the prephilosophical mythical form. The mythic elements in philosophy remain sufficiently intact so that Voegelin states his conclusion boldly: "Our knowledge of order remains primarily mythic, even after the noetic experience has differentiated the

16. Plato, *Republic*, 518D–E; Voegelin, *Order and History*, III, 68, and *Anamnesis*, 311, 328. Voegelin has recently carried this argument much farther, as we shall presently see. On the stunning analysis of the noetic structure of the movement in the soul, which climaxes in the death and resurrection of Christ, and its essential continuity with Classical philosophy, see Voegelin, "The Gospel and Culture," 59–101.

realm of consciousness and noetic exegesis has made its Logos explicitly clear" (A, 290).

It is precisely this interpenetration of the noetic mode with the mythic experience on one side, and with pneumatic experience on the other, which compels consideration of the derailment of philosophy. Before pursuing this thread, however, the general consequences of the differentiation of experience through the leap in being must be clarified.

A decisive consequence of the leap in being, whether occurring in the pneumatic or noetic mode—through revelation or through philosophy—is the radical *de*-divinization of the world.[17] The new locus of the divine is a "beyond" of existence, a reality experienced as transcending the visible reality. The structure of being itself thereby changes through dissociation and now receives the spatial-metaphorical linguistic indices, *immanent* and *transcendent* (OH, I, 10–11; A, 141, 275, 316–17, 322–23). The new task faced is relating man's existence, in a world now free of gods, to the divine Ground of being "located" in the beyond of transcendence. It is at least in part to meet this demand that Greek philosophy developed the symbol *participation*, in Plato *methexis*, Aristotle *metalepsis* (A, 290ff, 307ff).[18]

Through the experience of transcendent Being symbolized in revelation and philosophy, men gain release from the old imperial order in the cosmological form. The divine source of being lies in a transcendental beyond, and no earthly divinity mediates its efficacy. The Chosen People of Israel are free. They stand collectively in the present under God, and this immediacy carries over into Christianity where it is the individual human person who stands in freedom in immediacy to God. The very form of philosophy develops in the awareness of the autonomy of the individual soul. It arises through the opposition of solitary thinkers to the disorder of corrupt public order, expressed in the conventions of the polis, and to the dogmatic vulgarity of the sophists, for whom mere "man is the measure" (OH, II, 169, 273–74; A, 117–33). Philosophy thereby affirms the con-

17. Cf. Voegelin, *The New Science of Politics*, 106ff; see also his "World Empire and the Unity of Mankind," (1962), 176ff; "What Is Nature?" in *Anamnesis*, 134–52.
18. On the Platonic *metaxy*, see Voegelin, *Anamnesis*, 266ff, 317.

stitutive centrality of freedom both to itself and to man. Freedom is understood to be an essential condition for the realization of the specific nature or essence of man through the contemplative life. Plato found it to be the one good thing about democracy. For Plato, of course, knew that in his new found freedom man can rebel and reject the truth of being. He can form conceptions of order built out of the diseased motivations of self-love, the unreality of dreams, or the *libido dominandi* and, so, effectively ignore the divine Ground of being altogether—as in the case of the modern ideological systems and the empires they dogmatically order.[19]

III

The discussion at this point opens on a field of formidable questions that are explored in rich detail in *Anamnesis*.[20] What is the noetic experience and science—*Noesis* as Voegelin terms it—which symbolically forms as true philosophy? How is noetic knowledge of reality related to the nonnoetic modes of experience and symbolization and the whole of man's knowledge of reality? What is the derailment suffered by philosophy and how is it to be remedied? We shall briefly address each of these questions.

The terms *noesis, noetic experience, noetic interpretation* and the like derive from the technical vocabulary of Classical philosophy, specifically from the term *Nous* which means severally reason, intelligence, and mind. Aristotle contrasts intelligence (*nous*) with calculative or discursive reasoning (*dianoia* or *logos*) in the *Nicomachean Ethics*. It may be understood, in its highest aspect, as the intuitive property of rationality (in Bergson's sense) by which fundamental principles of science are grasped without intermediary steps of ratiocination, either deductive or inductive. Insofar as Voegelin specifically defines political science as the noetic interpretation of political reality, the concrete meaning of the expression can be suggested by saying that *Noesis* is an interpretation of political reality substantially like that given by Plato and Aristotle.[21]

19. Plato, *Republic*, 557B, 562B–566; Voegelin, *Anamnesis*, 223–53.
20. See especially Voegelin's concluding essay, "What is Political Reality?" *Anamnesis*, 283–354.
21. Aristotle, *Nicomachean Ethics*, VI, 6, 1140b31–1141a8; *Posterior Analytics*,

This preliminary information is not without significance, since it immediately precludes the understanding of political science as a systematizing science of phenomena which models itself methodologically on the natural and mathematical sciences of the external world.[22] The noetic interpretation of political reality, on the contrary, arises out of the tension in existence that forms between the historically grown self-understanding of a society (as found in its laws, customs, institutions, literature, formulations of its political leadership) and the reflective, self-conscious man's experience of existential order (A, 285). The tension in political reality, therefore, is not an external object of experience. Rather, it is an inner experience or apperception in the concrete consciousness of specific individual persons who find themselves at odds with society regarding fundamental issues of existence. This existential tension arises out of the palpable conflict between conventional and noetic truth. The resultant anxiety to live in order, then, provides the impetus for a rational search of the truth of being—the reflective search for the true order of man's existence within the world, society, history, and divine reality. This search—Socrates' *zetema* in the *Republic*, for example—is conducted into the vertical dimension of existence, into the depths and heights of consciousness. It seeks to uncover, through a meditative sifting of the contents of experience, the source or configuration of ultimate reality and its order. This introspective quest Voegelin terms the "search of the Ground"—the *aition, arche*—or ultimate cause (A, 288, 287–315 *passim*, 148ff).

The meditative search of the divine Ground brings to essential clarity awareness of a further existential tension, that between the man and the divine Ground itself. This may be seen superficially as the life of reason as it seeks to justify man's opposition to the in-

---

II, 19, 100b5–14; Voegelin, *Anamnesis*, 284, 286–87. Cf. Stanley Rosen, *Nihilism: A Philosophical Essay* (New Haven and London: Yale University Press, 1969), 7ff, 151–58, 187–90. See also the discussion in my "Beyond Behavioralism: The Philosophical Science of Politics," in George J. Graham, Jr., and George W. Carey (eds.), *The Post Behavioral Era: Perspectives on Political Science* (New York: David McKay, 1972), 285–305.

22. Cf. Voegelin, *Anamnesis*, 283ff, 318; *The New Science of Politics*, 3ff; *Science, Politics, and Gnosticism*, (1968), 15–22; "Reason: The Classic Experience," (1974). See also Leszek Kolakowski, *The Alienation of Reason: A History of Positivist Thought*, trans. N. Guterman (Garden City, N.Y.: Doubleday, Anchor Books, 1969).

roads into the psyche of disorders prevalent in society by appeal to such principles of order as abstract ideas or philosophical absolutes. Such an intellectualized characterization of the process, however, though partially valid, is insufficient and, in the long run, a major source of error about the philosophical inquiry and the nature of philosophy itself. For it is the *experiential*, rather than the merely ideational, dimension of the activity that is decisive. Philosophy is born out of the travail of the anxiety of existence. It finds the way toward truth by a search of the divine Ground whose ontological direction is known through a man's experience of participation in the community of being (A, 289). Distinctive to the philosophical effort is the identification and evocation of reason—*logos, nous, ratio*—as the specific nature of man. It is reason, so understood, that 1) illuminates consciousness; 2) directs, controls, and guides man's search for truth; and 3) possesses an intrinsic affinity for (and decisive kinship with) the divine Ground.

results of the noetic act = political science

Among the results of the noetic act, therefore, the following may be noticed especially: 1) differentiation in the experiential mode of participation of reason (*Nous*) to the extent that it is apperceived as the intelligible core of divine Being, the source of all order and truth and the ultimate Ground of being itself; 2) the differentiation of human reason in the symbolic mode of self-reflective cognitive inquiry (*zetesis*) called philosophy, which illuminates with intelligence the loving search of the divine Ground; 3) the development of conceptual instruments that are both the outcome and the means of the noetic exegesis, that symbolically "fix" the content of the inquiry in its experiential and conceptual aspects in the consciousness, and that, when taken all together, comprise a fabric of critically authenticated knowledge with convincing claim to objective scientific truth, thus becoming "political science" and "philosophy" regarded as subject fields. *Nous* is, by Voegelin's account, both the directional factor of consciousness and the substantial structure or order of consciousness. Rationality in existence, therefore, may be identified with what Bergson called the "openness" of the soul and irrationality with the closure of the soul against (or mistakenness about) the Ground (A, 152, 289, 296).

The foregoing account of *Noesis* is clarified when placed in the context of Aristotle's *Metaphysics*, as analyzed by Voegelin. The first sentence of the *Metaphysics* becomes intelligible in a new sense: "All men by nature desire to know [the Ground]" (980a).[23] Aristotle developed the noetic exegesis of this perceived desire for the Ground, as well as of the Ground's actualizing attractiveness, through the symbol of the participation (*metalepsis*) in one another of two entities bearing the name *Nous* (1072b20ff). By *Nous* he designated both the human capacity for intelligent search of the Ground as well as the Ground of being itself—that which is experienced as the Mover who gives direction to the inquiry. For Aristotle, the first to differentiate concepts out of mythic symbols, *synonymity* of expression means to be of the same kind, or sameness through generation (*genesis*). He wrote: "We must next observe that every thing (*ousia*) is generated from that which has the same name (*ek synonymou*)" (1070a4f). "That thing which communicates to other things the same name (*to synonymon*) is in relation to them itself the highest thing of that kind (*malista auto*)" (993b20ff). The synonymity of noetic entities implies, therefore, the origin of human reason in the divine *Nous*. In terms of the mythical symbolism of synonymity-through-genesis, Aristotle understood the tension of consciousness as the reciprocal participation (*metalepsis*) of two entities of *Nous* in one another. "From the side of the human *nous*, the knowing questions and questioning knowledge (*wissende Fragen und fragende Wissen*), that is the noetic act (*noesis*), is cognitive participation in the Ground of being; the noetic participation, however, is possible because it is preceded by participation of the divine in the human *nous*" (A, 290, 150–52).

Voegelin's discovery of the retention in Aristotle's ontology of the mythic experience of substantive participation of man in the divine—and of the divine in man—is of great importance. It enables one to see more clearly the relation of philosophical experience and symbolization to the matrix out of which they differentiated: it exhibits the dependence of philosophy upon the more compact experience of the divinity of the cosmos in decisive respects. Aristotle's participation (*metalepsis*) is neither merely a metaphor nor merely a means of designating parallel attributes in man and the divine. Rather, it is the noetic expansion of the mythic insight that man's

23. Cf. Voegelin, *Anamnesis*, 323; the balance of this paragraph is a close paraphrase of page 290.

participation in the divine is *constitutive* of man's being in its specific essence, *i.e.*, in the rational dimension. The philosophical anthropology developed in the *Ethics* can then be read in a new light. Aristotle's famous analysis that the highest part of man is his active reason—and that man's most perfect happiness is the contemplative life because the noetic activity called "philosophic wisdom" is the highest virtue of man's highest part and, therefore, most proper to him—climaxes in the description of such a life as more than merely human. "For it is not insofar as he is man that he will live so, but insofar as something divine is present in him." Then, paradoxically, Aristotle specifically identifies the very nature of man with reason: *Nous is* each man himself, the noetic life *is* the life of man's true self, and hence also the happiest. The paradox dissolves only if proper weight is accorded Aristotelian participation in its full experiential dimension. Man is not as he appears. The core and constitutive factor of the human essence is his "immortalizing (*athanatizein*)" participation through reason in the divine *Nous* or Ground of being. Apart from this man falls short of his own humanity.[24]

The experience of the consubstantiality of the community of being is neither destroyed nor negated through philosophical differentiation. Rather, it is intensified, achieving analytical clarity. Yet this process entails abstraction which, though an advance, ironically contributes to the subsequent loss of awareness of the engendering experiences articulated in the noetic concepts. From this situation, Voegelin asserts, the derailment of philosophy after Aristotle occurred. The whole new philosophical vocabulary was permeated at the time of its differentiation (especially by Socrates, Plato, and Aristotle) by the experience it explicates. But this immediacy soon was lost.

[margin note: Derailment of philosophy after Aristotle]

The process of noetic exegesis and the verifying experiences upon which truth depends arose out of myth and the primary experience of the divine cosmos. The noetic exegesis supplied a differen-

24. Cf. *ibid.*, 340, for the specific and synthetic (or composite) essence of man. See Aristotle, *Nicomachean Ethics*, 1177b26–1178a3. For the analysis of the passage cited from the *Nicomachean Ethics*, see Voegelin, "Immortality: Experience and Symbol," 272–73, where he classifies *athanatizein*, *phronesis*, and *philia* as "existential virtues"—a third category supplementing the ethical and *dianoetic* (intellectual) virtues named by Aristotle himself. Cf. Voegelin, *Anamnesis*, 124–33; see the exploration of this problem in Voegelin, "Reason: The Classic Experience," 251–60.

tiated corrective of the earlier more compact knowledge, but it did not and cannot totally supplant that knowledge. The key concept, human nature, for example, was not developed through inductive logic but as the term for the "nonexistent reality" of man—*i.e.*, neither a thing nor divinity, but an "In-Between" (*metaxy*) of consciousness—which loves the divine Ground of being. The term arose from the concrete experience of a philosophizing man seeking to designate the essence of his humanity.[25] What is true of the philosophical experience of human nature, similarly, is also true of the experience of a man's presence under God, which the Israelite prophet pneumatically apperceives concretely to be his essence or specific humanity.

The proposition that all men *qua* men equally possess such a nature and are thus essentially the same—regardless of whether they vividly experience their specific humanity in the full light of differentiated consciousness—is not a product of the specific experience of this or that prophet or theorist. Rather, the insight arises from the primary experience of the cosmos in which each being participates in due measure, the men as men, God as God; it rests upon this fundamental experience as a starting supposition. The insights of a philosopher can thereby be advanced as universally valid knowledge or science, as representative truth that is consequential for the order of personal lives, society, and history. The Hellenic philosophers developed specific symbols to express the primordial experience of the community of being and the uniquely political communality of a mankind that partakes of being. Heraclitus spoke of the *Logos* as the common (*xynon*) in man, as that in which all men *qua* men participate and which becomes the existential source of order insofar as men consciously agree in it (*homologia*). For Aristotle the common is the *Nous*, the divine element shared by man and God; and his symbol for the ordering of society through participation of all men in love (*philia*) of the *Nous* is the *homonoia*—a term which found its way into Saint Paul's vocabulary as the designation of the Christian community bound together in likemindedness (A, 291; OH, II, 179f, 231, 237).[26]

25. Voegelin, *Anamnesis*, 40, 266ff, 291, 300, 304ff; "Immortality: Experience and Symbol," 251, 261, 274; and "Gospel and Culture," 63ff, 71–75.

26. See G. S. Kirk and J. E. Raven, *The Pre-Socratic Philosophers: A Critical His-*

The phenomenon confronted in *Noesis*, then, is the differentiation of the specifically rational component of the mythic experience and its identification as noetic through the conceptual language of philosophy. The *Bakchos* of the mystery religions, which is equally the god and the god-related man, becomes for Plato the divine *Sophon* and the philosophical life that partakes of it; and it becomes for Aristotle the *Nous*, which is both divine and the essence of man, for man's very humanity is measured by the degree of his participation in the divine Reason. In Voegelin the mythical symbolism is pushed still farther into the background when, instead of speaking of *Bakchos* or *Nous*, he speaks of "tension to the Ground." Yet the process of bringing to optimal clarity through dissociation the various realms of being must not be one in which the sense of their identity is either negated or lost; for this consubstantiality, first apprehended in the primary experience of the compact consciousness, remains an insight of permanent validity, the matrix of man's understanding of the embracing intelligible order (A, 291–92).

IV

The derailment (*parekbasis*) of philosophy in the wake of Aristotle occurred primarily because the *experience* of which philosophy is the symbolic form was not itself made central (A, 313ff). The obscurity of the engendering experiences when approached through the symbols employed by Aristotle has been suggested by the foregoing discussion of participation. Why the experience was not made more clearly central may be explained by the fact that Aristotle's philosophizing lay in such proximity to the myth that he perhaps failed to anticipate the possibility of the abstraction of the philosophical symbols from their experiential context. Such a detachment, however, did occur historically, Voegelin contends, resulting in a fundamental misunderstanding of philosophy that persists to this day.[27]

In the detachment of the symbols from their evocative experi-

---

tory with a Selection of Texts (Cambridge, Eng.: Cambridge University Press, 1960), 187ff. Aristotle, *Nicomachean Ethics*, VIII, 1155a22; IX, 1167a22, 1177a12–18; 1177b26–1178a1; cf. *Politics*, II, 1262b7, 1263b38. See also Rom. 15:5; Phil. 2:2, 20; cf. 1 Cor. 1:10, Phil. 1:27.

27. See *Anamnesis*, 325ff, for a historical sketch of the derailment.

ences, the language the philosopher used to explicate his relation to the transcendent Ground was regarded as propositional assertions about the external world, or simply as *topoi*—speculation without reference to any experiential criterion apart from the internal consistency demanded of a logical construct. In either case, the fallacious result is an *ignoratio elenchi* by which "philosophical" argument becomes irrelevant—splitting *dianoia* from *noesis* and identifying reason with the former, irrationality with the latter. The cultural monument to this deformation is the "Enlightenment," which might as easily be named the "Age of Unreason." The result is the truncation of reason and a grotesque parody of philosophy, eventuating in the latter's wholesale explicit abandonment in favor of modern natural science as a more effective means of grasping external reality and (at the same time) the dogmatic assertion of "truth" from the standpoints of contending systems that range from left-wing Hegelianism to neo-Thomism.[28] The humane disciplines were left to oscillate between these polarities. And contemporary political science is "theorized" from "positions" that range from dogmatic positivism to dogmatic metaphysics by "theorists" who display the full fury of the *odium theologicum* implicit in their mutually exclusive dogmatisms. The resultant confusion was well captioned by Voegelin's blunt response when asked his opinion of Arnold Brecht's encyclopedic study of twentieth-century political theory: "There hasn't been any" (A, 313).[29]

Voegelin's point is that the *episteme politike* was lost long before Comte and Marx made their ostentatious exodus from philosophy, as Comte himself very nearly understood. The morass of relativism and contentious dogmatism—compromising a veritable "*Dogmatomachy*" (A, 328ff) as it were—into which political science fell has ruined the discipline and been destructive of political existence itself. That the damage in America has not been even greater than it has may be mainly ascribed to two reciprocating factors: the general

28. *Ibid.*, 302–303, 313. Cf. Rosen, *Nihilism*, Chap. 5. On Voegelin's treatment of "dogmatism," see John A. Gueguen, "Voegelin's *From Enlightenment to Revolution*: A Review Article," *Thomist*, XLII (1978), 123–34.

29. The volume in question is Brecht, *Political Theory: The Foundations of Twentieth Century Political Thought* (Princeton, N.J.: Princeton University Press, 1959).

theoretical soundness of the Anglo-American political tradition, and the good common sense of political scientists who spurn "theory" and content themselves with making political processes and the institutional operations of government intelligible (A, 351ff, 354; NSP, 187ff). In the commonsense rejection of ideology and its attendant destruction of reality, Voegelin sees a genuine residue of *Noesis*, a sign of spiritual and intellectual health and existential resistance to contemporary disorder that can become the rallying point for the reconstitution of a sound philosophical science of politics. Common sense, as was noticed earlier and bears repeating here, has its philosophical representative in the eighteenth-century Scottish school of that name. It was defined by Thomas Reid as that "certain degree" of rationality "which is necessary to our being subjects of law and government, capable of managing our own affairs, and answerable for our conduct toward others. This is called common sense, because it is common to all men with whom we can transact business, or call to account for their conduct."[30] "Common sense is a compact type of rationality," Voegelin adds. "The civilized *homo politicus* does not need to be a philosopher, but he must have common sense" (A, 352–53).

The restoration of political science and of philosophy cannot be effected simply by correctly understanding Aristotle; but this is, indeed, a necessary first step. Aristotle clearly knew the achievement and the nature of philosophy; since this clarity is not today generally appreciated, it must briefly be reflected upon. Philosophy through the distinctive noetic experience and the inferential and noetic powers of intelligence differentiated the primary cosmic experience. In the place of a cosmos full of gods, there emerged a de-divinized world and, correlative to it, divinity concentrated in the world-transcendent Ground of being. The realms of being under the post-noetic dispensation could be designated by the spatial-metaphorical indices of immanent and transcendent that correspond, respectively, to the world of things in space and time and to the divine Being of the world-Ground "beyond" space and time. The residue of myth in Aristotle, especially in the cosmology, was no decisive handicap to

30. Thomas Reid, *Essays on the Intellectual Powers of Man* (1785), Essay VI, Chap. 2 (repr. ed.; Cambridge, Mass.: MIT University Press, 1969), 559, quoted in Voegelin, *Anamnesis*, 352.

the prospering of philosophy after his time. The real obstacle lay, rather, in the incomplete condition in which he left the philosophical vocabulary. He did not provide conceptual instruments adequate to cope in requisite precision with the highly diverse content of the noetic experience and to make the new theoretic structure of being clear.

It was, for example, plainly the intention of Aristotle that the expression *being (ousia)* should generally designate the whole range of reality. To fulfill this intention and avoid subsequent misunderstandings, it would then have been necessary to create a vocabulary that specified the several modes of being with unmistakable clarity. This Aristotle failed to do. Hence Voegelin, as he engages in the task of establishing a noetic science of man satisfactory in the light of present knowledge, takes hold of the Aristotelian ontology and epistemology at just this point; and he proceeds in *Anamnesis* and in more recent works to develop a full-scale theory of the modes of being. The principal modes of reality are: 1) the Mode of thingness, of existence in space and time; 2) the Mode of divine Being beyond time and space; and 3) the Mode of the In-Between, the nonobjective reality of consciousness, its tensions and dimensions—i.e., the noetic reality itself. (A, 300). Since *whatever* man knows of reality he knows in his consciousness, the core of the endeavor is the creation of the philosophy of consciousness.

The noetic interpretation of reality is, of course, not the only one thrown up by men in their anxiety of existence, nor is it the socially dominant one. Indeed, all that men say about the ultimate meaning of existence is finally traceable either to this fundamental anxiety or to the experience of alienation. The characteristic response to these experiences is to seek the Ground. The symbolisms of the myth of the divine cosmos that precede the specific differentiation of *Nous* by the philosophers display a rational component of search of the ultimate cause; and the evinced presence of this process permits classification of many ancient myths under the categories of theogony, cosmogony, anthropogeny, and historiogenesis, for example (A, 299, 322 and *passim*; OH, IV, 59–113). The classification depends upon identification within the myths of connective quasi-etiological chains that derive the experienced reality of the separate participants of the community of being from an ultimate Ground, or first cause. The rational concern of men in the cosmological civilizations to comprehend the source and structure of being and its order is thereby evidenced. In addition, various types of pneumatic experiences as represented in the great world religions compete with *noesis* as authoritative symbolizations of existential truth.

Philosophy is, in short, but one of the sources of man's knowledge of reality (A, 333–40). It cannot even claim to be the most profound mode of experience. The prophet and the mystic speak with an authority that exceeds the grasp of the philosopher in the experiential dimension, as well as in impact upon the order of concrete societies, insofar as the issue is nascent or renascent "religion." Philosophy is the form of existence of no society in history up until now, Voegelin notes more than once. The mystic's quest for the divine Ground takes him into the divine presence and into the ineffable Tremendum of apophatic contemplation and mystical theology. His quest achieves encounter with reality at a depth that appears to transcend reason itself; and it is not subject even to analogical communication in either rational discourse or mythopoeic representation, but finds utterance only through the irrational rationale of paradox and in the ultimate silence of the contemplative who beholds the ineffable and unfathomable mystery of Being.

This is to say neither that mysticism is to be depreciated nor that philosophy is a subordinate mode of knowing. Mysticism—along with revelation and myth—is a great source of man's knowledge of divine Being, and philosophy has no quarrel with it: "Classical *noesis* and mysticism are the two predogmatic realms of knowledge (*Wissensrealitaeten*) in which the *Logos* of consciousness was optimally differentiated" (A, 333, 346, 48).[31] Yet the mystical eschatology of Plato, it is instructive to note, is concentrated in the myth that then serves as a more differentiated symbolism. The truth of myth clearly is affirmed by Plato. But it is a pneumatic truth that defies adequate conceptualization. It supplements the truth of philosophy, supports its orientation of man's existence toward the divine Ground, and even inspires the philosopher in his work. Still it cannot form the basis of noetic analysis and empirical assertions.

---

31. Cf. the discussion of faith in my *Political Apocalypse: A Study of Dostoevsky's Grand Inquisitor* (Baton Rouge, Louisiana State University Press, 1971), Chap. 2.

Like cosmic myth, mysticism is a great and unique mode of human knowledge. Philosophy, Voegelin wrote in 1943, through the noetic act achieved in meditation, penetrates to the point where consciousness experiences the proximity of the divine Ground and so formulates the ontological hypothesis of transcendent Being; but it cannot go out of the beyond of the finite and draw the strictly transcendent and infinite into consciousness as a datum of immanent experience (A, 56–57, 42).

V

The philosophy of consciousness is both the core and most difficult, technically, part of Voegelin's political theory. Moreover, while the 1943 formulations are presupposed in the subsequent work, they are not final statements; and even the further differentiations expressed in the 1965 essay, "What is Political Reality?," have been modified in important respects by more recent publications. Subsequent developments will be considered in the next chapter.

In foregoing pages of this chapter, like a cat circling a dish of hot milk, we have worked around the theory of consciousness itself. The discussion has attempted to clarify the questions which, apart from that central one, have greatest prominence in Voegelin's later work—questions which comprise the foundations of his thought and ramify through everything he had so far written. This accords with Voegelin's own procedure, since it was only in 1966 that he published the underlying theory of consciousness that he had tested and refined over the preceding decades.

In the memorial that prefaces the 1943 letter to his dear friend Alfred Schutz, Voegelin blocked out the major dimensions of his own work as it was to appear over the next thirty years. As we have seen, the neo-Kantian methodology and the defective instrumentarium supplied by modern philosophy as developed from René Descartes to Max Weber and Edmund Husserl had largely to be set aside. A new start was made from the foundation (*Grundlage*), but not last word, laid down by Plato and Aristotle of a philosophy of social order. After this decisive break with the main currents of modern thought, then, the restoration of a sound theory of politics followed two principal lines. The first was the interpretation of the network of rationally purposive and planned world-immanent action, especially on the basis of theoretical work done by Schutz, whom Voegelin describes as being, since the former's death in 1959, "the silent partner of my thought." The second was the investigation of experiences and of the central issue of the general relationship between experience and symbolization. Since the accent of reality falls on experience, Voegelin determined, as we have seen, that his "History of Political Ideas" must be jettisoned as obsolete, to be supplanted by the philosophy of consciousness and symbolic forms. This undertaking was articulated into explorations of the experiences of order, their symbolic expression, the consolidating institutions that concretely foster order in history, and the order of consciousness itself (A, 17–20).[32] The outlined program corresponds to what Voegelin has been doing since the 1940s. Perhaps the milk has now cooled enough for us to try a frontal assault on the theory of consciousness itself, the procedure to be primarily synoptic, with only a glance in the direction of the unfolding of the theory.

Voegelin describes his attention to the philosophy of consciousness from the 1920s onward in this passage from the "Autobiographical Memoir."

An important development in my understanding of the problems that worried me throughout the 1940s, and well into the writing of *Order and History*, was marked by my correspondence with Alfred Schutz on the problems of consciousness. They were not published at the time but only in 1966 as the first part of my volume on *Anamnesis*. The correspondence with Schutz was precipitated by the reading of Edmund Husserl's "Krisis der Europaeischen Wissenschaften" (1936). Husserl's study interested me greatly because of its magnificent sweep of history from Descartes to his own work. It also irritated me considerably because of the somewhat naive arrogance of a philosopher who believed that his method of phenomenology had at last opened what he called the apodictic horizon of philosophy and that from now on everybody who wanted to be a solid philosopher had to be a follower of Husserl. This arrogance reminded me a bit too strongly of various other final philosophies like those of Hegel and Marx, and also of the

32. The old "History of Political Ideas" is a typescript of about 4,000 pages that I was first privileged to read in Munich in 1965. On its qualities see the remarks of William C. Havard, "The Changing Pattern of Voegelin's Conception of History and Consciousness," *Southern Review*, n.s., VII (1971), 62, expanded and reprinted in Stephen A. McKnight (ed.), *Eric Voegelin's Search for Order in History* (Baton Rouge & London: Louisiana State University Press, 1978), 1–25.

conviction of National Socialists that theirs was the ultimate truth. I was especially disgusted by Husserl's language presumption in speaking of himself as the functionary of the spirit, because such language reminded me of recent experiences with functionaries of another sort. In continuation of my earlier analysis of consciousness in *On the Form of the American Mind* I now went into an elaborate criticism of Husserl's conception of consciousness, the decisive point being that his model of consciousness was the sense perception of objects in the external world. Although one could agree to the sophistications of analysis that he brought to bear on this model of perception, it seemed to me ridiculous to pretend that there was nothing to consciousness but the consciousness of objects of the external world. By that time, in 1942, I knew already enough about Classic, Patristic, and Scholastic philosophy to be aware that the philosophers who had founded philosophy on an analysis of consciousness were analyzing a few phenomena of consciousness besides the perception of objects in the external world. I went, therefore, into the question of what really were the experiences which form a man's consciousness and I did that by an *anamnesis*, a recollection of decisive experiences of my childhood. As a matter of fact I wrote twenty brief sketches, each giving such an early experience, so that they added up to something like an intellectual autobiography up to the age of ten.

The phenomena described were definitely phenomena of consciousness, because they described my consciousness of various areas of reality as a child. And these experiences had very little to do with objects of sense perception. For instance, one of the experiences that had stuck firmly enough to be recollected forty years later was the Monk of Heisterbach. Heisterbach was the ruin of some medieval monastery in the neighborhood of Koenigswinter where we frequently went for a Sunday excursion. The Monk of Heisterbach was the monk who got lost, to return only after a thousand years and discover that these thousand years had passed for him like a day. Such time concentrations and shortenings, though obviously not problems of sense perception, constitute very relevant parts at least of my consciousness, even if they don't of Husserl's. In this manner I went through such experiences as the anxieties and fascinations aroused by standing on the border of the known world, with Andersen in his fairytales, and looking north into a mysterious horizon of infinity. Or experiences of festival movements in the life of man, when I watched passing steamers on the Rhine with their night-parties. These types of experience constitute consciousness; and this is the real consciousness a man has, unless somebody wants to insist that my childhood was entirely different from that of any other child in the history of mankind. The experiences of participation in various areas of reality constitute the horizon of existence in the world. The stress lies on experiences of reality in the plural, being open to all of them and keeping them in balance. That is what I understood as the philosopher's attitude; and that is the attitude I found in the open existence of all great philosophers who by that time had come to my attention. Restoring this openness to reality appeared to be the principal task of philosophy.

The analysis of the experiences required a technical vocabulary. Fortunately I did not have to develop it from scratch, but rather to learn it gradually from other philosophers who had gone through the same process and already found the terms by which they could signify the analytical steps in the exploration of their experiences. At the center of consciousness I found the experience of participation, meaning thereby the reality of being in contact with reality outside myself. This awareness of participation as the central problem was fortified by the analysis of the myth conducted by the members of the Chicago Oriental Institute under the category of consubstantiality, developed by Mr. and Mrs. Henri Frankfort and probably taken over from Lucien Lévy-Bruhl. If man were not consubstantial with the reality he experiences, he could not experience it. Among the philosophers I found important confirmation from the radical empiricism of William James. James's study on the question—"Does 'Consciousness' Exist?" (1904)— struck me at the time, and still strikes me, as one of the most important philosophical documents of the twentieth century. In developing his concept of the pure experience, William James has put his finger on the reality of the consciousness of participation, inasmuch as what he calls pure experience is the something that can be put into the context *either* of the subject's stream of consciousness *or* of objects in the external world. This fundamental insight of William James identifies the something that lies between the subject and object of participation as the experience. Later I found that the same type of analysis had been conducted on a much vaster scale by Plato, resulting in his concept of the *metaxy*, the In-Between. The experience is neither in the subject nor in the world of objects but In-Between, and that means In-Between the poles of man and of the reality he experiences.

The In-Between character of experience becomes of particular importance in understanding response to the movements of divine presence, for the experience of such movements is not precisely located in man's stream of consciousness, in the immanentist sense, but in the In-Between of the divine and the human. The experience is the reality of both divine and human presence, and only after it has happened can it be allocated either to man's consciousness or to the context of divinity under the name of revelation. A good number of problems which plague the history of philosophy now become clear, as hypostases of the poles of a pure experience in the sense of William James, or of the *metaxy* experiences of Plato. By hypostases I mean the fallacious assumption that the poles of the participatory experience are self-contained entities that form a mysterious contact on occasion of an experience. A mystery is there, to be sure, but even a mystery can be clearly expressed by stressing the participatory reality of the experience as the site of consciousness and understanding the poles of the experience as its poles and not as self-contained entities. The problem of reality experienced thus becomes the problem of a flow of participatory reality, in which reality becomes luminous to itself in the case of human consciousness. The term *consciousness*, therefore, could no longer mean to me a human consciousness which is conscious of a reality outside man's consciousness, but had to mean the In-Between reality of the participatory pure experience which then analytically can be characterized through such terms as the poles of the experiential tension and the reality of the experiential tension in the *metaxy*. The term *luminosity of consciousness*, which I use increasingly, tries to stress this In-Between character of the experience as against the immanentizing language of a human consciousness which, as a subject, is opposed to an object of experience.

This understanding of the In-Between character of consciousness, as well as of its luminosity—which is the luminosity not of a subjective consciousness but of the reality that from both sides enters into the experience—resulted in a better understanding of the problem of symbols: Symbols are the language phenomena engendered by the process of participatory experience. The language symbols expressing an experience are not inventions of an immanentist human consciousness; rather, they are engendered in the process of participation itself. Language, therefore, participates in the *metaxy* character of consciousness. A symbol is neither a human conventional sign signifying a reality outside consciousness nor, as in certain theological constructions, a word of God conveniently transmitted in the language the recipient can understand. It is engendered by the divine-human encounter and participates, therefore, as much in divine as in human reality. This seems to me, for the moment at least, the best formulation of the problem that plagues various symbolist philosophers, the problem that symbols do not simply signify a divine reality beyond consciousness but are somehow the divine reality in its presence itself. But I am afraid I have not completely worked out yet the details of this participatory philosophy of symbolism. (AM, 70–75)[33]

From the beginning of this study I have stressed the significance of the American experience and of common sense for a proper understanding of Eric Voegelin. It is impossible to read William James's late work, his *Essays in Radical Empiricism* and his *A Pluralistic*

33. The analysis of William James's writings is thematic in the first chapter of Voegelin, *Ueber die Form des amerikanischen Geistes*, esp. 41–52. Cf. James, *Essays in Radical Empiricism* [and] *A Pluralistic Universe* (2 vols. in 1; repr. ed.; Gloucester, Mass.: Peter Smith, 1967), I, 1–37. For a relevant discussion of Husserl, see I. M. Bochenski, *Contemporary European Philosophy*, trans. Donald Nicholl and Karl Aschenbrenner (Berkeley & Los Angeles: University of California Press, 1969), 131–40.

Universe, without being constantly reminded of Voegelin's own attitude toward philosophy as reflected in his most recent work. Voegelin's debt is acknowledged in the passage just quoted as well as elsewhere. Perusal of *On the Form of the American Mind,* moreover, shows that Voegelin's grasp of James's work was already comprehensive in 1928, and already set in the context of a detailed consideration of the whole development of English and American philosophy from Locke to Dewey as that development bears on the understanding of experience, consciousness, theory of knowledge, and ontology. Simply said, there is a great deal about Voegelin that is Jamesian: the evidence appears in his first book and is still apparent fifty years later in *The Ecumenic Age* and subsequent work.

As always, of course, it is James modified and adapted in ways not unlike those reflected in the development of James's own thought under the impress of such thinkers as Gustav Theodor Fechner and Henri Bergson. This process of adaptation and expansion reflects the substance of Voegelin's critical method. Matters only hinted in James are developed in Voegelin, and it is a James reconciled to Plato and Aristotle who is found in Voegelin's pages, as the passage pertaining to consciousness shows. But the disdain for systems in philosophy and for dogmatism, the disparagement of what James called the "thinness" of "vicious intellectualism," and the correlative preference for the "thickness" of the whole of experience as the indispensable foundation of philosophizing are traits common to James as well as to Voegelin.[34] The central thrust of James's effort was to break "the reality of concepts" so as to arrive at "concrete experience."[35] With reference to Bergson, he approvingly wrote: "The only way to apprehend reality's thickness is either to experience it directly by being a part of reality one's self, or to evoke it in imagination by sympathetically divining some one else's inner life." By its failure to rely on concrete experience because of a fascination with conceptual schemes and intellectual constructs, "philosophy [has] been on a false scent ever since the days of Socrates and Plato." While concerned in the first instance to explain "pure experience" as the yet-to-be-named *that* of immediate perception, which only

34. James, *Essays in Radical Empiricism* [and] *A Pluralistic Universe,* II, 60, 212, 309.
35. *Ibid.,* 261, 257.

becomes a *what* when "taken" a second time, James clearly extends
his radical empiricism not only to the connections that form relationships within phenomenal experience, but also to "ordinary religious experience."[36]

Such "religious" experience is "fragmentary" and "discontinu-
ous" with our experience of nature, he notes. This leads him to argue that religious experiences evidence a continuity "with a wider
self from which saving experiences flow in." Therefore, there is
some "direct empirical verification" of divine reality, and James expresses surprise that "philosophers of the absolute" have paid so little attention to the fact, "even when it seemed obvious that personal
experience of some kind must have made their confidence in their
own vision so strong. . . . They have preferred the thinner to the
thicker method, dialectical abstraction being so much more digni-
fied and academic than the confused and unwholesome facts of personal biography." James then continues with the famous statement:
"We may be in the universe as dogs and cats are in our libraries,
seeing the books and hearing the conversation, but having no inkling of the meaning of it all."[37]

By James's account, consciousness as an entity does not exist.
What exists as the world-stuff or reality is pure experience, of which
knower and known are part and parcel. Thus, there is no material
reality to which mind reality (or consciousness) can be contrasted.
There is only the homogenous reality of experience, the *that* immediately apprehended in the flux of existence as first taken in common experience. It is only by a second "taking" that "pure experience" is further experienced as object and subject, as known and
knower, and identified through the other categories of conceptualization in a process of sorting and partitioning. The *materia prima*
of pure experience, however, knows nothing of this whatness. But if
consciousness is nonexistent as an entity, this is not to say that the
word does not stand for something; and that something is a *function*. Thoughts do exist, and the function they serve in experience is
knowing. Consciousness is the name for that function, for the expe-

36. *Ibid.*, II, 250–51, 291; I, 23, 44, 52; II, 38–40, 299. Cf. Voegelin, *Ueber die
Form des amerikanischen Geistes*, 43, 48.
37. James, *Essays in Radical Empiricism* [and] *A Pluralistic Universe*, II, 308–
309. Cf. Voegelin, *Ueber die Form des amerikanischen Geistes*, 50–51.

rience "that things not only are, but get reported, are known."[38] But even this attentuated meaning of consciousness is spurned by James. For if *consciousness* is understood as "a kind of external relation, and does not denote a special stuff or way of being," then the quality of being conscious of experiences can better be *"explained by their relations—these relations themselves being [further] experiences—to one another."*[39]

What does this mean? It means that the primal stuff of "pure experience," whose reality is immediately apprehended, is *known* through the relationships it immediately has with different "portions" of the pure experience. These relations are merely dimensions of a unified pure experience: "one of its 'terms' becomes the subject or bearer of the knowledge, the knower, the other becomes the object known." In other words, it is *in* the experience itself that reality and its interrelationships are known in the instant of its presence, at the level of pure experience; and this analysis applies to the thing known as well as to the subject who knows: the relationship of knowing and consciousness are, then, parts of the *that* of pure experience, and at least the latter is a superfluous term. Moreover, the analysis applies to nonperceptual experiences no less than to perceptual ones. "The instant field of the present is at all times what I call the 'pure' experience. It is only virtually or potentially either object or subject as yet. For the time being, it is plain, unqualified actuality, or existence, a simple *that.* . . . The doubling of it in retrospection into a state of mind and a reality intended thereby, is just one of the acts."[40]

In its pure state, or when isolated, there is no self-splitting of [pure experience] into consciousness and what the consciousness is "of." Its subjectivity and objectivity are functional attributes solely, realized only when the experience is "taken," *i.e.,* talked-of, twice, considered along with its two differing contexts [of thoughts and things] respectively, by a new retrospective experience, of which that whole past complication [associated with circumstance and biography] now forms the fresh content.[41]

38. James, *Essays in Radical Empiricism* [and] *A Pluralistic Universe,* I, 3–4, 138, 145, 160, 185; II, 280.
39. *Ibid.,* I, 25. Emphasis as in original.
40. *Ibid.,* 4, 16–18, 23–24.
41. *Ibid.,* 23.

Distinctive to radical empiricism is James's insistence (against the whole argument of Hume and his successors) that relationship aspects of reality experienced are every bit as authentic as things experienced. Thus he insists that, "To be radical, an empiricism must neither admit into its constructions any element that is not directly experienced, nor exclude from them any element that is directly experienced. For such a philosophy, the relations that connect experiences must themselves be experienced relations, and any kind of relation experienced must be accounted as 'real' as anything else in the system."[42]

This means, in contrast to ordinary empiricism, that conjunctive and disjunctive relations are integral to pure experience. "Prepositions, copulas, and conjunctions, 'is,' 'isn't,' 'then,' 'before,' 'in,' 'on,' 'beside,' 'between,' 'next,' 'like,' 'unlike,' 'as,' 'but,' flower out of the stream of pure experience, the stream of concretes or the sensational stream, as naturally as nouns and adjectives do, and they melt into it again as fluidly when we apply them to a new portion of the stream."[43] Or, again: "Every examiner of the sensible life *in concreto* must see that relations of every sort, of time, space, difference, likeness, change, rate, cause, or what not, are just as integral members of the flux as disjunctive relations are. . . . With, near, next, like, from, towards, against, because, for, through, my—these words designate types of conjunctive relation arranged in a roughly ascending order of intimacy and inclusiveness."[44]

For James, then, thoughts in the concrete are both fully real and made of the same stuff as things—pure experience. His insistence on the multifaceted intimacy of men's normal sympathetic relationship to the universe led Voegelin in 1928 to coin the term *open self*, to symbolize the person who flees from the isolation and loneliness of his merely private existence as an atomized individual to embrace the mysterious togetherness of reality disclosed in pure experience. This *with*ness and interpenetrating otherness argued in James's analysis of experience, then, points toward the converging of his and

42. *Ibid.*, 42.
43. *Ibid.*, 95.
44. *Ibid.*, II, 279–80; I, 45. Cf. Voegelin, *Ueber die Form des amerikanischen Geistes*, 47.

Plato's meditations in Voegelin's later account. Plato, Bergson, and James all intend the same reality. The symbolisms of intimacy, responsiveness, pulling, withness, otherness blend in Voegelin's symbolisms: participation; attunement to the lasting and passing in the hierarchy of existence; consubstantiality of being disclosed in the primordial experience of the divine cosmos; and the mystery of man's articulation in the In-Between of symbolisms engendered out of a self-reflective awareness of conscious participation as he is drawn to search the Ground of being in the loving quest for truth called philosophy.[45]

To the final objection that intuition shows consciousness to exist through the palpable experience of the flowing of thought within us, in absolute contrast to objects external to us, James retorts that he, too, must follow intuition. This flowing of thought-consciousness is no more than "a careless name for what, when scrutinized, reveals itself to consist chiefly of the stream of my breathing." It is the physiology of breathing, he is persuaded, that is "the essence out of which philosophers have constructed the entity known to them as consciousness."[46] As James subsequently said, "Souls have worn out both themselves and their welcome, that is the plain truth." *Soul, psyche,* and *consciousness* are equivalent terms in philosophy. And James added this afterthought: "But if the belief in the soul ever does come to life after the many funeral-discourses which Humian and Kantian criticism have preached over it, I am sure it will be only when some one has found in the term a pragmatic significance that has hitherto eluded observation. When that champion speaks, as he well may speak some day, it will be time to consider souls more seriously."[47]

That "champion" has appeared in Voegelin, for while he accepts virtually all of James's analysis (including the nonexistence of consciousness-soul), yet the latter comes to life nonetheless in his theory of consciousness, which rests on the analysis of experience

45. James, *Essays in Radical Empiricism* [and] *A Pluralistic Universe*, I, 42, 44, 49, 181, 196, 202; II, 20−25, 33−35, 40, 44, 64, 271, 277−90, 325, 329. Voegelin, *Ueber die Form des amerikanischen Geistes*, 49, 51−52.
46. James, *Essays in Radical Empiricism* [and] *A Pluralistic Universe*, I, 36−37. Cf. Voegelin, *Ueber die Form des amerikanischen Geistes*, 46.
47. James, *Essays in Radical Empiricism* [and] *A Pluralistic Universe*, II, 210−11.

showing consciousness-soul as a dimension of nonexistent *reality*. We may now turn directly to Voegelin's theory of consciousness.

VI

The theory of consciousness presented in *Anamnesis* is not a propositional account of a previously "given" structure that can validly be stated once and for all. The consciousness, as James had argued, is no object of external perception, is not *per se* either object or subject of any experience of any class whatever. The consciousness can only be the concrete consciousness of an individual person; its functions and reality are ascertainable strictly in relation to experience and solely through introspective awarenesses of various kinds. Voegelin's theory, therefore, is the articulation of the content of certain traits of a meditative analysis, one which is permeated by the experiences symbolized and which can be verified by critical comparison with accounts given by other philosophers.

It is to be noticed that the substantial *unity* of human experience is not itself experienceable. That the "knowledge" gained and expressed as a theory has universal applicability to every man is no more empirically warrantable or demonstrable than is (for example) the assertion that every being called man possesses a common human nature and is, therefore, in that sense equal to every other man. This claim to validity is an act of trust or faith (*pistis*), one that bridges the gulf separating assertions made on the empirical basis of inner experience or apperceptions of *a* man and carrying claim to universal truth. Nor does the difficulty attach only to inner experience—for all experience is, in a sense, inner. The sceptic and positivistic pitfall of solipsism is avoidable in the physical sciences, for example, only through the postulation for practical methodological purposes of the uniformity of nature. And if one seeks to look behind that postulate for reassurance in matters of the present kind, then the ground of universal statements is "belief in the premise that a truth concerning the reality of man found by one man concretely does, indeed, apply to every man. The faith in this premise, however, is not engendered by an additional experience . . . but by the primordial experience of reality as endowed with the constancy and lastingness of structure that we symbolize as the Cosmos. The trust in the Cosmos and its depth is the source of the premises . . . that we accept as the context of meaning for our concrete engagement in the search of truth."[48]

Finally, whether the theoretical account finds expression in the mythic language of entities (such as God, man, soul, Cosmos) or in the more abstract philosophic language of tensions (such as the field of consciousness, polarities, immanence, transcendence, divine reality, the Ground), no objectivation or reification is entailed. Rather the terms are merely indicative of the experienced dimensions of the nonexistent reality of consciousness itself. The spatial-temporal vocabulary of the immanent reality of things is employed in the figurative sense compelled by the fact that men have no other language in which discursively to express themselves. So much for the epistemological considerations.

The transition from the Jamesian to the Platonic analysis is made by Voegelin as follows: "The consciousness, then, is not a given that can be described from without, but an experience of participation in the Ground of being whose Logos can only be brought to clarity through the meditative exegesis of itself." The consciousness is a process of ever-deepening insight into its own *Logos* attained through meditation. It is the center radiating the concrete order of human existence in society and history.

A philosophy of politics is empirical—in the pregnant sense of an investigation of experiences which penetrate the whole realm of ordered human existence. It requires . . . rigorous reciprocating examination of concrete phenomena of order and analysis of the consciousness, by which means alone the human order in society and history becomes understandable. . . . [Since] the consciousness is the center from which the concrete order of human existence in society and history radiates . . . the empirical study of social and historical phenomena of order interpenetrates with the empirical study of the consciousness and its experiences of participation. (A, 8–9, 275–76)

The interpenetration of the experiences symbolized in the field of history and those symbolized in the inner experience of participa-

48. See Voegelin, *Anamnesis,* 7, 52, 55–58, 286, 353. Quotation from "Equivalences of Experience," 234. On the positivist critique of universal propositions, see Kolakowski, *Alienation of Reason,* 5, 176. On the uniformity of nature, see A. E. Taylor, *Elements of Metaphysics* (repr. ed.; New York: Barnes & Noble, University Paperback, n.d.), 222–33.

tion as expressive of the field of consciousness has been the basis for our presentation of Voegelin's account: participation *is* consciousness itself. The principal philosophical symbolisms may briefly be recalled. The consciousness is a process of participation in the In-Between of the reality of things and the divine Ground of being. The process of consciousness forms around the tension of awareness of the Ground of being, which the Hellenic philosophers articulated as the rational search of the Ground; and the Ground itself moves (*kinesis*) the consciousness through actualizing attractiveness to seek It as the common substance of Reason. The beckoning from the divine pole of reality also was symbolized as the pull (*helkein*) of the divine Ground. The name found by Plato and Aristotle for that dimension of consciousness which participates most intimately in transcendent divine Being is Reason; and the exegetical accounts of men's loving participation in the Ground comprises philosophy.

The tension of participation may further be described metaphorically by the directional indices of immanent and transcendent poles of being. The range of experience is seen to be coextensive with the range of known reality and to be articulated in correlation with the several modes of reality: thingness—experienced through perception; nonexistent reality of consciousness itself—experienced as self-reflective participation in the In-Between; the divine reality of the Ground—experienced noetically as the actualizing *Nous*, pneumatically as the attracting, pulling, drawing Creator-Savior God. It is to be noticed, however, that the drawing of the Ground is a property of the noetic experience as portrayed in the *Republic* and the *Laws*, as well as in the pneumatic experience represented in the Gospel of John, where identical language is used. Hence, the experiences can properly be assimilated to each other in certain essential respects. Whether faith has thereby become reason, Voegelin does not here say. But he does make unmistakably clear that the neat distinction between noetic and pneumatic experience and symbolization is obliterated in the instances cited (A, 126, 266ff, 289).[49]

Some further details of the analysis of consciousness may now be sketched. Voegelin resumed exploration of his consciousness in the

---

49. Cf. Voegelin, "The Gospel and Culture," *passim.*

1940s, as we have seen, through anamnestic experiments for the purpose of discovering the experiences that motivate a philosopher's quest. That class of experiences is most fully identified and analyzed in the essay just cited; and to judge from the published materials, he could hardly have found the answer before the mid-1960s. The tendency of his thought in this major dimension is suggested, for example, by the 1943 essay in which he quoted from a fourteenth-century meditation, *The Cloud of Unknowing*: "It is needful for thee to bury in a cloud of forgetting all creatures that ever God made, that you mayest direct thine intent to God Himself." He then commented: "The purpose of meditation is the annihilation of the content of the world *per gradus*, from the corporeal world through the spiritual, so as to reach the point of transcendence in which the soul, to speak with Augustine, can turn in the *intentio* to God." He identified the question of transcendence as the decisive problem of philosophy and philosophizing about time and existence (addressed in the first chapter of *On the Form of the American Mind*), as the modern equivalent of the Christian mystic's meditation. By approaching consciousness through the experiences of hearing, seeing, and even smelling, he arrived at the view akin to James's, that consciousness does not itself "stream"—except as a peripheral or border experience constituted in the consciousness itself, not as constituting the consciousness. Sensory perception, however, could not provide an adequate starting point for a theory of consciousness; rather, the different mode of apperception or inner experience also had to be examined. The speculative phenomenology of Husserl, for example, could serve as a substitute for meditation because it, too, sought the "existential assurance" of transcendence:

Both processes have the function of transcending the consciousness, the one into the individuated body, the other into the world Ground[;] both processes lead to a "point of transitoriness" (*"Fluechtigkeitspunkt"*) in the sense that the transcendent cannot itself become a datum of consciousness, but that the processes lead only to the border and make possible the instantaneous border experience that may empirically last only a few seconds. (A, 14, 33, 36, 37, 41, 42)[50]

50. Cf. William Johnston (ed.), *The Cloud of Unknowing and the Book of Privy Counseling* (Garden City, N.Y.: Doubleday & Co., 1973), 48.

The specific experiential starting point for the theory of consciousness as advanced in 1943 is the phenomenon of attention and the turning of attention (A, 43).[51] When thus approached, the consciousness displays four prominent traits: 1) It possesses a center of energy that can be directed in various ways and degrees of intensity to different dimensions of reality. 2) It exhibits itself as a process. 3) The process of consciousness is, throughout, internally luminous. 4) The luminous dimensions of the process called consciousness range from past to future, not as empty spaces, but as the structure of a finite process bounded by birth and death. The experienced finitude of the process of consciousness inevitably supplies the model for all process and for the conceptual apparatus with which the mind operates, including its reflections on the consciousness-transcending processes of the infinite and the divine. And this leads to such difficult problem areas of prominence in the history of thought as the Kantian logical and cosmological antinomies of quantity (endlessness and eternity), the mythic symbolization of transcendent Being through finite representations (the "fundamental function" of myth), the process theology from the Pythagorian *tetraktys* to Schelling's *Potenzenlehre*, and the ontological imagery described in A. O. Lovejoy's *Great Chain of Being* (A, 11, 43–53).

What can be observed as lacking in this earlier account of consciousness are the features discovered through decades of attention to the Classical texts and prominent in the earlier sections of this chapter. The key insights are the discovery of consciousness as the In-Between of immanent and transcendent being, so that it participates experientially in both; and the discovery that the experience which motivates philosophizing is the movement of the soul through the pull of divine reality when this is actualized in the response of the philosophical man (Aristotle's *spoudaios*, Plato's *daimonios aner*) through the desire to know that forms as love of Wisdom.

The "present" in the luminous process of consciousness that extends from past to future is, in the 1943 essay, the complex interpretive result of radically immanent moment-images that comprise the stuff of experience. Through the later revision of the account of ex-

51. Cf. James, *Essays in Radical Empiricism* [and] *A Pluralistic Universe*, II, 269–73.

perience and of consciousness as the nonexistent reality of the In-Between which is the site of experiences, the present is expanded to comprehend not only the moments of past and future, but also the "flowing present" of the Eternal. The philosophical experience of the Eternal encountered in the tension between the poles of time and eternity is stated as follows: "We remain in the 'In-Between,' in a temporal flowing of experience in which however Eternity is present, in a flowing that certainly cannot be dissolved into the past, present, and future of world-time because in every point of flow it carries the tension of trans-temporal eternal Being." This appercep-tion of the Eternal present in time clearly outstrips in profundity the *intentio* of *The Cloud of Unknowing* quoted by Voegelin earlier, al-though the continuities of the analysis are apparent.

The problem of transcendence central to all philosophy is like-wise transformed: "in the center of philosophizing stands the experi-ence of the tension to Being from which radiates the truth of order into the [various] complexes of reality by way of the indices [of being: Being, immanent-transcendent, world]." Where there is the light of the experience of Being, there is also an independent world of things, and there is God. For without an understanding of world-transcendent reality there is, indeed, no immanent world of nature and things; and there where God and world meet through the experi-ence of Being and are bound together, there is the realm of man—"he who with the experience of himself, as the one experiencing order, enters into the knowing Truth of his own order [*der mit der Erfahrung seiner selbst als des Ordnung Erfahrenden in die wis-sende Wahrheit seiner eigenen Ordnung eintritt*]. Such a com-prehensive range of problems appears to me to be the historically constituted heart of all philosophizing" (A, 286, 319, 55, 273–76).

The modes of consciousness are knowledge, forgottenness, and recollection, Plato's *anamnesis*. What is remembered, however, is what has been forgotten; and the troublesome task of recollecting the forgotten must be assayed because it should not remain forgot-ten. Through recollection of the forgotten that which ought to be remembered is brought to the present of knowledge; and the tension to knowledge shows forgottenness to be the situation of not-know-ing, the ignorance (*agnoia*) of the soul in Plato's sense. Knowledge and not-knowing are situations of existential order and disorder.

What is forgotten can, however, only be remembered because it is a knowledge in the mode of forgottenness whose presence in forgottenness stirs existential discontent in a man, and this discontent presses toward conscious knowledge. From the mode of forgottenness recollection retrieves what ought to be known into the present in the mode of knowledge. Recollection is, therefore, the activity of the consciousness through forgottenness; and this means that the latent knowledge of the unconscious is aroused through recollection and returned in an observable manner into specific presence in consciousness where it is articulated. Articulation is fixed through language by the emergence in consciousness of linguistic vessels bearing the content of previously forgotten and inarticulate knowledge. Lastly, whether the recollection proceeds out of the resources of personal experiences, or out of meditation on the historiographically evinced experiences of men of distant generations, what is recollected that preeminently ought to be known (and not remain forgotten) is the source of man's humanity and of the order of society and history *in participatory attunement to the divine reality of the Ground* (A, 11).

VII

Philosophical or noetic science, by Voegelin's account, is both a means of salvation whereby reason directs man toward the source of being and a means of critically appraising the truth of symbolisms that compete with it as authoritative expressions of man's understanding of reality (A, 325; OH, III, 68–69). In its critical aspect the science serves to identify mistaken, pernicious, and destructive views of reality and to discredit and correct them through rational assessment. It thereby assists in preserving the order of human existence and man's attunement to the truth of being in the face of the exigencies of life in the world. That truth does not always persuade is a fact to be borne as a mystery of existence. Philosophy operates in the fertile field of historical existence, perennially beset by Bacon's Idols and the ideological systems that divert men from *ennui*, anxiety, and alienation into prisons of their own making—prisons which too often form not only in the minds and souls of individual persons but, driven by the *libido* for power, penetrate entire societies and threaten to engulf living mankind itself in a totalitarian hell of this or that complexion.[52]

The search of philosophy is the search of the Ground in a differentiated mode. In this search the knowledge of revelation and mysticism are allies against the common enemy, dogmatism (A, 327–33). And myth, in its concreteness, lies ready to hand as the tales out of which can ever arise the reorientation of men in existence and their attunement to the truth of divine Being. It is well to remember, the *Ground* of twentieth-century philosophy is the *aition* of Hesiod.

The foregoing analysis may, then, be summarized in the following way.

1. Whatever man knows of reality he knows through experience. The experiences of reality occur in a wide range of modes and find expression in a corresponding variety of symbolization. Experience and symbolization "happen" together in the consciousness of individual men. Consciousness so functions as to lay hold of reality and make it intelligible. Intelligibility is achieved through the articulation of symbols whose meaning can only be understood in their proper or engendering experiential context. It is critically important that symbols not be divorced from the experiences that have engendered them and that, in turn, they are meant to evoke.

2. Myth, philosophy, revelation, and mysticism are symbolic forms of human existence that optimally express distinctively different, though related, kinds of experiences and communicate ordering knowledge of reality. The *truth* of them all lies at the level of the experiences they articulate, not at the level of the symbols themselves. The myth is expressive of the primary or primordial experience of the oneness of all that is. It centers in the representation of the divinity of the cosmos, with its interpenetrating community of men, gods, world, and society constituted through participation.

3. Mythic participation is compact, in the sense that it comprehensively embraces at least latently the whole range of reality

52. On the unscientific or derailed status of "systems" and systematic philosophy, see Voegelin, *Science, Politics, and Gnosticism*, 40ff; "On Hegel: A Study in Sorcery," 342ff. For Pascal's *divertissement*, see the *Pensées*, Nos. 139 *et seqq.*, 166, 168. Cf. Gerhart Niemeyer, *Between Nothingness and Paradise* (Baton Rouge: Louisiana State University Press, 1971), esp. Chap. 4.

experienced by men. The compactness of mythic participation is shattered through the differentiation or dissociation of modes of experience held together in incipiency in it. This dissociation of modes of experience, in two instances, takes the form of noetic experience productive of philosophy in ancient Hellas and of pneumatic experience in the several forms of revelation in Israel and mysticism in the horizons of Hellas, Christendom, and elsewhere. The experience of participation is, in its compact as well as differentiated modes, attended by anxiety of a fall from existence into the nothingness of the nonexistence encompassing the reality of man and all that is. Myth, philosophy, revelation, and mysticism all assuage this anxiety by rendering partially intelligible the mystery of the structure and order of being and by attuning human existence to it in their unique ways. To repeat: "Our knowledge of order remains primarily mythic, even after the noetic experience has differentiated the realm of consciousness and the noetic exegesis has made its Logos explicit" (A, 290).

4. Philosophy is the symbolic form *par excellence* of the noetic mode of participation. It is distinguished by the philosopher's discovery of the self-reflective reason as the specific essence of man and the substance of the *psyche* (or consciousness), which knows both itself and its affinity with the ultimate divine reality that is its cause, fulfillment, and the Ground of all being. The philosophers' inquiry is the loving search by reason of the divine Reason in which it participates and to which it seeks more perfectly to attune itself in the reciprocal relationship of knower and known, lover and beloved. The core of the philosophical effort, then—and of human nature itself—is openness to the Ground as the vertical tension of existence rendered intelligible through the symbols of rational exegesis called *noesis*.

5. The deformation or derailment of philosophical science occurs whenever the symbols found by reason to express the experience of participation in the noetic mode are severed from their engendering experiential context and treated as speculative topics—or as referring to subordinate realms of being, or as arising out of modes of experience other than noetic participation. Such deformations, by Voegelin's account of the matter, have been a predominant characteristic of the history of philosophizing and remain so today.

derailment of philosophy

restoration of philosophy

6. The restoration of the philosophical science of man entails: a) the rediscovery of the technique of noetic meditation through a study of the writings of those philosophers who were its masters, and b) the elaboration of a philosophy of consciousness and an ontology out of the revitalized noetic or theoretic activity as informed by philosophical resources available in the contemporary horizon. That these tasks are well advanced, the richness of *Anamnesis* alone attests.

7. The new ontology that emerges from Voegelin's analysis as presented in *Anamnesis* is founded in the reality of experience in the In-Between of participatory consciousness. Reality is "no closed rational system"; neither idealism nor materialism provide satisfactory accounts of it.[53] Voegelin tends to avoid the terms *metaphysics* and *ontology*, as well as *being* and *becoming*, because of the connotations these terms carry. He prefers simply to speak of *reality* when symbolizing the comprehensive range of the Is. The theory of knowledge and the science of reality tend to merge in his account, for what *is* is strictly what is experienced by the reality called "man," in the participation in the In-Between called "consciousness," within which the tensional awarenesses of realities encountered and expressed in language are engendered.

Voegelin's account is radically empirical in William James's sense, and it blends the language of James's "each-form" (in preference to the "all-form" of the absolutists) with Plato's meditative analysis to present a pluralistic account of reality.[54] The plural field of reality is articulated tensionally through its symbolic indices (which are themselves part of the reality of experience) into thingness, the self-reflective consciousness as its articulately rational center, and the divine Ground. These and other terms express the *tensional* polarities of experiences that concretely happen in the participatory consciousness of concrete persons. The analysis of engendering experiences shows reality to be a process in the form of the process of consciousness, one which differentiates from a compactness to a more articulate insight into its own luminous structure. "Reality is therefore not constant" (A, 306).

The empirical concreteness of the account is to be stressed:

53. Voegelin, *Ueber die Form des amerikanischen Geistes*, 20; *Anamnesis*, 57.
54. James, *Essays in Radical Empiricism* [and] *A Pluralistic Universe*, II, 324.

"Consciousness is always consciousness-of-something," Voegelin insists, and not a hovering over-soul or separate entity. Moreover, in his strictly empirical account, there is *no* other reality than the one men experience through their existential tension to the Ground luminous with reason (A, 309–11). The exploration of the participatory experiences of the In-Between through the self-reflective consciousness whose cognitive structure is reason is not one perspective among others. Rather it is the sole perspective available to men as they seek an objective and scientifically valid account of their existence and articulate the truth of the reality of which they are an ineluctable part. The *language* in which the search of reality finds expression, no less than the engendering experiences themselves, composes the texture of the participatory reality when present to itself in the mode of the self-reflective consciousness called *Noesis*. The symbolic indices of experiences are themselves the realities of the In-Between of participation-consciousness. "The philosophy of order is the process in which we as men find the order of our existence in the order of consciousness" (A, 11).

8. The work of restoration of philosophy and of political science must not be mistaken for the proclamation of a definitive or ultimate truth in an apocalyptic manner. Voegelin claims to have detected and rectified an error of consequence with respect to the nature of philosophical thought, its meaning and truth. The claim is urged with scholarly precision and sobriety. Despite the magnitude of the claim, one is compelled to say that there is none of the enthusiasm or millenarian overtone in it that characterized Hegel, for example. Voegelin does not even faintly pretend that his work will free men of error in the future, that either philosophy or history climaxes in his work; nor is he sanguine in the hope that his analysis will be persuasive to this or a subsequent generation. Indeed, he appears to be pessimistic in all of these regards. He claims only that, as far as he can see, both the diagnosis and the therapy are sound. In so claiming, he remains philosopher and physician and declines to become prophet and healer.

CHAPTER 7

Principia Noetica:
The Voegelinian Revolution—
1981 and Beyond

The picture of Voegelin's work that emerges from
the foregoing analysis of it adds up to a revolution in the science of
man comparable in magnitude (if not in style) to the revolutions of
Copernicus and Newton in mathematical astronomy, cosmology,
and physics. That Voegelin's work effects a radical break with dominant contemporary schools of thought and philosophical movements
has been clear from the outset of our account. The Voegelinian revolution, though, is more than a new science of politics. It is a comprehensive new science of man which, when drawn together from
the array of theoretical insights dispersed over the extensive work of
a lifetime, may be said to compose a *Philosophiae Hominis Principia Noetica*, a turning point in man's understanding of himself and
the truth of existence.

As in the case of other scientific revolutions of the first magnitude, it is impossible for human understanding to be the same after
Voegelin as before him. The new noetic science of man articulated
in his thought effects a further differentiation of reality, for reality
takes on meaning and luminosity altering its process and structure
through the advance of self-reflective rationality achieved concretely
in the experiences symbolized in the reality of the concrete existence of the concrete person, the man Eric Voegelin. To be sure, no
Truth to end the quest for truth in the mysterious process of reality
is found or proclaimed, after the fashion of those who have before
pronounced apodictic Answers to the riddle of existence and pro-

pounded them in a System to end all systems. To the contrary, the core of the Voegelinian revolution is to show (among other things) the defectiveness of all such "stop history" Answers as imposing fallacious second realities; and, in counterpoint to them, he undertakes the science of *man-as-participant* in the Mystery of history and reality. Voegelin achieves this by reformulating the Question pervading the millennial quest of men for knowledge of the whole and by laying before us his response to that Question. In the long perspective, attainable today as it was in antiquity by Plato through the art of measurement (*techne metretike*), it is not so much the answers as the modes of asking the Question that assume millennial importance. There are answers aplenty in Voegelin's closely reasoned philosophy, but no doctrine, ultimate teaching, or ultimate Word is to be extracted from it. As he rémarks on the way to formulating the Question in its newly differentiated mode:

History . . . has a long breath. . . . The feeling [that there is nothing new under the sun] has its importance as a safeguard against the human weakness of elevating one's own present into the purpose of history. It will always be a wholesome exercise to reflect that 2,500 years from our own time [we] will belong to as remote a past as that of Heraclitus, the Buddha, and Confucius in relation to our present. The further reflection on what will be worth remembering about our present, and why, will establish the perspective in which it must be placed: Our present, like any present, is a phase in the flux of divine presence in which we, as all men before us, and after us, participate. The horizon of the Mystery in time that opens with the ecumenic expansion in space [during the Ecumenic Age] is still the Question that presents itself to the presently living; and what will be worth remembering about the present, will be the mode of consciousness in our response to the Question. (OH, IV, 331)[1]

1. On the *techne metretike*, see *Order and History*, III, 92, 129, 158. That a revolution is afoot in Voegelin's work is modestly hinted, not only in the quoted passage, which contains a veiled comparison of the present with the epoch in history identified by Karl Jaspers as its "Axis-time," but also in the 1977 introduction to the American edition of *Anamnesis*, trans. and ed. Gerhart Niemeyer (Notre Dame & London: University of Notre Dame Press, 1978), Chap. 1, entitled "Remembrance of Things Past," wherein Voegelin discusses the intellectual and spiritual "revolt" against the "revolt" against reason and philosophy embodied in conventional modern thought. That reality itself changes through scientific advances is noticed by the historian of science, Thomas S. Kuhn, although the theoretical implications are not elaborated: "I have so far argued only that paradigms of science are constitutive of science. Now I wish to display a sense in which they are constitutive of nature as well. . . . Examin-

The "mode of consciousness" exhibited in Voegelin's work and symbolized in the Question is *itself* the operative new paradigm of the science of man. The copestone is provided in *The Ecumenic Age* (1974) and further elaborated in shorter pieces published since the 1970s to pull together the principal lines of the paradigm.

I

Of what does the Voegelinian revolution consist? Viewed *negatively* it entails very nearly a clean sweep of the major intellectual structures of the modern world that constitute the dominant climate of opinion he so often deprecates. Most especially the clean sweep thrusts aside the whole of ideological thought as deformed and doctrinaire: *i.e.*, the leading currents of radical modernity as expressed most especially in Marxism, Freudianism, and positivism. These above all (together with Hegelianism) have generated the debilitating "dogmatomachy of 'answers'" that forms as contending "systems of science," each claiming a monopoly on truth, but each obscuring (rather than illuminating) reality and capable of surviving with a show of intellectual validity only because of its interdict on the asking of the Question. The obscuring of reality through systems (*scotosis*) and the prohibition against the asking of the Question as a principle of the systems are, thus, the twin marks of the deforming contemporary reductionist climate of opinion marking our age. Consequently, the life of the spirit and the life of reason are virtually impossible—if not completely destroyed, at least lacking a proper public forum. The desert of the spirit thereby identified is, in principle, the one bluntly indicated by the exiled Solzhenitsyn to his Harvard audience on June 9, 1978: "There is a disaster, however,

---

ing the record of past research from the vantage of contemporary historiography, the historian of [natural] science may be tempted to exclaim that when paradigms change, the world itself changes with them." Kuhn, *The Structure of Scientific Revolutions* (2nd ed., enlarged; Chicago: University of Chicago Press, 1970), 110, 111. Kuhn also observes, one should note, the decisive role of noetic intuition in engendering the luminous insights that constitute science as discovery, for example: "Scientists . . . often speak of the 'scales falling from their eyes' or of the 'lightning flash' that 'inundates' a previously obscure puzzle, enabling its components to be seen in a new way that for the first time permits its solution. On other occasions the relevant illumination comes in sleep. No ordinary sense of the term 'interpretation' fits these flashes of intuition through which a new paradigm is born." *Ibid.*, 122–23.

which has already been under way for quite some time. I am referring to the calamity of a despiritualized and irreligious humanistic consciousness. To such consciousness, man is the touchstone in judging and evaluating everything on earth. Imperfect man. . . . We have lost the concept of a Supreme Complete Entity which used to restrain our passions and our irresponsibility. . . . This is the real crisis."[2]

Solzhenitsyn's perspective is of interest because, viewed *positively*, the Voegelinian revolution, too, is an act of concrete resistance against a climate of opinion that massively obscures reality and with murderous insistence mutilates man's humanity.[3] The individual's existential response can be seen, in Voegelin's case, as equivalent to the responses of Socrates-Plato in antiquity and of Camus and Solzhenitsyn in the contemporary world. Resolute resistance to untruth is the indispensable first act in the reorientation of existence in openness toward truth in the lives of every spiritually sensitive man, whether a Plato or a Paul or a contemporary victim of a deadly climate of opinion, totalitarian or otherwise. And the movement of resistance, if it amounts to more than mere nay-saying at the level of overt articulation or to merely adding one more voice to the cacophony of dogmatic strife, can form in the consciousness of a man searching the truth of the Question the responsive symbolisms found in myth, philosophy, revelation, literature, and the fine arts.

Voegelin finds the Question a constant structure in the process of reality becoming luminous which *is* science as discovery. The Question, then, is the question of the truth of the reason of things, the search of the mysterious Ground of all reality, manifest in the compact myth of the cosmological form no less than in the more differentiated responses of philosophers, prophets, mystics, and sages of all times and places. There is, however, no ultimate Answer to the Question, because all of the answers must finally confront their limits in the "Mystery of Reality" engendering them (OH, IV, 230, 326, 329; I, 2). The fundamental experience of reality, in early cosmological societies no less than in later ones, including our own, is the mystery of existence out of nothing. Indeed, Voegelin now finds that

2. Quoted from the Dallas *Morning News*, July 6, 1978, p. D2.
3. Voegelin, "Reason: The Classic Experience," *Southern Review*, n.s., X (1974), 237–64, at 241.

the Mystery is central to the primary experience of the cosmos, thereby modifying his earlier analysis. He writes:

Existence out of nothing as the primary experience of early societies might be suspect because it reminds one of modern existentialism. The parallel is well observed, but the suspicion of modernistic interpretation of ancient materials is unfounded. Rather, inversely, the resemblance is caused by a consciousness of groundless existence acutely reawakening among modern thinkers who have rejected doctrinal metaphysics and theology without being able to recapture nondoctrinal trust [*pistis*: faith] in cosmic-divine order. . . . The experience of a cosmos existing in precarious balance on the edge of emergence from nothing and return to nothing must be acknowledged, therefore, as lying at the center of the primary experience of the cosmos. (OH, IV, 73, 77)

The fundamental tension of experienced reality is the mysterious tension of existence out of nonexistence. The fundamental tension is symbolized in the cosmos itself in early myth. The cosmos is not a thing among others; rather it is the embracing whole and "background of reality against which all existent things exist" *including* the quaternarian structure of reality in the mode of existence articulated as God, man, world, and society. Symbolized as intracosmic areas of reality, their truth "derives from the experience of an underlying, intangible embracingness, from a something that can supply existence, consubstantiality, and order to all areas of reality even though it does not itself belong as an existent thing to any one of these areas." *Not* as an existent thing among others, but as the "background of reality against which all existent things exist," thus, the *cosmos* "has reality in the *mode of nonexistence*" (OH, IV, 72–73).[4] There are, then, two modes of reality: "Reality in the mode of existence is experienced as immersed in reality in the mode of nonexistence and, inversely, nonexistence reaches into existence. The process has the character of an In-Between reality, governed by the tension of life and death" (OH, IV, 174).

Here we have Voegelin's exegesis of the earliest extant pronouncements by philosophers "on the process of reality and its structure," those by Anaximander (*fl.* 560 B.C.), and Heraclitus (*fl.*

4. Emphasis added. Cf. Voegelin, *Order and History*, IV, I, 1, and Voegelin, "Equivalences of Experience," 227.

500 B.C.). In Anaximander's words: "'The origin (*arche*) of things is the *Apeiron* [Depth; Boundless]. . . . It is necessary for things to perish into that from which they were born, for they pay one another penalty for their injustice (*adikia*) according to the ordinance of Time.'" Reality experienced and so symbolized in Anaximander is a cosmic process in which things emerge from, only to disappear again into, the nonexistent reality of the Depth (*Apeiron*). Things do not owe their existence to themselves; they exist for a time and lapse back into the nonexistence out of which their existence came. "Hence, to exist means to participate in two modes of reality: (1) In the Apeiron as the timeless *arche* of things and (2) in the ordered succession of things as the manifestation of the Apeiron in time." In the terse language of the mysteries, Heraclitus subsequently expressed the dual participation of things in reality in this way:

> "Immortals mortals
> mortals immortals
> live the others' death
> the others' life die."[5]

Voegelin's unfolding of the new science of man is spun around the meditative exploration of these insights that stand at the head of the practice of noetic science and its articulation of the Question in symbols arising as "experiential analysis." The philosophic differentiation of the truth of existence takes its rise from such experiences as those compactly symbolized by Anaximander and Heraclitus to the point that their very language became the articulating language of philosophical science itself "that has remained a constant to this day" (OH, IV, 175).

The noetic science consists in the exploration of experience from the perspective of participation as its empirical basis; it sets aside the mathematizing method of the natural sciences and of conventional (or positivist) social science, as well as the extraneous language of subject-object, the dogmatic fact-value dichotomy, and the contraction of scientifically relevant "experience" to the world of sense perception as the controlling (if not sole) reality screening sci-

5. Anaximander A 9 and B 1, and Heraclitus B62, as quoted by Voegelin, *Order and History*, IV, 174.

194 THE VOEGELINIAN REVOLUTION

entific questions from pseudo-questions (*Scheinprobleme*) (OH, IV, 316–17).[6] Not to do so would be to abandon reality *as experienced*, thereby destroying the very possibility of an empirically grounded science of man. Voegelin's noetic science rests squarely on reality experienced not as an abstract position or principle, but as a necessity dictated by the facts themselves. The reality of the discussion is the comprehensive reality of science, delimited by the insight that the only reality is the one known experientially or imaginatively extrapolated from direct experience. The symbolisms of *noesis*, he repeatedly stresses, are not something found floating in thin air. Rather they are tied to (engendered by) specific events reported by specific men in whom the experiences occur. We have knowledge of these experiences only because such men tell us in the explicative symbolisms given in responsive answer to the Question as integral to the quest as it is lived. For this reason Voegelin's work is laden with the historiographic materials through which his "experiential analysis" (which contrasts with phenotypical analysis) proceeds in the back-and-forth zigzag of reiteration and reflective reconsideration of texts and problems. Only through lovingly attentive exploration of the materials supplied through his own experiences and those of other men can a *science* of man and reality be pursued along a path, both tortuous and joyful, of self-interpretation of reality.

Thus, for example, he writes: "There is no reality of order in history except the reality experienced and symbolized by the noetic consciousness of the participants—there would be no Ecumenic Age identified by its problems of order, unless they had been identified through symbols by somebody who had experienced them" (OH, IV, 145). In the context of Plato's *Symposium* and an analysis of the "symbolization of the erotic tension in man's existence as an In-Between reality," Voegelin stresses the essential points:

The truth of existence in erotic tension [as] conveyed by the prophetess Diotima to Socrates . . . [in the dialogue] is not an information about reality but the event in which the process of reality becomes luminous to itself. It is not an information received, but an insight arising from the dialogue of the

6. See also my "Philosophical Science Beyond Behavioralism," in George J. Graham, Jr., and George W. Carey (eds.), *The Post-Behavioral Era: Perspectives on Political Science* (New York: David McKay Co., Inc., 1972), 285–305.

soul when it "dialectically" investigates its own suspense "between knowledge and ignorance." When the insight arises, it has the character of the "truth," because it is the exegesis of the erotic tension experienced; but it does arise only when the tension is experienced in such a manner that it breaks forth in its own dialogical exegesis. There is no erotic tension lying around somewhere to be investigated by someone who stumbles on it. The subject-object dichotomy, which is modeled after the cognitive relation between man and things in the external world, does not apply to the event of an "experience-articulating-itself". . . . [Rather, in the context of the dialogue, it is] the "event" in which the erotic tension in a man's soul struggles to achieve the articulate luminosity of its own reality. Hence, the dialogue of the soul is not locked up as an event in one person who, after it has happened, informs the rest of mankind of its results as a new doctrine. Though the dialogue occurs in one man's soul, it is not "one man's idea about reality," but an event in the Metaxy where man has "converse" with the divine ground of the process that is common to all men. Because of the divine presence in the dialogue of the *daimonios aner* [spiritual man], the event has a social and historical dimension. The Socratic soul draws into its dialogue the companions and, beyond the immediate companions, all those who are eager to have these dialogues reported to them. The *Symposion* presents itself as the report of a report over intervals of years; and the reporting continues to this day. (OH, IV, 186)

The truth of reality yielded in responses to the Question in a variety of modes over millennia from distant antiquity to the present intimates the "sameness of being and thinking, of the *logos* of discourse with the *logos* of being." But this complementary and simultaneous differentiation of the truth of the structures and processes of reality and consciousness occurs, not to all men at all times, but in the process of the quest of the Ground to particular men at particular times and places. That this is so is itself part of the Mystery of Reality. The cognitive and ontic dimensions of the meditative process arise together on concrete occasions and in specific historical contexts as theophanies. Thus, "We have immediate knowledge of the process [of the search and of the reality it discloses] only in its presence. A man whom we can name concretely—a Heraclitus, Plato, Plotinus, or St. Augustine—experiences the process in its mode of presence." The "process as a moving presence," understood whenever it is experienced as the search of being-truth that yields knowledge of reality, makes sense only under this assumption:

that the truth brought up from the depth of his psyche by man, though it is not the ultimate truth of reality, is representative of the truth in the divine depth of the Cosmos. Behind every equivalent symbol in the historical field stands the man who has engendered it in the course of his search as representative of a truth that is more than equivalent. The search that [can render] no more than equivalent truth rests ultimately on the faith that, by engaging in it, man participates representatively in the divine drama of truth becoming luminous.[7]

In sum: "The divine-human In-Between of historically differentiating experience is founded in the consciousness of concrete human beings in concrete bodies on the concrete earth in the concrete universe"—and nowhere else (OH, IV, 333).[8]

II

The Question of the truth-reality of history is only a dimension of the Question of the truth-reality of the Whole of which history is part. In polemical and doctrinal starkness, Leibniz formulated the Question in 1714 in these words: "(1) Why is there something, why not nothing? and (2) Why do things have to be as they are and not different?" The questions as formulated, despite their doctrinal statement by a physicist-metaphysician engaged in propositional metaphysics (a deformation of philosophy, by Voegelin's account), nonetheless are aroused by the experience of reality as a tension between existence and nonexistence. And Leibniz answered: "This ultimate reason of things is called *God*" (OH, IV, 73–74).[9]

The Question as a "structure inherent to the experience of reality" (OH, IV, 317) takes a variety of forms and may be explicit (as in

7. Voegelin, "Equivalences of Experience," 224, 233–34.
8. Cf. Voegelin, "The Concrete Consciousness," in *Anamnesis*, ed. and trans., Gerhart Niemeyer, Chap. 11.
9. Quoting Leibniz; emphasis added. But cf. G. W. von Leibniz, "The Principles of Nature and of Grace, Based on Reason," 7–8, in Philip Wiener (ed.), *Leibniz: Selections* (New York: Charles Scribner's Sons, 1951), 522–33, at 527–28. Leibniz' questions were pursued by Max Scheler, whose terminology of *tensions* and of *participation* as central categories in philosophy were taken over and greatly developed by Voegelin. See Scheler, "The Nature of Philosophy and the Moral Preconditions of Philosophical Knowledge," in *On the Eternal in Man*, trans. Bernard Noble (New York: Harper & Bros., 1960), Pt. 4, pp. 90, 98–104; see also Scheler, *Man's Place in Nature*, trans., with intro., by Hans Meyerhoff (1928; New York: Noonday Press, 1961), 70, 88–95.

Leibniz) or implicit (as in Anaximander and Heraclitus) when only answers were given. In its various modes, it structures the process of the search of the Ground of being; and its very asking implies an Answer just as answers given imply the Question, even if the responsive answers of men out of the several experiential horizons of myth, philosophy, revelation, and the meditative styles of India and China provide in their equivalence no more than representative truth. It is through the differentiation of the Question that compact truth dissolves to differentiate as the advance of truth in history. History is thus understood to be the dimension of reality in the In-Between in which the luminosity of the meaning of the Whole increases and in which the process of the Whole is experienced as moving in the direction of "eminent reality." The process of differentiation and its ramifications will concern us in greater detail shortly.

For the moment, however, other aspects of the Question may be summarized. In the first place, as we saw, the Question symbolizes the experience of the Mystery of Reality as existence out of nonexistence. It yields understanding of the In-Between reality of the existence of things in the cosmos *as* the In-Between reality in precarious balance, partaking of nonexistence because under sentence of being born to perish "according to the ordinance of Time" (Anaximander). Secondly, however, the Question as a reflective movement in the process of consciousness in a man has direction toward eminent reality, *e.g.*, in the sense of the mortal whose quest is immortality (Heraclitus/Aristotle). Thirdly, the philosophical process of immortalizing in the In-Between, forming through erotic tension as the "desire" to know the Ground and more perfectly participate in its Reason through attunement, is experienced as a passion and as a cooperative divine-human enterprise decisively structured by the actualizing attractiveness of the divine *Nous* (Plato/Aristotle). The differentiated process of the Question is the process of direction-giving *ratio*, of insightful knowing questions and questioning answers,[10] through which the self-reflective meditation of a questing or "spiritual" man moves because he feels drawn (hence directed) toward the transcendent divine Ground variously experienced-symbolized as the Beyond of existence that is the Good (*Republic*) or the Beauti-

10. Cf. Voegelin, *Anamnesis*, 50–54, 151, 289–90. See also the discussion in Voegelin, "Reason: The Classic Experience," 241–46.

ful (*Symposium*) or the Third God *Nous* who pulls the golden cord of reason in human consciousness (*Laws*). Finally, the process of consciousness of a man as he quests is experienced-symbolized as a structure of faith in search of understanding, as the *fides quaerens intellectum* of Anselm's language presupposed by Leibniz' "answer," for instance. Even in distant antiquity, however, the Question is complete. In the myth of the cosmos, which is the immediate background of Anaximander's pronouncements, the *Apeiron* of non-existence is not merely a negative dimension of the Whole but the reality that is the creative origin or Beginning of existent things, including the life and order of the "things" called men. Hence, the trust (*pistis*) in the truth-reality of the Depth, symbolized as the cosmos whose undergirding and overarching order pervasively interpenetrates things in existence, is the mysterious source of the reason of things no less than of their reality. Faith in the reason of the Whole is thus the foundation of all inquiry. The first principles or basic assumptions of all science rest on faith, the dimension of *Nous* that embraces *pistis*. To repeat Voegelin's formulation:

We share with Aristotle the belief in the premise that a truth concerning the reality of man found by one man concretely does, indeed, apply to every man. The faith in this premise, however, is . . . engendered by . . . the primordial experience of reality as endowed with the constancy and lastingness of structure that we symbolize as the Cosmos. The trust in the Cosmos and its depth is the source of the premises—be it the generality of human nature or, in our case, the reality of the process as a moving presence—that we accept as the context of meaning for our concrete engagement in the search of truth. The search for truth makes sense only under the assumption that the truth brought up from the depth of his psyche by man, though it is not the ultimate truth of reality, is representative of the truth in the divine depth of the Cosmos.[11]

11. Voegelin, "Equivalences of Experience," 234. For the *fides quaerens intellectum* in this context, see Voegelin, *The Beginning and the Beyond: A Meditation on Truth* (Milwaukee, Wisc.: Marquette University Press, forthcoming). See also Voegelin, "Wisdom and the Magic of the Extreme: A Meditation," *Southern Review*, n.s., XVII, 2, pp. 255, 271. Cf. Michael Polanyi, *Science, Faith, and Society* (Chicago: University of Chicago Press, 1946), 45 and *passim*. Related to the issue at this point in the text is Thomas Kuhn's judgment: "The transfer of allegiance from scientific paradigm to paradigm is a conversion experience that cannot be forced. . . . A decision of that kind can only be made on faith." Kuhn, *Structure of Scientific Revolutions*, 151, 158. See also the discussion of "Where does . . . regularity and order come from?" in F. Sherwood Taylor, *A Short History of Science and Scientific Thought* (New York:

It will have become clear by now that the core of Voegelin's noetic science of man is not a set of axioms, principles, hypotheses,
or laws susceptible of statement as a system of science or even as
one among successive paradigms of science in the sense of Thomas
Kuhn's utilization of the term in his historical account of the turns
from "normal" to "revolutionary" interpretations of the world
through the natural sciences and their analytical schemata.[12] Although summarizing propositional statement has its legitimate
place in noetic science as a means of supplying guideposts, it is a
measure of the revolution worked by Voegelin's effort over the past
half-century that noetic science stands in stark contrast to the dominant modes of scientific thinking that form as a succession of systematic paradigms of greater or lesser utility for interpreting reality
on the pattern of what philosophers of science may assert to be the
methodology of the natural sciences. Noetic science signals the
abandonment of the sciences of the external world as the model of
the science of man. It proffers science in a new mode.

At its center lies the Question, not as an arbitrary alternative, but
as the existentially grounded symbolism engendered by the Mystery
of Reality and empirically evidenced by every great exploration of
the In-Between of reality from prehistoric times into the present.
There is no final Answer to the Question, other than the Mystery
whose meaning becomes more luminous through the process of
questioning itself. And the luminosity of the Mystery and depth of
its mysteriousness are enhanced by the process of questioning, both
through the advances in understanding gained in the differentiation
of truth from the primordial compactness of experiences of men
questing in the In-Between of reality *and* through the deformations
and contractions of reality engendered by men who turn from open
participation in the process of reality and history to the closure

---

W. W. Norton & Co., 1963), 341. Cf. Maurice Merleau-Ponty, *The Visible and the In-
visible,* ed. Claude Lefort, trans. Alphonso Lingis (Evanston, Ill.: Northwestern University Press, 1968), Chap. 1. Aristotle's statement of the issue is given in a brief paragraph that concludes: "We are left with the conclusion that it is intelligence [*Nous*]
that apprehends fundamental principles." Aristotle, *Nicomachean Ethics,* Bk. 6,
Chap. 6, 1141a8, p. 155; cf. *Posterior Analytics,* Bk. 2, Chap. 19, 100b5–14.
    12. "Why not" is explained by Voegelin in "What Is Political Reality?" *Anam-
nesis,* 283–85; the passage in Niemeyer's edition is at pp. 143–46. See Kuhn, *Structure of Scientific Revolutions,* Chaps. 2, 5, 10, and *passim.*

against the divine Ground (or, alternatively, against the cosmos in which reality is founded) to the fragmented hypostases of reality that emerge as second realities in several modes of restriction. For the truth of consciousness-reality, gained in the joyful willingness to apperceive that engenders the great pneumatic and noetic theophanies in men open to the horizon of reality, has its counterpart in the contrapuntal closure against the open horizon of experience and the attendant deformations, reductionisms, doctrinalizations, and perversions of differentiated truth found at every step of the way. And these latter—interpreted as the concupiscential exoduses from the Whole into the prison of a part, or as the egophany of the contracted self in contrast to the theophany of differentiating consciousness-reality—by their abundance and massive presence distorting reality and dominating the pragmatic and spiritual life of men in existence, compose no insignificant part of the Mystery of personal, social, and historical existence itself. They set the problem of the philosopher, no less than of everyman, who struggles to find his humanity and the order of existence amidst the welter of disordering forces. They periodically and repeatedly run amok to compound the misery of existence, as through the systems of "science" armed as ideologies for the manipulation of mankind by megalomaniacs driven to create the prisons of existence through radical closure enforced by limitless pride, the *libido dominandi* of Classical and Christian philosophy. The problem is to resist and so survive. And to do that requires the analysis of the truth and order of reality that arises only after a man discerns the untruth of the restricted and potentially murderous horizon of intellectual and political practitioners of egophanic revolt.[13]

III

What is paradigmatic in the new science, then, is twofold. Primarily, it is the exemplification of the contemplative life in the person and quest of Eric Voegelin in the "act of open participation in the process of both history and the Whole" (OH, IV, 335), so that what noetic

13. Cf. Voegelin, *Order and History*, IV, 330–35; *Anamnesis*, trans. and ed., Niemeyer, Chap. 1. On the "joyous willingness to apperceive" as emblematic of the desire to know and openness to reality, see *Order and History*, IV, 237; "Reason: The Classic Experience," 257; *Anamnesis*, trans. and ed., Niemeyer, 11.

science *is* can best be answered by pointing to the concrete instance of a life and its work. The paradigm of the new science is thereby given in much the same way that in the differentiating horizon of antiquity what philosophy is could be indicated by pointing to the paradigmatic Socrates, thereby defining philosophy existentially *in actu* as an *imitatio Socratis,* a definition that seventy generations of men by now have found of value. This book is to be read as a gloss on that paradigm. Secondarily, the paradigm is discernible in questions asked and answers given in openness to reality as this concretely forms the wealth of scholarly information and analysis in published work. This composes the scientific corpus of knowledge of human reality in the modalities of response to the Question provided the public in the critical work of Voegelin and in the myriad sources upon which his interpretations draw.

Can the paradigm of the noetic science therewith pointed to in a twofold way be more closely circumscribed? Can the "principles" of the inquiry and the "findings" of study be given summary statement in some useful fashion? I think the answer to these questions is yes, provided elementary precautions are taken to guard against misconceiving the attempt. There are principles basic to Voegelin's work, and there are results that carry human understanding of itself and reality at large beyond what it was without Voegelin's monumental effort to understand. Voegelin himself provides key formulations of "principles." In considering the following summary of the noetic science in the language of discovery-results, these cautions will be observed:

1. Although the language of principles, discovery, and results is employed, the usage must be placed in the *context* of the enterprise from which the summarizing statements are drawn.

2. More specifically, the language (and its affinity with propositional science in the positivist sense, with propositional metaphysics in the Scholastic sense, and with the mathematizing sciences of nature) does *not* delineate a system of science or a collection of axioms from which either a valid methodology of scientific inquiry or a definitive body of doctrinal truth can be deduced as a system of science or as expressive of a body of knowledge on the pattern, say, of Bertrand Russell's and Alfred North Whitehead's *Principia Mathematica* (1903).

3. Hence, the "cautions" in this list immediately confront a principle of noetic science itself, one negatively expressed and with implications to be considered subsequently. It is that the noetic science of man cannot be assimilated to the models of mathematics and physics conventionally taken to be the models of science *per se*. At this point all that needs to be stressed is the negative: the phenomena of human existence "cannot be dealt with according to the natural science model of science and object" (A, 286; Niemeyer ed., 145).

4. The summarizing statements are not doctrines which state in concise fashion the teaching or conclusions of a philosophizing scientist. Rather, they are guideposts. They are intended to introduce a highly complex body of thought to those who desire to become better acquainted with it, after this first approach, through study of the original sources. They constitute a bridge-building—not a substitute for *noesis* itself, but rather a means of orientation that attempts to identify salient structures in Voegelin's thought.

5. Finally, no pretense of completeness is to be imputed to the summary. A complete account of the process of discovery would entail a full-scale logic of *Noesis* that would comprise a separate book as large or larger than the present volume. (Voegelin has for decades toyed with the idea of writing such a logic, but so far there has been only an array of published hints.) This compilation of "results" is fragmentary, also, because the work is still in progress and, more importantly, because a raw inventory of "results" would subvert the philosopher's enterprise as he himself presents it.

"Results" return us to the perverse understanding of the science of things human as a body of knowledge about objective reality *qua* science on the defective model of subjects of cognition and objects in phenomenal reality; or, alternatively, on the model of philosophy as a propositional or doctrinal account of speculative *topoi* which refer to the phenomenal reality of sense perception—the origin of the derailment of noetic science in antiquity. But it is the very core of the revolution worked by the noetic science to understand that knowledge of reality is inseparable from the process of experience-symbolization in the In-Between attained in the ineluctable perspective of a man's participation in that same reality which, on specific occasions of specific events in the consciousness of individual men, becomes luminous with its meaning. To speak of "results," without strict attention to these decisive considerations, would be to commit precisely the basic fallacy Voegelin energetically cautions against: "To submit an experience of participation in the primordial field, of emergent truth, and of its meditative articulation through symbols to this butchery would destroy the reality of the experience as experienced."[14]

Taken together, these cautions form, in preliminary statement, certain of the key principles to understanding the noetic science in the dimensions of discovery-results. Particularly, the fifth item in the list will suggest that the exercise is dubious, to the extent that it flies in the face of a major thrust of the noetic science itself and opens it to the misunderstanding most frequently encountered in critical reactions to Voegelin's work. At best, our summary will be a kind of high-wire act conducted in imminent peril of falling. But the hazard is worth the candle if it succeeds in making the noetic science accessible to readers for whom propositional summary works but who would reject the appeal as tendered in the language of experiential analysis itself. In short, the endeavor appears justified if it at least partially succeeds in rendering more intelligible these fundamental insights into science and reality without too badly deforming them in the process.

IV

The principles of discovery are those of the inquiry (*zetema*) itself and will already be largely familiar to the reader of foregoing parts of this book. Perhaps more novel will be this statement of results, since it will concentrate on the modification of earlier insights by recapitulating the outcome of the latest work done by Eric Voegelin. For full understanding, these conclusions must be read in the context of the entire study and in the context of its sources.

This enumeration of principles of noetic science is by and large, of course, a partial compilation of those given by Voegelin in explaining the process of his thought. Inevitably, the principles are not

14. Voegelin, "Equivalences of Experience," 232; cf. "Reason: The Classic Experience," 94; see also *Order and History*, III, 277–79.

merely logical or methodological, but epistemological and ontological as well, since the act of philosophizing is not susceptible of dissection into discrete parts.

1. PARTICIPATION

The principle of participation is central to noetic science. It forms the existential basis of man's self-understanding insofar as from earliest times onward men are aware of participating in a structured reality of which they are but a part, one ontologically articulated by the symbolisms man, God, world, and society—the primordial quaternarian structure of being reflected in the earliest cosmological myths. Participation forms, therefore, as both the essence of the knower and the knowable and the inevitable perspective of the inquiry into reality. There is no Archimedean point outside of reality-as-participation available to men. Accordingly, it supplants the subject-object categories of cognition and ontology.

1.A. *Fundamental tension.* The participation of men in reality is not diffuse and random but forms directionally toward ultimate or eminent reality. This eminent reality (*realissimum*) is called God, and by various other names that symbolically designate the experience of the divinity of the ultimate reality, or Ground of being. The fundamental tension as stated abstractly is experienced concretely in a variety of modes, such as the philosophers' erotic tension toward the Ground which forms as the love of Wisdom in Plato; the Heraclitean and Pauline love, faith, and hope; the immortalizing quest of the mortal in Heraclitus and Aristotle; the restless wondering that stirs the questioning consciousness into the desire to know in all men and rises to the joyous willingness to apperceive in the spiritually sensitive and mature men of Plato and Aristotle; the *amor Dei* and *intentio animi* in Augustine; the faith in search of understanding in the mystic's experience articulated in Anselm.

1.B. *Hierarchy.* The search of the Ground in participation is structured by its insight into the hierarchical structure of reality and the self-reflective discovery of questioning reason of the range of participation as layered in ascending grades of greater reality from the physical to the spiritual, rational, and divine. The insight into the hierarchical structure-order of reality is, at the same time, an insight into the hierarchical structure-order of the psyche or consciousness of the self-reflective man whose composite nature is understood as the epitome of all the realms of being and whose specific nature is *Nous*. Further, *Nous* is identified both as the site of the experiences of participation in the Ground of being and also, somehow, as the same as the divine Ground experienced in Aristotle.

1.C. *Question*. The Question is "a constant structure in the experience of reality" (OH, IV, 326). The search of the Ground, in cosmological myth no less than in philosophy and revelation, forms in the directions of attunement to the truth of the Ground and of questioning about the truth of reality, including the Ground of eminent reality, mysteriously poised in existence out of nonexistence (Anaximander and Plato).

1.D. *Direction*. Directional indices of the quest arise in the process of questing in the language of the men who ask the Question: *Beginning*, when the quest for the Ground is extrapolated to an absolute point in the past (Genesis); *Depth*, when the quest seeks the Ground of things present in existence (Anaximander); *Beyond*, when the quest is pursued through the hierarchy of being to a point above the cosmos in the leap in being that discloses transcendent Being in the God of the Beyond (Moses, Plato, the anonymous author of the *Apocalypse of Abraham*) (OH, IV, 322–26); *End*, when the quest for the Ground in the mode of pneumatic vision is extrapolated to an absolute point of the future time, as an eschatological fulfillment perfecting and redeeming man and the world through the Parousia marking the culmination of time (Paul). To these may be added the summarizing, abstract spatial-metaphorical linguistic indices of transcendent-immanent as symbolizing the tensional relationship of the eminent reality and the reality of things, of the Creator and the creation, of the timeless Beyond and the realm of temporal-spatial reality, of Being and becoming.

2. DIFFERENTIATION

The answers to the Question are not all on a level. Some are superior to others in penetration, luminosity, and completeness. That superiority is achieved through a process of differentiation. The principle is basic to the inquiry called *Order and History* by the man called Eric Voegelin. As he retrospectively stated it in 1974, with reference to the formulation given in 1956:

"The order of history emerges from the history of order." History was conceived as a process of increasingly differentiated insight into the order of being in which man participates by his existence. Such order as can be discerned in the process, including digressions and regressions from the increasing differentiation, would emerge, if the principal types of man's existence in society, as well as the corresponding symbolisms of order, were presented in their historical succession. . . . [Nothing] was wrong with the principle of the study. (OH, IV, 1, 2)[15]

Differentiation was clarified in the form of three principles in the first volume of *Order and History*, it may be recalled, in these words: "(1) The nature of man is constant. (2) The range of human experience is always present in the fullness of its dimensions. (3) The structure of the range varies from compactness to differentiation" (OH, I, 60).

The principle of differentiation, then, designates a developmental or evolutionary process in the structures of consciousness-reality. Early myth understood as consciousness-reality experienced-symbolized is less differentiated (*i.e.*, more compact) than are philosophy and revelation, as leading symbolic forms articulating profounder experiences (hence understanding) of eminent reality, and therewith also of the Whole. The breakthroughs to more differentiated insights are designated "leaps in being" in the first three volumes of *Order and History*, but Voegelin prefers "spiritual outbursts" or "theophanies" in later work, though the earlier term is not discarded. Because not all insights into reality that differentiate are on a level, and degrees of penetration, luminosity, and completeness are discernible, the insights must be critically assessed and ranked:

A philosophy of history cannot be an amiable record of memorabilia . . . [but] must be a critical study of the authoritative structure in the history of mankind. Neither can the authoritative communications of truth about order, as they have sprung up in the course of history, be sympathetically accepted on an equal footing—for that would submerge us in the evils of historicism, skepticism and relativism; nor can they be rejected by the standards of an ultimate truth, whether such ultimacy be attributed to a truth of the past or a new one discovered by ourselves—for such absolutism would involve us in the gnostic fallacy of declaring the end of history. A study that wants to be critical must take seriously the fact that the truth about the

15. Internal quotation from *Order and History*, I, ix.

order of being emerges in the order of history. The Logos of history itself provides the instruments for the critical testing and ranking of the authoritative structure. . . . The principles which I have just attempted to formulate are supposed to furnish the critical foundation for the study *Order and History.* (OH, II, 7)

2.A. *Knowledge.* The process of differentiation is itself the *exclusive* source of knowledge of consciousness-reality—that is, of the knowledge attained through (and as) the noetic science *qua* science. Acceptance of this principle means, "negatively, to renounce all pretense to an observer's position outside the process. Positively, it means to enter the process and to participate both in its formal structure and the concrete tasks imposed on the thinker by his situation in it." What differentiates to become known as a new discovery is consciousness of a *structure* in reality that was present before it was experienced-symbolized in the differentiation of consciousness-reality and that will be present after the event. But, in addition, the differentiation that brings to view the structure also concretely brings to view the *process* of consciousness-reality in which "all men, past, present, and future participate" in the differentiated mode of a "new consciousness" with personal, social and historical dimensions (OH, IV, 314–15).[16]

2.B. *Contraction.* The countermovements in consciousness-reality to those of differentiation attained through openness to the Ground may be designated by the principle of contraction through closure against the Ground. The language is supplemented by such descriptive terms as rebellion, revolt, deformation, reduction, metastatic faith, magic, apocalypse, concupiscential exodus, bad faith, refusal to apperceive, alienation, contempt for Reason, egophany, derailment, defection from reality. The enriched vocabulary emerges in the course of the detailed analyses that articulate the inquiry in specific contexts. Taken together, they circumscribe critically the many ways in which the differentiated insights as symbolized are perverted, dogmatized, doctrinalized, obscured through systems, or otherwise torn from their experiential contexts so as to obfuscate insight with misleading screens, thereby restricting the horizon which

16. The details of the analysis in the context of the key instance of the "epoch" marking the Ecumenic Age in history should be consulted directly.

originally became more luminous through increased differentiation of consciousness-reality. Gnosticism is a special instance of contraction and spiritual disease (Plato's *nosos*, Schelling's pneumopathology) because of its great career over two millennia.

3. EXPERIENCE-SYMBOLIZATION

Experience is basic to all science. But the experience basic to noetic science is not primarily the perception of external things in phenomenal reality but the apperception of the structure and processes of the participatory reality of consciousness in existential tension to the Ground. In noetic science, experience so understood engenders the symbolisms that let it articulate itself. Experience-symbolism, thus, is a unit: without the experience there is no symbolism, without the symbolism no articulate experience. Both arise at once in the participatory search of the Ground, which differentiates the structure and process of consciousness-reality. The process of search or questing and its attendant symbolization of experience in the movement of differentiation stresses the cognitive and ontic perspective of participatory luminosity, in contrast to the subject-object dichotomy of science as knowledge of objects intentionally investigated by the scientist on the model of natural science. That this is the reality of the process of search of the Ground in *all* its modes is strenuously urged on the basis of critical assessment of the vast source material. That noetic science has *not*, since antiquity, been so understood is the root of the derailment of philosophy into topical speculation after Aristotle—derailment that continues into the present. From this fundamental mistake about the character of philosophizing arose (in part) such phenomena of world-historic significance as propositional metaphysics, the repudiation of philosophy in early modernity, and its subsequent "ruin" (Whitehead) through perversion at the hands (among others) of German Idealists, Hegel's "system of science," Marxism, positivism, and the other nineteenth-century "isms" that debouch into the dogmatomachy of contending ideologies underlying the terror of existence in the twentieth century.

3.A. *Equivalences.* The corollary principle of equivalence arises from the recognition that the same reality, its structure and process, is intended by the highly varied symbolisms left as the trail of history over the millennia from Stone Age petroglyphs to an Upanishad to a Platonic dialogue to the twentieth-century philosophizing of a James, a Bergson, or a Whitehead. Thus the discovery of "new" truth through a thinker's experiential descent into the depth of the psyche will be tempered by the recognition that it is not entirely new, but equivalently present in the more compact form of the old truth, just as Aristotle recognized the equivalence of the insights symbolized in myth to those symbolized in the more differentiated form of philosophy. And he could, therefore, equate the lover of myth (*philomythos*) with the lover of wisdom (*philosophos*) as men in search of the same truth.

Further illustrations may be given of equivalence of experience and symbolization that will clarify the central issue of noetic science, *i.e.*, the experience of participation and the paradox of its necessary epistemological consequence, namely "the identity and nonidentity of the knower with the known."

That being and thinking are the same was the insight of Parmenides; that the *logos* of his discourse was the same as the *logos* of reality expressed by the discourse, the insight of Heraclitus. The symbolism of participation, of *methexis* or *metalepsis*, is both classic and scholastic. *Aletheia*, with its double meaning of truth and reality, is Platonic-Aristotelian. The identity and nonidentity of the knower with the known has its equivalent in Hegel's sophisticated definition of absolute reality as the identity of identity and non-identity—though in this case our agreement must be qualified because of Hegel's lapse from the analysis of a structure of consciousness into the construction of a system. The process of reality is the equivalent of Whitehead's conception of the experience. The In-Between of man's existence, then, is Plato's *metaxy*. And the virtues of existential tension [toward the Ground]—love, hope, and faith—are constant symbols from the pre-Socratic and classic philosophers, through St. Paul and St. Augustine, to the present. The symbols of alienation, finally, that can be found in the Hellenic poets and philosophers were collected by Clement of Alexandria on occasion of his struggle with the Gnostic response to alienation, and new varieties of the symbolism were developed by Christians and neo-Platonists. In our own search today, thus, we are indeed engaged in the same search in which our predecessors were engaged in their day.[17]

17. Voegelin, "Equivalences of Experience," 223.

4. REASON

That science is a rational structure and reason a principle of science, including the noetic or philosophical science of man, is not remarkable in itself. Moreover, that reason is the constituent of man and the specifically human in him is equally commonplace. He is regularly designated a rational animal or a creature with intelligence or consciousness, the summarizing definitional expressions which have since antiquity been applied to him as a *zoon noetikon* translated into Latin as the *animal rationale* (echoed in the biological designation coined in 1859, *Homo sapiens*) or, in Aristotle's formulation, as the living being that possesses reason (*nous*), the *zoon noun echon*. But the Reason of noetic science and its meaning as the something that constitutes man in his humanity as recovered through, explored by, and differentiated in the new science reaches far beyond the unremarkable and commonplace conventional understanding. Differentiated Reason lies at the heart of noetic science as knowledge (*episteme*) about human things gained in the In-Between of participatory reality through critical self-reflective experiential analysis.

What is it? It is the *Nous* meditatively discovered in antiquity by the mystic philosophers, differentiated in the Classical period by Plato and Aristotle, and now further differentiated in the thought of Voegelin. In its widest perspective it is, in its several dimensions, concretely discovered to be the First Principle common to being, man, and science. Since our interest here is to accent its place in science, attention will focus primarily on that aspect of the subject rather than on the other two. Still the perspective of the whole symbolism alone makes the present synopsis fully intelligible.[18]

Reason is *the* principle of science, because it is a principle of both reality and consciousness; and, in the analysis of the Classical experience, reason is shown to be the highest principle common to man and divine Being. The recovery of the full meaning of *Nous* (Reason, Mind, Intelligence, Thought, as it is translated in various contexts) is itself a major achievement of Voegelin's work, one with which he remained occupied in 1981. Reason, as a principle of the noetic science, is both a structure and a process. It is both formal and substan-

18. The major source of the discussion is Voegelin, "Reason: The Classic Experience," in *Anamnesis*, trans. and ed., Niemeyer, 89–115.

tive. It determines the form of the inquiry as the structure of man's participation in the *metaxy* of existence as that inquiry explores the tension toward the divine Ground of reality. Its content is attunement to the truth of reality experienced, which manifests itself in personal, social, and historical order and in resistance to disorder in the several dimensions of human existence.

Reason, then, is the principle of existence in the mode of truth. Its discovery in antiquity, and its renewed vitality as manifested in noetic science, Voegelin shows, arises in the experience of *resistance* to disorder and untruth. Without accenting this existential core of Reason, as it arises in the psyche of men engaged in the combat (*agon*) of existence in the concrete horizon of the Hellenic philosophers' resistance to the untruth of the Sophists, or the contemporary philosophers' resistance to the untruth of the ideologues, its meaning cannot be grasped. Reason achieves the status of abstract "principle" only at a second or third remove from its genesis in the experience of resistance to untruth or, alternatively, in the experience of restless ignorance about truth that ought to be known. Reason, thus, is not an idea or a tradition or merely a human faculty, but an event whose discovery constitutes an epoch in the history of mankind. Through its discovery in a sequence of increasingly more differentiated participatory acts by philosophers resisting untruth and exploring truth out of an awareness of their own ignorance, the specifically human nature is constituted whose reality becomes transparent for its truth as a structure of Reason.

The key is not the finished experience symbolized in *Nous*. Rather, it is the origin of the discovery from which the differentiation arises. The origin lies in a man's experience of restless wondering as that is pulled toward the eminent reality that stirs the man to restlessness and wondering as the first act of the meditative ascent of *Noesis* or philosophizing. At this level, reason is the "something" in man that experiences shame in the recognition of his ignorance *or* that resists through as-yet-unclear motives the deformation of his own existence and that of other men by destructive forces in the social field. The "something" in this tension of ignorance or resistance has its setting in the thing called man and in the part of man called *psyche*, the soul or consciousness. Consciousness is the site of the experiences of restless wondering and ignorance; and the sensorium that reflects on its wondering and ignorance and asks questions about them in the analytical rise of successive wondering, questioning, and answering is, then, further circumscribed to be named Reason. Recognition of direction in the experience is especially significant. For the process of questing as a movement in the soul is not entirely self-induced by man. It is experienced as an attraction toward higher reality that is prefiguratively known in the restlessness of wondering itself and in the awareness of ignorance about what ought to be known. These "knowing" dimensions of the experiences, then, move to clarity in the differentiating rise of the philosopher to the point of the outburst of the symbolism in articulation of the name. That higher something is the divine *Nous* or Ground (*arche, aition*), experienced as the controlling reality to which the *nous* in man is responsive.

The discovery of *Nous*, then, is the revelation of the divine Ground. Occurring within the horizon of Hellenic philosophy, it symbolizes a now-understood-to-be noetic experience disclosing the Divine Ground of Being in a manner comparable in detail to the disclosures in the Israelite and Christian horizons. It is a theophanic event whose content is equivalent in Classical experience to the theophanies of Moses and Paul in their respective revelatory experiences of the I AM WHO I AM and of the Resurrected in the Vision on the road to Damascus. As in the latter instances of divine disclosure, the decisive accent lies on the movement of the divine partner in being. It is He who moves the man in the process of restless questioning to ask the questions that incipiently comprehend the knowledge gained in the answers to them. The exuberant joy of apperception in the philosophers' rise to the contemplative vision[19] of the divine *Nous*, then, has its explanation in their awareness of participating, as far as men are able to, in the process of immortalizing in the In-Between, through experience of the actualizing presence of the divine of the Beyond whom they touch in the culmination of their meditations. It is, for instance, the exuberance of genuine theophany that suffuses the usually staid language of Aristotle when, in

19. *Opsis* in Plato, *Republic*, 507–509, with reference to the *Agathon*; *Timaeus* 47, with respect to the cosmos, for example; see, for further elaboration, Voegelin, *Order and History*, IV, 241–47, beginning with section on "Noetic and Pneumatic Theophany." See also Voegelin, *The Beginning and the Beyond*, ms. pp. 66–70.

a precious and remarkable passage partially quoted in the preceding chapter, he admonishes men in their resistance: "not [to] follow those who advise us to have human thoughts, since we are [only] men, and mortal thoughts as mortals should; [but] on the contrary, [to] try to become immortal as far as that is possible and [to] do our utmost to live in accordance with what is highest in us." And he continues his exhortation with great emphasis in these words:

For though this [nous] is small in bulk, it far surpasses everything else in power and value. One might even regard it as each man's true self, since it is the controlling and better part. It would, therefore, be strange if a man chose not to live his own life but someone else's. . . . In other words, a life guided by intelligence [nous] is best and most pleasant for man, inasmuch as intelligence [nous] above all else, is man. Consequently, this kind of life is the happiest.[20]

Although the full details of Voegelin's revolutionary analysis of Reason as a *revelation* in the horizon of Classic philosophy cannot be entered into here, it is vital that we hear him carefully on the subject.

The Classic, especially the Aristotelian, unrest is distinctly joyful because the questioning has direction; the unrest is experienced as the beginning of the theophanic event in which the *nous* reveals itself as the divine ordering force in the *psyche* of the questioner and the cosmos at large; it is an invitation to pursue its meaning into the actualization of noetic consciousness.
. . . .
With their discovery of man as the *zoon noun echon* [the living being that possesses *nous*], the Classic philosophers have discovered man to be more than a *thnetos*, a mortal: he is an unfinished being, moving from the imperfection of death in this life to the perfection of life in death.[21]

In a summarizing commentary on a sentence from Aristotle, the cognitive participation of man in the divine is articulated:

The critical sentence . . . is the following: "Thought (nous) thinks itself through participation (metalepsis) in the object of thought (noeton); for it becomes the object of thought through being touched (thigganon) and

20. Aristotle, *Nicomachean Ethics*, Bk. 10, chap. 7, 1177b32–1178a5. See Voegelin's comments on this passage from Aristotle in "Reason: The Classic Experience," in *Anamnesis*, trans. and ed., Niemeyer, 103–104.
21. Voegelin, "Reason: The Classic Experience," in *Anamnesis*, trans. and ed., Niemeyer, 101, 104.

thought (*noon*), so that thought (*nous*) and . . . what is thought (*noeton*) are the same (*Met.* 1072b20ss)." When read in the Aristotelian context, the sentence articulates the dynamics of sameness and difference of the knower and the known in the act of noetic participation, [and] the joy of momentary sameness with the divine.[22]

And, finally, the far-reaching consequences of Voegelin's explorations of men's experiences of divine reality in the rich variety of their modalities and symbolisms are reflected in this summarizing passage:

The one truth of reality, as it emerges from the Metaxy, is in danger of dissociating into the two verities of Faith and Reason. . . . [But we can now] no longer ignore that *the symbols of "Faith" express the responsive quest of man just as much as the revelatory appeal, and that the symbols of "Philosophy" express the revelatory appeal just as much as the responsive quest.* We must further acknowledge that the medieval tension between Faith and Reason derives from the origins of these symbols in the two different ethnic cultures of Israel and Hellas, that in the consciousness of Israelite prophets and Hellenic philosophers the differentiating experience of the divine Beyond was respectively focused on the revelatory appeal and the human quest, and that the two types of consciousness had to face new problems when the political events of the Ecumenic Age cut them loose from their moorings in the ethnic cultures and forced their confrontation under the multicivilizational conditions of an ecumenic empire.[23]

It is clear by now that major "results" have invaded this account of "principles" in the attempt to formulate the groundwork of the noetic science. This was inevitable if the principle of reason itself was to be clearly understood operationally. There is an operational side that arises on the basis of the foregoing discussion of reason in context, and it is at least partially susceptible of brief formulation. Fortunately, Voegelin has done this work for us himself.

The science which as knowledge of reality arose as the exegesis of the philosophers' experiences of reality has educational, diagnostic, and therapeutic functions; and it applies to the whole range of

22. *Ibid.,* 108. The ellipsis in the sentence quoted from the *Metaphysics* marks the omission of *that* which seems to be a printer's error. For the perversion of the text by Hegel see the discussion by Voegelin at pp. 108–109, the context in which Aristotle is being quoted.
23. Voegelin, *The Beginning and the Beyond,* ms. pp. 45–46. Emphasis added.

FIGURE 1

	PERSON	SOCIETY	HISTORY
Divine Nous			
Psyche–Noetic			
Psyche–Passions			
Animal Nature			
Vegetative Nature			
Inorganic Nature			
Apeiron–Depth			

the study of human affairs (Aristotle's *peri ta anthropina*): personal, social, and historical. It is presented schematically in Figure 1.

The diagram's explanation and the corollaries of the principle of reason are succinctly stated by Voegelin in the following language.

The left vertical column lists the levels in the hierarchy of being from the *nous* to the *apeiron*. Man participates in all of them; his nature is an epitome of the hierarchy of being. The arrow pointing down indicates the order of formation from the top down. The arrow pointing up indicates the order of foundation from the bottom up.

The top horizontal column lists the dimensions of man's existence as a person in society and history. The arrow pointing to the right indicates the order of foundation.

Principle of completeness: A philosophy *peri ta anthropina* must cover the grid determined by the two coordinates. No part of the grid must be hypostatized into an autonomous entity, neglecting the context.

Principle of Formation and Foundation: The order of formation and foundation must not be inverted or otherwise distorted, as for instance by its transformation into a causality working from the top or the bottom. Specifically, all constructions of phenomena on a higher level as epiphenomena of processes on a lower one, the so-called reductionist fallacies, are excluded as false. This rule, however, does not affect the conditioning causality which is the very essence of foundation. Neither are inversions of the order of foundation in the horizontal column permitted. Specifically, all "philosophies of history" which hypostatize society or history as an absolute, eclipsing personal existence and its meaning, are excluded as false.

Principle of metaxy *reality*: The reality determined by the coordinates is the in-between reality, intelligible as such by the consciousness of *nous* and *apeiron* as its limiting poles. All "eristic phantasies" which try to convert the limits of the *metaxy*, be it the noetic height or the apeirontic depth, into a phenomenon within the *metaxy* are to be excluded as false. This rule does not affect genuine eschatological or apocalyptic symbolisms which imaginatively express the experience of a movement within reality toward a beyond of the *metaxy*, such as the experiences of mortality and immortality.

The diagram has proved of particular value for students because it gives them a minimum body of objective criteria for "true" and "false" in their struggle with the flood of contemporary opinion literature. With the help of the diagram it is possible to classify false theoretical propositions by assigning them their place in the grid. On occasion it has become an exciting game for the students to place ideas which enjoy the popularity of the moment in one of the twenty-one squares. Beyond its function as a technical aid in mastering contemporary phenomena of intellectual disorder, the diagram had the important psychological effect of overcoming the students' sense of disorientation and lostness in the unmanageable flood of false opinions that presses in on them every day.[24]

24. The foregoing paragraphs, Figure 1, and the quoted explanation that follows are paraphrased and taken from Voegelin, "Reason: The Classic Experience," *Southern Review*, n.s., X (1974), 260–64.

CHAPTER 8

The Vision of the Whole

William James, the most eminent American philosopher before Voegelin, reminded us of the ancient wisdom that,
"Where there is no vision the people perish."[1] He believed that "a
philosopher's vision and the technique he uses in proof of it are two
different things," and that "philosophy is more a matter of passion-
ate vision than of logic."

> Place yourself . . . at the centre of a man's philosophic vision and you [will]
> understand at once all the different things it makes him write or say. But
> keep outside, use your post-mortem method, try to build the philosophy up
> out of the single phrases, taking first one and then another and seeking to
> make them fit, and of course you fail. You crawl over the thing like a myopic
> ant over a building, tumbling into every microscopic crack or fissure, find-
> ing nothing but inconsistencies, and never suspecting that a centre exists.
> . . . What really *exists* is not things made but things in the making.

To which he later adds, as we noted earlier, "that personal experience of some kind must have made [philosophers'] confidence in
their own vision so strong."[2]

   If we pursue the Jamesian tack in summing up the Voegelinian
"results," what can be said about the philosopher's vision and its
"personal" engendering experience? Is there a center and, if so, what
is it? How does it relate to his technique of proof? Let us now turn to
these questions in a selective and illustrative conclusion of our

---

   1. William James, *Essays in Radical Empiricism* [and] *A Pluralistic Universe*
(2 vols., in 1; repr. ed., Gloucester, Mass.: Peter Smith, 1967), II, 165. Cf. Prov. 29:18.
   2. *Ibid.*, II, 85, 176, 263, 308, respectively; cf. 328–30.

study which is calculated to throw into relief what Voegelin's philosophy comes down to, what it is and what it is not.

I

About the center of Voegelin's thought, the personal experience that animates its every word and the vision that radiates from it, there can be no doubt at all: it is (in his own statement) "the love of being through love of divine Being as the source of its order" (OH, I, xiv).[3] The magnificent power and sensitivity of his thought attest on every page of his work, and most especially in the work of the last quarter-century, this great-spirited love that marks him as a philosopher worthy of his calling and one worth heeding. The veil of technical terminology, Greek words, range of strange and familiar sources and documents through which he carefully pursues his anamnestic quest should not be permitted to obscure the extraordinary lucidity of his language and expository technique. What is difficult about Voegelin's writing is the subject matter he explores, not the stylistic eccentricities of an author. His subject matter ranges over the height and depth of the human mind's encounters with the divine and perverse in many modes of experience and a variety of temporal and cultural horizons. The magisterial clarity, precision, and luminosity with which this range of material is handled by Voegelin is rivaled in elegance in twentieth-century philosophy only by James, Bergson, and Whitehead, and only the latter approached the range of thought one meets with in Voegelin.

What of the vision? *Vision* is an ambiguous, even loaded word, especially in this day of exotic visionaries. The obvious must be stressed: Voegelin's vision does indeed rise to the contemplative heights of the true mystic, but its ascent is founded in the painstaking sifting of the empirical materials of men's experiences of reality in the strict discipline of science. His vision is won through critical experiential analysis and is, therefore, well prepared to withstand

3. The theme was amplified by Voegelin in 1981 in a profound exploration of the relationship of Vision and *Noesis*, with attention to the Classical, Christian, and contemporary differentiations. He there wrote of "'The god' to whose presence and appeal in the erotically cognitive Metaxy man responds, the god who changes the meaning of mortal and immortal." Voegelin, "Wisdom and the Magic of the Extreme: A Meditation," *Southern Review*, n.s., XVII (1981), pp. 235–87, at 275.

scholarly and technical critique. His work is solidly built on his command of the primary and secondary source materials and a philologist's mastery of languages. From this foundation, a connoisseur's theoretically competent account of human affairs in the contemporary horizon emerges in his work. Hence, he with good justification offers us his vision as that of a philosophizing scientist—and as nothing else. To hold otherwise is to mistake and misrepresent the sobriety of a lifetime's disciplined effort.

The vision itself, I have argued, articulates a new science, a revolution in man's understanding of himself. Since new sciences and intellectual revolutions are a dime a dozen in the debased coinage of modern hyperbole, Madison Avenue style, thoughtful persons may be excused doubts similar to those of the villagers who heard the shepherd boy cry wolf one time too often when none was there. In this story, too, however, there really is a wolf, but this one is not the hound of hell but the shepherd's faithful friend. For Voegelin's vision provides both a new science and a new meaning of science. Its content is clarifying, diagnostic, and therapeutic. In facing Voegelin's work we are in much the same situation as that indicated by Werner Heisenberg: "Whenever we proceed from the known into the unknown we may hope to understand, but we may have to learn at the same time a new meaning of the word 'understanding.' We know that any understanding must be based finally upon the natural [*i.e.*, not scientific] language because it is only there that we can be certain to touch reality."[4] A new meaning of "understanding," together with a new understanding, is communicated in the new science of human affairs. This is the nub of the Voegelinian revolution under consideration here. Noetic science not only embraces the analytical *dianoia* of discursive rationality, but finds its center in *noesis* as the

4. Werner Heisenberg, *Physics & Philosophy: The Revolution in Modern Science* (1958, repr. ed.; New York: Harper & Row, Harper Torchbooks, 1962), 201. For the meaning of "understanding" as *dianoia* in Plato's sense, see Heisenberg, *Philosophic Problems in Nuclear Science*, trans. F. C. Hays (1952, repr. ed.; New York: Fawcett Premier Book, 1966), 35–44. Heisenberg also relevantly states: "We are now more conscious that there is no definite initial point of view [or methodology] from which radiate routes into all fields of the perceptible, but that all perception must, so to speak, be suspended over an unfathomable depth. . . . Even the most concise systems of concepts satisfying all demands of logical and mathematical precision can only be tentative efforts of finding our way in limited fields of reality." Heisenberg, *Philosophic Problems*, 106; cf. pp. 104–105.

consistent basis of its claim to scientific knowledge in the study of man and reality. It does so in the only posture in which such a claim can legitimately be asserted: *i.e.*, in the posture of participatory openness to the Mystery of Reality where the responsive answers of the inquirer into the In-Between of reality continually pose in new ways the Question of the reason of things. Although man cannot without patent absurdity claim to know more than can be known by a finite intelligence, even when he knows that he touches the infinite and divine in participation, still he can find through attentive listening and a sifting of the contents of experience that what he knows is more than was known in closure against the Ground or in ignorance and more even than was known by those men who asked the Question in less differentiated modes of consciousness. It is *only* in the sense suggested by these reflections that there can truly be a science of man worthy of the name: neither the noetic science of antiquity (whose insights were ranked as *episteme*, and so superior to mere opinion) nor the modern science of human affairs asserts a claim to absolute knowledge of either the part or the Whole. To the contrary, such a claim is unequivocally rejected as a sign of the derailment and egophanic deformation of man, science, and reality themselves. The divine-human encounter in the In-Between, though real and productive of new insight with the status of scientific knowledge, as we have said, neither renders a truth to end the search for truth nor abolishes the fundamental tension of the participatory reality of the In-Between itself nor makes man God in a transmogrifying apocalypse ending history and the human condition as the experienced imperfection of existence in the act of differentiation. In short, the noetic science *is* philosophy; and *philosophy* remains today as in Hellas the love of Wisdom in a differentiated mode, not the possession of the exhaustive or transmogrifying Truth of a system propositionally stated.

It will have become evident that the theoretical analysis through which Voegelin presents his vision is comprehensive to the extent of covering the whole range of reality from the *Apeirontic* Depth through the hierarchy of being to the Divine, and of exploring the personal, social, and historical dimensions of man's existence. Moreover, the exploration does not proceed on the basis of abstract speculation, for example, on the topics of man, history, consciousness, politics, and being. Rather, it proceeds on the basis of detailed consideration of the empirical materials known to the historical sciences from the Stone Age to the present and from Western Europe to China and America. Finally, it is to be noticed that the self-interpretations of those who articulate the experiences' engendering symbolisms of order play the decisive (though not exclusive) role in finding the truth of reality insofar as that is differentiated historically.

This calls attention to the centrality of *language* to the overall endeavor of exploring the order of history and reality: the indispensable points of ingress are the experiences symbolized. In precisely the linguistic symbols that arise on the occasion, the man who has undergone the experience tells what it is. The language and its meaning emerge together in the experience, becoming articulate in the context of a specific event in the In-Between. Furthermore, since the divine-human encounter in the In-Between is just that, the language symbols are themselves divine-human. They are, in other words, not merely the intentional contrivances of an articulate human being somehow "experiencing reality" from some imaginary vantage point outside the participatory reality of the In-Between. Emergent truth, therefore, is neither man's truth about God nor God's truth about man conveniently spoken in a language the man understands. Rather, it is the divine-human truth of the response of a man open to the divine Ground who lets the truth emerge in the experience-become-articulate. Truth-experience-symbol, then, form a unit of meaning within the In-Between, an illumination of reality whose structure and process themselves differentiate new truth in the course of the event itself. For these reasons, the linguistic "evidence" of the event and its meaning commands the utmost care and attention from the person who seeks to understand it as a part of his own meditative search of the Ground of being, one mindful of the trail of symbols left in history. Such is the search conducted by Voegelin and displayed in his work as the paradigm of such an effort in the contemporary horizon.

The Jamesian observation of "two different things" in a "philosopher's vision" and the "technique he uses in proof of it" can be sustained in Voegelin's case. But it is valid only in a qualified sense. In Voegelin's thought, vision and persuasive analysis are intimately intertwined because of the theory of language just presented. The division is, in principle, that between the act of *noesis* as it occurs in the event of experience-symbolization and the reflective *dianoia* as the discursive exegesis of the philosopher's understanding of the event and its persuasive embodiment in a text. But the discursive exegesis itself is an articulation of the experience of an encounter in the In-Between of the divine-human reality and, as such, partakes of the mutuality of the event in its exegetical presentment. One thereby understands that the "passion" of the engendering experience (vision, here in the sense of Plato's *opsis, hora*), characteristic of the meditative erotic tension toward the Ground, infuses *dianoia* no less than *noesis*, if the participatory dimension of philosophizing be given its due. Hence, the philosopher's admitted freedom in presenting the content and implications of experience symbolized is conditioned by the vision and also arises from it in expressive liberation. In other words, the exegetical freedom is itself the outcome of vision in a continuation of the divine-human collaboration experienced as a movement in the consciousness, a movement initiated by the pull of the divine Ground rather than by the autonomous activity of questing man rationally intending the object of his search and, then, dispassionately commenting upon its meaning in the subject-object posture. In the mutuality of the divine-human encounter, the experience *lets* the man *find* the language in which to symbolize and analyze the truth differentiated. The joy of apperceptive participation in theophany in the consciousness of a spiritual man, while exuberantly concentrated in the noetic act, equally suffuses the exegetical activity in a continuing afterglow of loving attentiveness to the truth apperceived in the divine encounter.

This progress of the desire of the philosophizing man from joy to joy in a continual renewal of insight and celebration is a decisive characteristic of the inquiry exhibited in *Order and History*, and in the dialogues of Plato or the mystic's meditative ascent so splendidly exemplified in Gregory of Nyssa where faith in search of understanding is a movement of the soul in which "every perfection (*telos*) is the beginning (*arche*) of a greater good:"

We see the soul as in the mounting of a ladder, guided by the Word, ascending toward holiness. Called to approach the light, it has become beautiful, taking in the light the form of the dove. Then, having participated in the good as much as it could, it is drawn once more by the Word to participate in supernatural beauty, as though it were still at the beginning and had had no part in it. Thus in proportion to its progress its desire increases for what is always manifested to it more—and because of the superabundance of goods that it never ceases to discover in the transcendent, it believes that it is only at the beginning of its ascension. That is why the Word says again: Arise, to the soul that is already arisen and: Come, to the soul that has already come. He, indeed, who really arises, must forever arise, and he who runs toward the Lord will never lack wide space. For one must always arise and never cease to run toward Him who says: Rise and come, and always gives one the strength to rise toward the better.[5]

Voegelin's vision as it articulates a philosophy of consciousness, politics, history, and being finds its gravitational center in experiences of the kind exemplified in the passage just quoted from Gregory of Nyssa. Herein lies the "centre" we have been urged to seek in a philosopher if we would understand him. "Grateful," as Voegelin directly tells us, for every scrap of testimony to the beauty and truth of man constituted in his participation in the Ground, and "for every appeal to expand the horizon, from whatever direction it may come," Voegelin concludes that it is "clear beyond a doubt that the center of a philosophy of politics [has] to be a theory of consciousness" (A, ed. Niemeyer, 3). This theory of consciousness could only come through the "discovery" of consciousness in the concrete existence of a man such as himself in the course of the anamnestic experiments recounted in *Anamnesis* and indicated as the background of the theory discussed in Chapter 6.

An analysis of consciousness . . . has no instrument other than the concrete consciousness of the analyst. The quality of this instrument, then, and consequently the quality of the results, will depend on what I have called the horizon of consciousness; and the quality of the horizon will depend on the analyst's willingness to reach out into all the dimensions of the reality in which his conscious existence is an event, it will depend on his desire to know. A consciousness of this kind is not an *a priori* structure, nor does it just happen, nor is its horizon a given. It rather is a ceaseless action of expanding, ordering, articulating, and correcting itself; it is an event in the reality of which as a part it partakes. It is a permanent effort at responsive openness to the appeal of reality, at bewaring of premature satisfaction, and

5. Jean Daniélou, "The Dove and the Darkness in Ancient Byzantine Mysticism," in Joseph Campbell (ed.), *Man and Transformation: Papers from the Eranos Yearbooks*, Bollingen Series, 30 (5 vols.; New York: Random House, Pantheon Books, 1964), V, 293–94.

above all at avoiding the self-destructive phantasy of believing the reality of which it is a part to be an object external to itself that can be mastered by bringing it into the form of a system. (A, ed. Niemeyer, 4)

This discovery of consciousness in the concrete as the "specifically human mode of participation in reality" of a man's personal, social, and historical existence, if it were to be persuasively "proved," had to find its empirical support in history as a part of man's comprehensive experience of truth attested over millennia.

The historical dimension at issue was not a piece of "past history" but the permanent presence of the process of reality in which man participates with his conscious existence. Reality, it is true, can move into the position of an object-of-thought intended by a subject-of-cognition, but before this can happen there must be a reality in which human beings with a consciousness occur. Moreover, by virtue of their consciousness these human beings are quite conscious of being parts of a comprehensive reality and express their awareness by the symbols of birth and death, of a cosmic whole structured by realms of being, of a world of external objects and the presence of divine reality in the cosmos, of mortality and immortality, of creation into the cosmic order and of salvation from its disorder, of descent into the depth of the *psyche* and meditative ascent toward its beyond. Within this rich field of reality-consciousness, finally, there occur the processes of wondering, questing, and seeking, of being moved and drawn into the search by a consciousness of ignorance, which, in order to be sensed as ignorance, requires an apprehension of something worthy to be known; of an appeal to which man can lovingly respond or not so lovingly deny himself; of the joy of finding and the despair of having lost the direction; of the advance of truth from the compact to differentiated experiences and symbols; and of the great breakthroughs of insight through visions of the prophetic, the philosophic, and the Christian-apostolic type. In brief, Man's conscious existence is an event within reality, and man's consciousness is quite conscious of being constituted by the reality of which it is conscious. The intentionality [therefore] is a substructure within the comprehensive consciousness of a reality that becomes luminous for its truth in the consciousness of man. (A, ed. Niemeyer, 4, 10–11)

Herein, then, lies Voegelin's vision and his own exegesis of it, and it can readily be seen that the passion of the vision is not abated in the abbreviated statement of its discursive unfolding. The Promethean "fire exceeding bright" found, too, in Gregory of Nyssa burns luminously in the work that lies before us as the animating center of *noesis* and *dianoia* alike in the new science of human affairs. Against the backdrop of these reflections on the character of Voegelin's vision and the status of the noetic science's claim to knowledge, the results of his inquiry can best be intimated by focusing attention on the symbolism *history and the Whole.*

The symbolism of history and the Whole articulates Voegelin's vision of reality as grasped at the pinnacle of his meditation on truth. At this apex he is moved to say: "Things do not happen in the astrophysical universe; the universe, together with all things founded in it, happens in God" (OH, IV, 334). The divine revelation of truth to man in history occurs in two fundamental modes of experience—in the mode of the Beginning, with its experience of the divine creativity in the cosmos, and in the mode of the Beyond, with its experience of the divine ordering presence in the soul. At the pinnacle of the meditation on truth theophany is the controlling event in the disclosure of the order of history that emerges from the history of order. These two modes, as expressed by their directional indices in the perspectives of the search of the Ground by man, find their millennial expressions in Genesis and in Plato's Myth of the Cave. These theophanic events establish the language of truth in the modes of myth, history, and philosophy.

The language of truth about reality tends historically to be recognized as the truth of language in reality. An important phase in this process is represented by the cosmogony of Genesis. The creation story lets the cosmos, with its hierarchy of being from the inorganic universe, through vegetable and animal life, to man be spoken into existence by God. Reality is a story spoken in the creative language of God; and in one of its figures, in man who is created in the image of God, reality responds to the mystery of the creative word with the truth of the creation story. Or inversely, from the human side, divine reality must be symbolized analogically as the creative word of God because the experience engenders for its expression the imaginative word of the cosmogonic myth. Reality is an act of divine mythopoesis that becomes luminous for its truth when it evokes the responsive myth from man's experience.[6]

Voegelin calls the process "the miracle of reality breaking forth into the language of its truth."[7] As his statements make clear, the quest

6. Voegelin, *The Beginning and the Beyond: A Meditation on Truth*, (Milwaukee, Wisc.: Marquette University Press, forthcoming), ms. pp. 1, 17.
7. Ibid., 17. Cf. *Order and History*, IV, 17.

226 THE VOEGELINIAN REVOLUTION

of the Ground in the mode of the Beginning in the instance of Genesis is at the same time structured by the experience of the Beyond,
which discloses the vertical axis of experience in the hierarchy of
being culminating in the Hellenic philosophers' symbolism of the
Beyond. Thus, though distinguishable directional indices may predominate in a symbolic form, the vertical and horizontal axes both
are present to myth, history, and philosophy as a mark of their balance and completeness in articulating the truth of reality in the language of truth. Wherever this balance and completeness is lost, a
partial or deformed representation of reality results.

Only the barest hint of the rich subtlety of the inquiry that rises
to the splendor of these insights is possible here. The vision of history is simultaneously a vision of the Whole of which history is a
part. It is the process of the differentiation of the truth of the Whole
that creates meaning *in* history and, thereby, constitutes history itself as the process in which reality and its order are established in
consciousness. The seventeen-year pause between publication of the
third and fourth volumes of *Order and History* found Voegelin seeking the form that a philosophy of history must take if it is to be adequate to the complexity of the subject. The unilinear path of his
inquiry as stated in the initial volumes had to be abandoned in a
bow to the evidence. The emergence of order in history as the movement of differentiation from the compactness of cosmological myth
through leaps in being in Israel and Hellas and subsequent differentiations in other cultural horizons up to mysticism in the West into
the present does not neatly occur on any time line at all. Rather,
there is the plurality of contemporaneous theophanies across the
whole ecumene, from the Near East to India and China, and the
linkage of these to the rise of historiography and the emergence of
new political entities in the imperial form of ecumenic empires that
supplant the old cosmological empires of the more compact experience, *i.e.*, the primordial experience of the divinity of the cosmos.
Parallel histories, equivalent theophanies, and emergent empires
form constellations of meaning as the decisive phenomena investigated in *The Ecumenic Age* as symbolized events, constituting in a
triadic structure the consciousness of *epoch* as the mark of the Age
itself.

The symbolism of *epoch*, and the establishment through experiential analysis of its meaning in the Ecumenic Age as the discovery of a new unit of meaning in history, thereby becomes the hub of Voegelin's philosophy of history. The elaboration of the consciousness of epoch is his critical revision of Hegel's symbolism of "the absolute epoch," with Christ as the "hinge of history," and of Karl Jaspers' symbolism of the "Axis-time" of human history, which covered the period from 800–200 B.C. with a concentration around 500 B.C. when Confucius, Buddha, and Heraclitus were contemporaries. The process of differentiation occurs, indeed, but it takes the form of a sheaf (to remember Bergson's expression), not a linear progress.

Just as in Hegel and Jaspers, then, there is the "'absolute epoch,'" which sets "the central issue of a philosophy of history" (OH, IV, 308–309).[8] The problem of the earlier thinkers is accepted as valid in principle, but the solution of the problem is new. The key to Voegelin's resolution of the problem is his rejection of the consciousness of epoch as *exclusively* determined either by the "spiritual process" marked by the rise of philosophy and the great world religions or by the Epiphany of Christ and its attendant transcendental understanding of man and of the structure of history radiating from these spiritual outbursts. Hegel's account is defective, because it claims absolute knowledge on the basis of the "key to world history" initially gained by Christians and now perfected by Hegel the paraclete through the merger of the noetic science of the Hellenic philosophers into his own "system of science" and thus providing definitive truth in the form of a declaration of the meaning *of* history. Jaspers' account is defective, because it not only failed to dissolve the merger, it ignored Christ through an odd doctrinization of Christian faith that takes no cognizance of the differentiation of eschatalogical consciousness in Jesus and Paul as the specific difference of the faith experience in their horizon.

The empirical basis and experiential analysis of noetic science supplies Voegelin's alternative to Hegel and Jaspers. Not spiritual process alone, but the "triad—Ecumenic Empire, Spiritual Outburst,

8. For the pertinent discussion in Karl Jaspers, see his *Vom Ursprung und Ziel der Geschichte* (Frankfort and Hamburg: Fischer Buecherei, 1955), 14–31.

Historiography" form the "unit in the process of differentiation and symbolization" from the equivalent compact symbolism of *oikoumene-okeanos* of the cosmological myth to mark the epoch in history called the Ecumenic Age.

At the present state of experiential analysis, I conclude, the concept of epoch or axis-time marked by the great spiritual outbursts alone is no longer tenable. Something "epochal" has occurred indeed; there is no reason why the adjective should be denied to the disintegration of the compact experience of the cosmos and the differentiation of the truth of existence. But the "epoch" involves, besides the spiritual outbursts, the ecumenic empires from the Atlantic to the Pacific and engenders the consciousness of history as the new horizon that surrounds with its divine mystery the existence of man in the habitat that has been opened by the concupiscence of power and knowledge. (OH, IV, 308, 313, 312, 201–10)

From the standpoint of experiential analysis, then, the misconstruing of the problem of epoch can be seen as rooted in the structure of consciousness. On one side, the "absolute epoch" cannot be marked by either ecumenic empires or spiritual outbursts alone, because there is no epoch without the historical consciousness of something epochal. On the other side, history conceived as the horizon of divine mystery surrounding the spatially open ecumene cannot rise to consciousness unless the ecumene actually opens up under the impact of concupiscential political-military expansion. And such expansion cannot be seen as more than the dynamics of power politics in the senseless rise and fall of peoples and their rulers unless historians consciously relate the events to the emergence of the truth of existence articulated in the spiritual outbursts. "There is no consciousness of epoch unless something that can be experienced as epochal is happening indeed in the process of reality." If the triadic unit is split up and hypostatized as the subject and object of knowledge with the historiographer the recording subject of an objective history, then "the reality that has become luminous as a process of transfiguration will evaporate" between the hypostatized poles of subject-object. (OH, IV, 313)

What is differentiated, then, is the new horizon of mystery of history and reality in the consciousness of epoch. The conventional understanding of the events in the field of history pose the same problem for historical consciousness as for the philosopher's noetic consciousness.

When the luminosity of noetic consciousness is deformed into an "anthropology" of intramundane man and a "theology" of a transmundane God, the theophanic event will be destroyed, and with it will be destroyed man's tension toward the divine ground of his existence and the experience of participation. In the same manner, when the symbolisms engendered in the Ecumenic Age, including historiography, are deformed into events in a "history" other than the history whose experience they articulate, the process with its eschatological tension will be lost. The impasse of such derailments can be avoided only if one acknowledges the process of differentiation itself as the exclusive source of our knowledge concerning the unit of experience that understands itself as historically epochal when it differentiates. (OH, IV, 313–14)

II

A complex of issues of critical importance for the philosophy of history comes to view in the question of the meaning *of* history as contrasted with meaning *in* history. Meaning *in* history there assuredly is, as Voegelin amply demonstrates in the course of his study of the Ecumenic Age against the background of the earlier volumes of *Order and History*. He finds these "dominant lines of meaning" moving through the web of events.

(1) The fundamental advance in consciousness from the compactness of the cosmological experience to differentiation in the pneumatic and noetic modes, arising in Israel and Hellas, productive of philosophy, revelation, and mysticism; and

(2) distributed over Israel and Hellas as a new historical consciousness, and from these centers over a wide span of other ethnic cultures.

(3) The outbreak of imperial conquest productive of the new ecumenic empires that reorganized the old ethnic cultures into new ecumenic societies forming a chain from the Mediterranean to the China Sea.

(4) The reactions of the ethnic cultures to this grinding process of imperialism (or "concupiscential exodus"), including the protective movement of doctrinalization of the differentiated insights—with,

however, the result that they at the same time were deformed and obscured by dogmatization.

(5) The emergence of historiography out of the speculative historiogenetic myth in the new ecumenic-imperial horizons by such persons as Herodotus and Thucydides, Polybius and Livy, the anonymous Israelite historians from the author of the David Memoirs to the Chronicler, and the great Chinese historian Sse-ma Ch'ien.

(6) The imperial conquests (such as those of Darius and Xerxes, Alexander the Great, of Maurya Asoka in India, of Caesar and Scipio in Rome, and of the Chinese Empire of Ch'in Shih-huang-ti) which were, then, interpreted by the historians, in the wake of the spiritual outbursts, as themselves carriers of a meaning of humanity beyond the meaning known at the tribal and ethnic level.

(7) The emergence of the Ecumenic Age itself as a unit of historical development in the time period from the rise of the Persian Empire (ca. 550 B.C.) to the fall of the Roman Empire in the West (476 A.D.); and

(8) The concomitant emergence of an ecumenic humanity, "which, with all its complications of meaning, reaches as a millennial constant into the modern Western civilization" (OH, IV, 57–58; cf. pp. 114–15, 207, 271, 312, and *passim*).

No less resolutely than in *The New Science of Politics* published twenty-two years earlier, however, Voegelin in *The Ecumenic Age* rejects the proclamation of a meaning *of* history as a Gnostic derailment, one widely prevalent in the ideological "philosophies of history" spawned in the eighteenth and nineteenth centuries down to the present under inspiration of the kind of speculations found centuries earlier in Otto of Freising (d. 1158) and Joachim of Flora (d. 1202) (NSP, Ch. 4; OH, IV, 266–71). Any such "stop-history" response to the mystery of man's existence in the In-Between, which supplants the mystery with a claim to knowledge of the essence and end of history, is a *prima facie* fallacy and deformation. Still, there is something to it and the general rejection, therefore, requires some qualification. Just *what* there is to it comes to view in the insights that arise in the horizons of both philosophy and the apocalyptic-eschatological strand of the Judaic-Christian revelation. These insights agree in understanding reality as a knowable structure in process of actually moving beyond its structure toward the perfection of transcendental fulfillment out of time. The history of order, as we have seen, is the history of the movement from compactness to more differentiated consciousness-reality in the In-Between of mortality and immortality discovered in the process of the movement. And that movement is not a movement toward nothing but toward more eminent reality. Thus the unsettling assertion in the first pages of *Order and History* (OH, I, 10–11) that the leaps in being effect a "change in being" itself, and not merely in man's awareness of its nature and order, is amplified in *The Ecumenic Age* as a major thesis. The ontological aspects of the problem must be considered along with the implications for the philosophy of history.

The theophanic or hierophanic events of philosophy and revelation engender the knowledge of man's existence in the divine In-Between and the language symbols in which the knowledge is articulate. They also engender the awareness of the Before and After of the events as generative of the sense of epoch that comes to view in the triad of Ecumenic Empire, Spiritual Outburst, and Historiography. But the consciousness of epoch also carries with its meaning as a *structure* in history an insight into the *process* of history as pointing toward "a fulfillment, toward an Eschaton, out of time." For this reason history is experienced "not [as] a stream of human beings and their actions in time, but [as] the process of man's participation in the flux of divine presence that has eschatological direction. . . . The process of history, and such order as can be discerned in it, is not a story to be told from the beginning to its happy, or unhappy, end; it is a mystery in process of revelation" (OH, IV, 6).

History, then, is the Mystery of Reality becoming luminous through the Question of the reason of things and of the destiny of man and the Whole, which Voegelin invokes as the valid substitute for the declared End of existence in the deformed philosophies of history. The movement and the process as transfigurative are acknowledged, however, and, against the background of their impenetrable mystery, elucidated.

The prospective transfiguration of man, history, and the Whole is not, then, a sole property of derailed accounts of reality, decisive though it is to those accounts. The legitimate source of the insight lies in the quest of the Ground in the mode of the philosophers' differentiation of the Beyond of the *Nous* (and the parallel Mosaic experience of the I AM in the pneumatic theophany) as the ordering height of reality, thereby distinguishing it from the more compact Depth experienced as the divine Ground in Anaximander's *Apeiron*, and the attendant discovery of the In-Between of noetic height and *Apeirontic* Depth as the reality of man forming the fundamental tension of reality. But the fundamental tension of reality, differentiated out of the inherent instability of the experience of the cosmos as existence out of nonexistence, was not the end of the matter. For Plato intimated the insight of the mystery of reality beyond *Nous*, and he utilized mythopoesis as a protective means to secure *Nous* from the further differentiating insight into the unfathomable mystery of its own background (OH, IV, 224–38). In Christianity, and most especially in Paul, however, the movement toward the beyond of divine presence in the mode of eschatology assumed dominant proportions. The tendency against which Plato and Aristotle successfully struggled in order to maintain the balance of structure and process in their accounts of order is shaken, if not lost, in Paul's exegesis of his Vision of the Resurrected.

The Platonic/Aristotelian discovery of the *"postulate of balance"* is "one of the principal events . . . in the history of mankind" (OH, IV, 228).[9] On the one side there was the epochal theophany itself: *i.e.*, the discovery of the constitution of reason through revelation, the understanding that the life of reason is rooted in revelation, and that revelation is the source of reason in existence. Here the point is driven home that the God who moves the philosophers in their search of the Ground, who elicits from a Parmenides "the exclamation 'Is!', was the same God who revealed himself to Moses as the 'I am who (or: what) I am,' as the God who is what he is in the concrete theophany to which man responds" (OH, IV, 229). The advances in depth to be traced in revelation in Israel, and the parallel developments in philosophy in Hellas in differentiation of the divine Ground of being, display the complexities of revelation as it discloses the actual movement of insight into the relation between God and man.

The core of the philosophers' theophany is the revelation of God

9. Emphasis added.

as the *Nous* common to both the cosmos and man. But the kind of instability that is evident in the movement of the process of differentiation from the compact experience of the divinity of the cosmos existing out of nonexistence to the revelation of Reason, and the consequent epoch of a Before and After, of an old truth now become untruth through the newly differentiated truth of the philosophers, attaches still to the differentiating quest even after the noetic theophany occurs. Its questing movement toward a Beyond beyond the Beyond "will not cease moving before it has sensed the truly Tremendum, the ultimate, non-present Beyond of all divine presence. In the case of the noetic theophany, the experience of a God who embodies his Nous in the cosmos, limited by Ananke [Necessity or Fate], cannot but point, by implication, toward the non-incarnate, acosmic abyss of the divine beyond the Demiurgic action" (OH, IV, 233). The exodus from less-differentiated to more-differentiated reality in the leap in being shows the paradoxical structure of the spiritual exodus in its accelerating tendency to move beyond itself in an annihilating transfiguration, not merely of the old truth into the new, or even the supersession of the new truth by a still newer truth of greater power and differentiation, but the transfiguration of the cosmos and man with it into the timeless reality of the "One beyond *Nous*" (Plotinus) who is revealed in limitless depth only intimated by the partial revelations of divine mystery bestowed upon men piecemeal (OH, IV, 231–33).

Hence, on the other side, the philosophers recoil from the plunge into the acosmic abyss in a leap out of existence as a danger to the newly discovered noetic order to be avoided at all cost. Their "postulate of balance" is embodied (in Plato) in the myth that surrounds the noetic theophany with a "belt of uncertainties" calculated to protect its truth. The divine Unknown must remain the mystery of the unknown it is until such time as it may be more fully known in a further theophany. God reveals himself, after all, when and where and to whom He pleases. The truth of reality disclosed in the divine-human encounter in the In-Between and symbolized as *Nous* (together with its positive insights into the order of history and the truth of the Whole) could not constitute new meaning *if* "the movement of the psyche toward the absolute Beyond were allowed to cast on all divine incarnation in the world the spell of daimonic evil"—

as was subsequently done in the Gnostic imaginings that entail the annihilation of the world itself as well as the structure in reality differentiated in the theophanic events (OH, IV, 234–35).

The Classical philosophers' postulate of balance arises, then, from their discovery of the paradox central to reality: reality is a "recognizably structured process that is recognizably moving beyond its structure." While the structure is sufficiently static to outlast the philosophers and to endure over the millennia to the present, it is nonetheless "dynamically alive with theophanic events which point toward an ultimate transfiguration of reality." The task of the philosopher, in executing the requirement of balance, is "to preserve the balance between the experienced lastingness [of reality] and the theophanic events in such a manner that the paradox becomes intelligible as the very structure of existence itself." This is the definition of the postulate (OH, IV, 227–28).

This task can be discharged, for instance, by stressing that the differentiating theophanies that constitute meaning in history are exoduses *within* reality and not exoduses *from* it; that the God of the Beginning whose creative act established the cosmos and maintains its order is the same as the God of the Beyond whose presence moves the philosopher's quest of the Ground in the process of differentiation climaxing in the discovery of the divine *Nous*; that the differentiated consciousness—whose reality of reason is both human and divine in the mode of participation (but *not* identification)—arises *in* the reality of the cosmos and its lasting order from the Beginning, not the cosmos and its order *from* consciousness. Moreover, the consciousness that experiences the divine Ground in a differentiating movement toward eminent reality is itself founded in the concrete existence of a concrete man in a concrete society in a concrete existence that is embraced by the lasting cosmos itself into whose depth the man will surely perish just as he has been born out of it. Such is the lot of men whose existence is in the imperfection of the In-Between. Still, the understanding of reality is not left in the bleak hopelessness of Anaximandrian compactness. For the balance of consciousness in its degree of contemporary theophanic differentiation demands, also, that men bear the awareness of "participation in the transfiguring movement, without [succumbing to the deforming egophanic expectation of] achieving its consummation in this world" (OH, IV, 271).

The postulate of balance will, then, serve as a prophylaxis against typical derailments that attempt to resolve the paradox of reality by attaching an index of superior reality to one dimension over the other. For example, in apocalyptic and Gnostic movements, the dimension of transfiguration of reality is the "truth" that overcomes the "untruth" of existence in the lasting cosmos, which may be discounted as ephemeral or as the handiwork of the evil creator god of the Beginning; *or* the Feuerbachian and Marxian projectionist psychologies find the "truth" of the lasting structure to be the explanation of the "untruth" of the projected transfigured reality that is, consequently, an illusion to be destroyed through critique and revolutionary action; *or*, as yet another possibility, the two experiences can be interpreted as a mutual cancellation of reality altogether, and the paradox of reality then degenerates into the meaningless void of existence, as it does in Sartre's existential nihilism (OH, IV, 228; cf. pp. 18–30).

III

Saint Paul's theophany fulfilled the noetic theophany of the philosophers, but it also induced, because of his "analytically defective interpretation" of the experience of transfiguration, an instability in the balance of reality that has remained "one of the great constants in history, spanning the period from the Ecumenic Age to Western modernity" (OH, IV, 251–60, 266–67). Paul was, of course, a saint and prophet of Christ, not a philosopher. His experience was not the vision (*opsis, hora*) of Plato arising in the culmination of the quest of the Ground begun in the noetic field constituted over a period of two centuries by Anaximander, Heraclitus, and Parmenides in the disclosure of the *Nous* as the Third God symbolizing the philosophers' theophany. Paul's Vision (*apokalypsis*, Galatians 1:12) of the Resurrected Christ on the road to Damascus, rather, occurred in the pneumatic field of faith constituted over two millennia from Jesus and the Apostles back through the prophets of Israel to Moses and, finally, to Abraham who was before the Law (Romans 4:3; Genesis

15:6). It is the faith of Abraham, "the father of us all," who in openness to theophany departed out of Haran for a land that God would show him (Genesis 12:1–5; Romans 4:16; Galatians 3:7), which is exegetically embodied in the differentiated symbolism of Paul's myth of the End (telos; telion) of history in the transfigured perfection of eternity to be marked by the Parousia. The Second Coming of Christ in power and glory is a process already begun in the Passion and the Resurrection and confirmed in the transfiguring vision in Paul himself (Galatians 1:11-17). There is little that is doctrinal or dogmatic about this subject matter as contained in Paul's recounting of it. Rather we are confronted with a theophany experienced and symbolized, as it was by Plato, in the medium of the myth, one presented this time not in a philosopher's dialectic, but in the epistles of the Apostle to the Nations.

"The truth of existence emerges from the theophanic events in history" (OH, IV, 251). In what Voegelin terms the "hard structure of truth" (as contrasted with its dubious penumbra) in the Pauline myth, the truth of existence that became visible in the philosophers' experience of man's immortalizing is consistently differentiated through the unfolding of its full meaning in Paul's vision and its exegesis. This "superior degree of differentiation" consists, first, in the differentiation of the truth of existence, which carries beyond the structure of creation to the divine love of the transcosmic Creator whose experienced ordering process is revealed to be the Agape or Love that moves the man to respond to the theophanic events that constitute meaning in history. The truth of existence thereby becomes the truth of God who, in His divine freedom, is no longer bound by Ananke. Second, the directional movement of reality as experienced more compactly by prophets and philosophers is fully differentiated through the articulation of its ultimate goal (telion) as imperishing (aphtharsia) beyond the Anaximandrian birth and perishing in time consumed in the Depth. The experiences symbolized in the Beginning and the Beyond must be augmented by the truth of the End. The divine creativity symbolized in Aristotle's noetic theophany in the prote arche is, in Paul's pneumatic theophany, differentiated in an eschatology that completes the drama of creation, fall, redemption, death, and resurrection to its End in the ultimate return of the creation to its intended imperishable glory. Third, Paul fully differentiates the experience that man is the site wherein the transforming movement of reality becomes consciously luminous in its actual occurrence. The victory of God over the forces of death is possible because His protagonist is the creature man in whom can be incarnated His own divinity in the transfiguring act of the sonship of God that emerges in the God-man (Colossians 2:9; Romans 8:22-23).

As Voegelin states it: "If any event in the Metaxy has [ever] constituted meaning in history, it is Paul's vision of the Resurrected" (OH, IV, 243). The theophanic experience extends from a pneumatic center to a noetic periphery. The Pauline experience is so decisively affected by the vision of God's way with man that existence in the In-Between recedes to comparative insignificance, however, and *participation* in divine reality that moves the recipient of theophany becomes the *anticipation* of the state of perfection—with the consequence that the symbols expressing existence in the Metaxy take on new dimensions of meaning as the result of Paul's intensive submersion in the movement of reality toward final fulfillment as assured in the transfiguring vision bestowed upon him as a divine gift. Voegelin writes:

When reading the First Letter to the Corinthians, I have always the feeling of traveling, with Paul, from *phthora* [perishing] to *aphtharsia* [imperishing] in a homogeneous medium of reality, from existence in the Metaxy as a way station to immortality as a goal, with death as a minor incident on the road. Death is indeed reduced to the "twinkling of an eye" in which reality switches from imperfection to perfection. (OH, IV, 247)

Participation *qua* anticipation, movement *qua* perfection, and the truth of existence *qua* the truth of God do more than theophanically differentiate meaning in history. They announce the meaning of history. The shift in accents from the philosophical theophany is decisive. Paul's assurance of the truth of reality bestowed in the gift of the vision centers in his prediction (*kerygma*) of resurrection, and the connection of the vision and his prediction is shown in First Corinthians 15:12–19: "If there is no resurrection of the dead, then Christ has not been raised; if Christ has not been raised, then your faith is vain" (16–17). "If Christ has not been raised, our preaching is empty and your faith is empty" (15). "If we have no more than hope in Christ in this life, then we are of all men the most pitiful" (19). The last sentence Voegelin sees as the key to understanding Paul's experience of reality. Mere hope in this life as existence in the In-Between is not enough. Indeed, it is worse than nothing, unless it rises to the assurance of transfiguration that derives from the vision, for the vision is more than a theophanic event in the In-Between: it is the actual renewal of the transfiguration of reality itself, begun in Christ and now continued in Paul. It is not the differentiated insights into reality that cause the difficulties in Paul's telling of the tale of death and resurrection to its end. Rather, it is the loss of the perspective of the In-Between of existence that permits the time of existence to be uncritically blended in the Time of the Tale, *i.e.*, of the Pauline myth itself. "The difference could become shadowy to Paul, because he was obsessed with the expectation that the men living in Christ, himself included, would not die at all but, in the wake of the Parousia, be transfigured in their lifetimes. The transfiguration, as it had begun in time through Jesus the Christ, would shortly be completed in the same time" (OH, IV, 247–49).[10]

The dubious penumbra of "analytically defective interpretation" in the Pauline myth arises from the obsession just identified as expressed in the concrete prediction of the imminent Second Coming of Christ. In fact, however, no Parousia occurred, nor has it yet occurred, despite Paul's fervid expectation. And those facts are of cardinal importance for the whole history of the Western mind. Paul opposed the philosophers' discovery of meaning in history through the noetic theophany, which disclosed the structure of reality to be in process of moving beyond itself in transforming immortalizing, with his meaning of history whose process of transformation is not only confirmed in the Vision of the Resurrected as actually occurring but whose eschatological End is known and concretely anticipated as near. Paul "knows the end of the story in the transfiguration that begins with the Resurrection." The two conceptions obviously do not contradict but complement one another. They can be seen to be rooted in the paradox of reality, *i.e.*, in the experience of reality as

10. The quotations from First Corinthians 15 are as given by Voegelin.

a structure in process of moving beyond itself in the participatory reality of men and God—not toward perdition, but toward a more eminent degree of reality through an exodus within reality.

The philosophers' concentration on structure no more abolishes the truth of *movement* beyond structure than Paul's concentration on transfiguring exodus abolishes the cosmos and its *structure*, however. The postulate of balance obtains. "When the paradox of reality becomes luminous to itself in consciousness, it creates the paradox of a history in suspense between the Ananke [Necessity; Fate] of the cosmos and the freedom of eschatological movement. . . . The process of history is a mystery as much as the reality that becomes luminous in it" (OH, IV, 258, 270–71). The flaw in Paul's account of his own experience, then, lies in his obsession with the End as near, which gave rise to "an inclination to abolish the *tension* between the eschatological *telos* of reality and the mystery of the transfiguration that is actually going on within historical reality. The Pauline myth of the struggle among the cosmic forces *validly* expresses the *telos* of the movement that is experienced in reality, but it becomes *invalid* when it is used to anticipate the concrete process of transfiguration within history" (OH, IV, 270).[11]

IV

The failure of the End to occur as predicted, however, opened the way over the millennia since its prediction for developments of a quite different order to occur. In an unbroken chain of speculations since the High Middle Ages the End of history has been proclaimed in a wide spectrum of sectarian, Gnostic, alchemic, apocalyptic, and ideological moods. In the eighteenth and nineteenth centuries the turbulence of theophany gives way to the turbulence of revolutionary egophany, eclipsing with imaginary second realities the reality illuminated in theophany. The symbol *egophany* means "the pathos of thinkers who exist in a state of alienation and libidinous obsession" (OH, IV, 260).[12] The participation of man in the In-Between of mortality and immortality is brutally compressed into the *identifi-*

11. Emphasis added.
12. See the section entitled "The Egophanic Revolt," 260–71.

cation of the divine with the human in the consciousness of the human speculator who effects therewith the Parousia in himself as the new Christ.

Transfigurative doctrines of the egophanic thinkers cannot be explored here beyond the notice of three salients in this field of deformed symbolisms. First, the egophanic outbursts do not fall on a line from compact to differentiated insight into the structure and process of history. Rather they make their way and brutally stake their sweeping claims through a deformation of the symbolisms of theophany, with the result that scotosis rather than illumination results, a phenomenon that finds its apogee in Hegel and Marx and their twentieth-century epigones. Second, the modern revolt is intelligible in all its variants as visibly traceable to the theme of transfiguration differentiated in Paul's eschatological myth as defectively interpreted in the apocalypse of the impending end of history in perfection. This insight is of considerable value since it enables one to classify the spectrum of "philosophies of history" as variants of Paul's myth in the mode of deformation, as Voegelin demonstrates in his detailed analysis especially of Hegel's speculative work in which participation is transmogrified into *identification* in revolutionary reconciliation destroying the Metaxy. He summarizes the point in these words:

The symbols developed by the egophanic thinkers in the self-interpretation of their work, such as "*Wissenschaftslehre*," "system of science," "philosophy of history," "*philosophie positive*," or "*wissenschaftlicher Sozialismus* [Scientific Socialism]," cannot be taken at their face value; they are not engendered by bona fide analytical efforts in the noetic and pneumatic fields; they rather must be recognized as mythical symbols in a mode of degradation [Mircea Eliade]. The "history" of the egophanic thinkers does not unfold in the Metaxy, *i. e.*, in the flux of divine presence, but in the Pauline Time of the Tale that has a beginning and an end. (OH, IV, 269)

Third, Gnosticism as a strand in radical modernity is a deformation of the reality constituted in the fields of noetic and pneumatic theophany, one whose distant origins antedate Christianity itself and lie in the experience of alienation from the world. The genesis of the attitude lies in the disorientation of existence experienced in the pragmatic destruction attendant on expansion of empire and the differentiation of consciousness in the Ecumenic Age. These traumatic events are responded to in the "syncretistic spiritualism" of Gnosis by contracting divine order to the personal existence of the alienated individual man. Ancient and modern Gnosis are, in principle, not different. In a long line of continuity reaching from Valentinius to Hegel and the modern systems, Gnosticism in its libertine and ascetic variants in antiquity and in the systems imposed on reality in modernity manifest the *libido dominandi* in splitting the reality of the divine Beginning and its assurance of cosmic order from the reality of the Beyond whose truth, then, is transmuted into a knowledge (*gnosis*) of world destruction as the inevitable price to be paid for man's redemption.

The "magnitude of insensitivity required in the construction of a Gnostic system" requires further explanation beyond mere alienation, however. The Gnostic must possess such a vivid consciousness of the movement toward the Beyond that its obsessive illumination blinds him to the "contextual structure of reality." He must ignore the fact that the cosmos does not emerge from his consciousness, but his consciousness from the cosmos. In so ignoring this fact, he inverts the relationship of the Beyond of consciousness (in its immediacy) to the Beginning (which is experienceable only through the mediation of the historical process) and thereby displays his unawareness of destroying the mystery of reality by his speculative inversion. His imaginative invention of the drama of the divine fall into the prison of the world and man, which is overcome to its redemptive end in the act of speculative Gnosis, is a libidinous act of self-salvation. The "strength and luminosity of eschatological consciousness necessary to make the Gnostic deformation intelligible," Voegelin is "inclined" to think, is explainable only if one recognizes "in the epiphany of Christ the great catalyst that made eschatological consciousness an historical force, both in forming and deforming humanity" (OH, IV, 20).[13]

By the Gnostics' perversion of the experience of reality as disclosed in theophany and by the rejection of balance in the assertion

13. On Voegelin's theory of Gnosticism and other of his themes see Peter J. Opitz and Gregor Sebba (eds.), *The Philosophy of Order: Essays on History, Consciousness, and Politics* [Festschrift for Eric Voegelin on his 80th birthday] (Stuttgart: Klett-Cotta Verlag, 1981); Eugene Webb, *Eric Voegelin: Philosopher of History* (Seattle and London: University of Washington Press, 1981); also Ellis Sandoz (ed.), *Eric Voegelin's Thought: A Critical Appraisal* (Durham, N.C.: Duke University Press, forthcoming).

of the split running through reality, existence in the world is represented as an absurdity, a "cosmic prison" to be broken out of through an "eschatological extravaganza" of transfiguration that overcomes the world, as in the Hegelian, Marxian, and Comtean systems and their proclamations of the God-man, New Men, the Final Age of the world in perfection. The specific fallacy of all Gnosticism is the obsession with the Beyond, of transcendence in antiquity, of the eschatological Future in modernity. It is, therefore, a concupiscential exodus *from* reality that "rejects the life of the spirit and reason under the conditions of the cosmos in which reality becomes luminous in pneumatic and noetic consciousness." As Voegelin formulated the issue in 1981: "At the time when the word spoke itself in the fullness of its clarity, in Christ, Gnostic thinkers would answer the question with the myth of a fall in the realm of divinity and attribute the creation of the world . . . to a Devil. This solution of the Platonic problem through a Satanistic vision has become a force in world history. . . . At the core of the vision lies the refusal to participate in the process of reality under the conditions of its mysterious structure."[14] The antidote for this "addiction" and attendant contraction and deformation of reality is the postulate of balance. The pneumopathology of the "process of contraction is a disturbance of consciousness through the loss of balance between the Beginning and the Beyond," which overcomes the experience of a "pragmatic reality devoid of meaning" with the "Gnosis of transmutation" richly interlaced with metastatic faith, apocalyptic expectations, and alchemistic magic denominated "science" and "reason" in the forms dominating the modern period (OH, IV, 17–28, 234–38, 266–71).

Transfiguration is a constant in human experience from Hellenic philosophy and Old Testament prophetism, through Christ and the Apostles, to Paul and his vision, to ancient Gnosticism, to the resurgence in the High Middle Ages, into the deformed speculations of Enlightenment thinkers from Voltaire to Condorcet, and the modern Gnostic-ideological speculators whose systems dominate the current climate of opinion in its deformity. There can be no doubt

---

14. Voegelin, "Wisdom and the Magic of the Extreme," 256.

about the constancy of the constant. Voegelin has shown the validity, as well as the sources and character of the invalidity, in this range of thought over the millennia as the core of his own philosophy of history, the first modern nonideological work of its kind. He has restored the postulate of balance to its central place in noetic science as that forms a philosophy of human affairs in its personal, social, and historical dimensions. His exploration of the In-Between of history as the site where the self-reflective consciousness differentiates the Question in men's experiences and symbolizations of the truth and order of reality yields a new understanding of philosophy and science themselves as well as of man, politics, history and the Whole, as I have attempted to show. Some of the implications for the theory of the Whole can now be drawn in conclusion.

V

Ontology no less than the philosophy of history takes new form as a result of Voegelin's painstaking attention to the language of truth as the truth of language in the In-Between reality. The revision of the problem of absolute epoch was necessitated by carefully weighing the empirical evidence. The entire range of human activities in the sphere of political endeavor in the mode of power and concupiscential exodus, the interpretative efforts of the historians in making sense of pragmatic as well as paradigmatic events, as well as the spiritual outbursts themselves in the theophanies of the noetic and pneumatic fields must all be considered in an analysis of the truth of the Whole. The radical empiricism of Voegelin's ontology, in other words, requires that the entire range of experienced reality, not just the spiritual process, be considered in the noetic science of being. And this can be done successfully, of course, only by one whose command of the sources is sufficient to place the vast pertinent evidence and the array of theoretical instruments developed over the centuries in its interpretation at his disposition. The requisite confluence is uniquely achieved in the body of work before us, and the result is the revolution in thought that we have discerned and sought to delineate.

The Question of the truth and order of the Whole is asked and responsively answered in the participatory acts of differentiation.

⌈There is no knowable reality apart from that experienced and sym-
│bolized in the divine-human encounters that structure the In-Be-
│tween in the process of differentiation itself; hence, there is no real-
│ity to be described and analyzed objectively by a knower external to
⌊the reality known. There is only the reality of consciousness in the
modes of presence, forgottenness, and memory (or recollection). The
ontological symbolisms, then, are themselves constituted in the
divine-human encounter as the language of truth. The truth of language constitutes both the truth of reality and the truth of consciousness in process of differentiating in the self-reflective reality of
men in whom the Whole becomes luminous for its truth. The human reality, therefore, is that dimension in reality in which the
Whole becomes self-conscious for its truth. This human reality of
participation is the tensionally structured In-Between of consciousness and of history. It is constituted in the modes of Beginning and
Beyond, the directional indices of the quest of the ground symbolized especially in historiogenetic myth and, preeminently, in the
theophanies which occur in the human response to divine initia-
tives that constitute the noetic and pneumatic fields of consciousness and, therewith, history and its meaning. The differentiating
process, however, is just that: the discovery of new structures of reality is a differentiation of structures already compactly present and
"new" only in the sense of rising into the clarity of consciousness in
the process of emergent truth-experience-symbol and, so, becoming
reality in a more meaningful luminosity.

The philosopher's debate about reality in the comprehensive
sense of the Whole moves in the noetic field of consciousness as first
constituted by Anaximander in his previously quoted dictum: "The
origin (*arche*) of things is the *Apeiron* (Depth *or* Boundless). . . . It is
necessary for things to perish into that from which they were born;
for they pay one another penalty for their injustice according to the
ordinance of time." The reality thus experienced-symbolized comprehends the divine Depth; the existing things; the relation between
the Depth and the things; and the relation among things. Not yet
articulate in the dictum is the noetic consciousness itself, the area
of reality in which the symbolisms emerge in their luminosity (OH,
IV, 215).

causally

Reality is thus symbolized not as a static field of homogeneous extension, but as aetiologically and directionally structured.

There is first of all the articulation of reality into the two modes of being, of the Apeiron and of thinghood, which are known to man inasmuch as he experiences himself as existing not completely in either the one or the other of the two modes but in the metaleptic reality of the Metaxy. Moreover, the two modes are experienced not as two indifferently different varieties of the genus "being," but as aetiologically and tensionally related, the one being the unlimited *arche*, the origin and ground of things, the other having the character of a limited thinghood that originates in the Apeiron and returns to it. Hence, there is a difference of rank between the two modes of being, with the Apeiron being "more real" than the things. This tension of existence toward reality in an eminent sense becomes conscious in the movements of attraction and search analyzed by Plato and Aristotle. And finally, the consciousness of tension is not an object given to a subject of cognition but the very process in which reality becomes luminous to itself. The Apeiron and the things are not two different realities in a static relationship one toward the other; they are experienced as modes of being, or as poles of a tension within the one, comprehensive reality. Reality in this comprehensive sense is experienced as engaged in a movement of transcending itself in the direction of eminent reality. Reality is in flux; and the flux has such directional structures as become manifest in the unfolding of the noetic field of consciousness from Anaximander's dictum to the philosophy of history of Plato and Aristotle.

The result of the analysis can be formulated in two propositions: (1) Reality in the comprehensive sense is recognizably engaged in a movement in the direction of eminent reality. Note: Reality as a whole, *not* the two modes of being separately. (2) Conquest and exodus [in the power fields formed by expansive ecumenic imperialism *and* in the Spiritual Outbursts considered as exoduses] symbolize enterprises of participation in the directional flux of reality. Note: Enterprises of participation, *not* autonomous human actions that could result in the conquest of, or exodus from, reality. The two propositions, together with their safeguards against fallacious deformation, circumscribe both the sense of the participatory enterprises and the limits to their sense on principle. (OH, IV, 216)

The central dimension of reality, then, is the participatory reality of the self-reflective consciousness in which truth emerges in the process of differentiation through individual men's personal responses to revelation. There is no human truth apart from the man's response to theophany, and there is no divine Truth apart from the

truth of language engendered in the response of man in the language
of truth. "The emergence of meaning in history must be taken seriously: The truth of the process need not emerge, if it were there
already; and when it emerges, it is not a possession beyond the process, but a light that casts the process in the role of the darkness
from which it emerges. What becomes manifest is not a truth on
which one can settle down forever after, but the tension of light and
darkness in the process of reality." To recall Plato's parable, the man
can ascend from the Cave into the light, but the ascent does not
abolish either the mystery in the process (of turning around and ascent) or the darkness of the Cave of existence, man's habitat symbolizing the In-Between of the *condicio humana* (OH, IV, 218).

The central property of reality is the process of movement toward
eminent reality in the emergence of truth-reality in men's responses
to theophany in the divine-human collaboration or partnership in
being. Being is essentially the process of transfiguration. The process
is not under human control, nor is emergent reality. The revelation
is as mysterious as is the fact of response or the failure to respond in
indifference or in resistance to reason. Paradox attaches to reality as
a knowable structure known to be a structure of movement beyond
itself. And the Paradox of Reality is reflected in the Question as it
differentiates in history when history is conceived as the unfolding
of the meaning of existence in the In-Between over time. For luminous truth is hedged-in on all sides by the Mystery of Reality that
rises above the mystery of history. The discovery of the truth of the
epochal structure in history leaves still unanswered Leibniz' Question in its differentiated form:

(1) Why should there be epochs of advancing insight at all? why is the
structure of reality not known in differentiated form at all times?
(2) Why must the insights be discovered by such rare individuals as
prophets, philosophers, and saints? why is not every man the recipient of
the insights?
(3) Why when the insights are gained, are they not generally accepted?
why must the epochal truth go through the historical torment of imperfect
articulation, evasion, skepticism, disbelief, rejection, deformation, and of
renaissances, renovations, rediscoveries, rearticulations, and further differentiations?
. . . The questions are not meant to be answered; on the contrary, they

symbolize the mystery in the structure of history by their unanswerability.
(OH, IV, 316)

The central property of reality as transfiguration is, however, ana-
lyzable experientially in terms of the tension of structure and process. No more in noetic science than in natural science is reality a
"given" beyond question. Rather the structures in reality as experienced raise the questions in search of answers. The structures include the existence of the cosmos; the hierarchy and diversification
of being; the experience of questioning as the constituent of humanity; the leap in existential truth through the noetic and pneumatic
illuminations of consciousness; the process of history in which the
differentiations of questioning consciousness and the leap in truth
occur; and the eschatological movement in the process beyond its
structure (OH, IV, 326). Although the catalog of experienced structures is not exhaustive, it does suggest the cardinal point of the
Question. The precariousness of existence out of nonexistence, of
there being something rather than nothing, and of things (including
structures experienced) being the way they are and not otherwise
pose questions which reveal that precariousness and the mysteries
of uncertainty attach not so much to the relatively secure and stable
cosmos and the natural order as to the social field as the part of the
cosmos that unfolds its meaning in history. The process of history,
then, can be seen to represent the process of reality in the preeminent sense, and "the events of history rather than of nature become
crucial as criteria of order and disorder in the cosmos" (OH, IV, 328).

The structure of reality that differentiates in history is the consciousness of structure. And the central structure that rises to consciousness is movement of reality beyond its structure. The gaining
of this insight is not a piece of random information, but is itself an
"eschatological event" that illuminates the process of man's humanity and shows it to be transfigurative, an event that also shows the
process of differentiation to be a movement toward eschatological
fulfillment as the horizon of divine mystery of historical existence.
The gaining of this epochal insight, however, is at the same time a
discovery of the process of reality in which all men—past, present,
and future—participate by virtue of their common humanity. The
"new center of consciousness" has a social and historical dimension

in the sense of being the consciousness not of one man or a few select men, but of a great many human beings in a wide geographic
and time expanse and in a wide variety of modes and degrees of differentiation. The movement from the truth of the cosmos to the
truth of existence as it concretely occurs in the Ecumenic Age brings
to light the stratification and diversification of consciousness empirically observable in responses to the theophanies. But it also brings
to light the common core of the responses that constitutes what is
universal about universal mankind and its history (OH, IV, 314–15).[15]

The analysis of reality in terms of structure and process, finally,
relates the theory to the problems of hierarchy and time as processes
of *foundation* and *formation* previously glimpsed in the discussion
of reason. As shown in Figure 1 (page 215, herein) the hierarchy of
being is to be analyzed in terms of the relationship of the strata to
one another in the order of foundation from the bottom up and in
the order of formation from the top down. There is no "time" in
which "history" happens, but there is the stratified hierarchy of
being in which the process of consciousness is founded. The flux of
divine presence in the In-Between is founded in the biological and
physical existence of man on earth and in the universe. The ultimate
foundation of reality is the physical universe and its time dimension
is the ultimately founding measure of the higher strata which participate in one another in the order of the cosmos and its founding
and conditioning causality, the lower strata reaching into the stratum of consciousness itself as the condition of its existence and
reality.

However, the ultimate reality of the Whole is not the physical
universe but the divine reality that is experienced in consciousness
as the forming constituent of humanity and of the Whole itself.

In man's consciousness, the foundational movement within reality from
the physical depth becomes luminous for the creative constitution of all reality from the height of the divine ground. As far as the modes of lasting are
concerned we have to state therefore: In the order of foundation from the
depth, the time dimension of the universe comprehends the time-dimensions of the other strata in the hierarchy of being; in the order of creation
from the height, the divine mode of lasting that we symbolize as eternity

15. For the notion that reality is not a "given" in natural science, see Kuhn, *The
Structure of Scientific Revolutions*, 126–30.

comprehends the time-dimensions of the other strata of reality, including the universe. (OH, IV, 334–35)

Man's "nature" as an epitome of being, then, is not the fixed entity that doctrinal metaphysics would have it be. Man as the epitome of the Whole partakes of the structure *and* process of the Whole in the dynamics of foundation from the Beginning and formation from the Beyond. Hence, the strata of reality in man and the Whole are not simply piled on top of each other in a static ranking of higher and lower degrees of reality. Rather, the hierarchy of being emerges as the "movement of reality from the apeirontic depth up to man, through as many levels of the hierarchy as can be discerned empirically, and as the countermovement of the creative organization from the divine height down, with the Metaxy of man's consciousness as the site where the movement of the Whole becomes luminous for its eschatological direction" (OH, IV, 335).[16] After history differentiates as a dimension of human existence the Question differentiates to address the historical process of the Whole, which becomes luminous with a directional movement that is inseparable from the Mystery of "a reality which brings forth the universe and the earth, plant and animal life on earth, and ultimately man and his consciousness" (OH, IV, 335).[17]

In Voegelin's Vision of the Whole, then, reality is a myth spoken by God and told by man. The process of transfiguration in reality is real, he assures us. Writing at age eighty he stresses (in concert with Plato of the *Laws*) the close connection between the lifelong study of the thinker, whose constant work constantly guided is an existential catharsis, and the suddenness of the visionary insight guiding it. "Under the formative presence of the Beyond illusions and opinions have to be shed, supposed knowledge has to be modified by further

16. The "philosophical language of 'natures' has become inadequate," OH, IV, 263; cf. 253, 258, 267.

17. On the problems hinted at in the text respecting the evolution of matter and the contemporary understanding of the history of the universe and its mystery of eschatological direction, see J. T. Fraser, *Of Time, Passion, and Knowledge: Reflections on the Strategy of Existence* (New York: George Braziller, 1975); and Jacques Merleau-Ponty, *Cosmologie du XXe siècle; étude épistémologique et historique des théories de la cosmologie contemporaine* (Paris: Gallimard, 1965). This was the subject of Voegelin's lecture (unpublished) to the Conference on Gnosticism and Modernity on April 29, 1978, at Vanderbilt University.

250 THE VOEGELINIAN REVOLUTION

experience, lines of work have to be abandoned and forgotten when new discoveries are made, until the Beyond itself shines forth as the light that guides the meditative process."[18]

The Hellenic and Judaic-Christian Visions are complementary in revealing the fundamental order of reality, but the truth of the order of reality is not the whole truth of reality. That truth of the Whole must be expressed by the complex meditative symbolism of "visionary revelation-struggle-salvation."[19] Complementarity is not identity, however, and the *Nous* of Plato is not a synonym for the *pneuma tou theou*, the spirit of God, who is the Christ of the New Testament —the *theotes* of the divine Beyond. The Vision of the New Testament symbolizes a deeper stratum of the appeal-response of the divine-human encounter that had differentiated in the noetic visions, namely the full meaning of the divine saving presence in Between existence. The stress, then, falls on "visionary revelation" and on "salvation" in the meditative complex rather than on the philosophers' "struggle."[20] The discontinuity of Plato's Vision, which revealed the noetic truth of existential consciousness in opposition to the anoetic untruth of the Cave, is embodied in the saving tale that "reveals revelation as an event of transfiguration; reality is really moving toward the *eschaton* of immortality." In Saint Paul the discontinuity induced by the overwhelming revelation of pleromatic presence in Christ tends to become more than the epochal event in history that it is. Rather, it tempts the pneumatic visionaries into the deformation of expecting the transfiguration of reality in the near future, thereby proclaiming the end of history at the expense of the balance of consciousness. It clearly sounds the theme of annihilating break signalled in the *"alle bisherige Geschichte"* of Marx's *Manifesto* 2,000 years later and of the other second realities of the modern centuries in the mode of deformed existence.[21]

18. Voegelin, "Wisdom and the Magic of the Extreme," 277.
19. *Ibid.*, 280.
20. *Ibid.*, 283.
21. *Ibid.*, 284–85. Voegelin's reference to *alle bisherige Geschichte* abbreviates the opening line of the first section of Marx's *Communist Manifesto*: "Die Geschichte aller bisherigan Gesellschaft ist die Geschichte von Klassenkaempfen [The history of all hitherto existing (or previous) society is the history of class struggles]." See Siegfried Landshut (ed.), Karl Marx, *Die Fruehschriften* (Stuttgart: Alfred Kroener Verlag, 1935), p. 524. The expression *mache athanatos* is drawn from Plato, *Laws* 906A.

The balance of consciousness requires that "struggle" be held at the center of the meditative's quest as the lot of man in history. The Vision of the Whole comprehends the truth of disorder no less than of order in human existence. Hence, the philosopher "is obliged to recognize the *mache athanatos* [undying struggle] as the movement toward the experienced *eschaton* of immortality and yet not to indulge in the dreamer's fantasy of an eschatological transfiguration to be pleromatically accomplished by his own dreams and actions."[22] Here is Voegelin's Vision and Saving Tale. The final word, then, will be this:

[The] eschatological tension of man's humanity, in its dimensions of person, society, and history, is more than a matter of theoretical insight for the philosopher. It is a practical question. . . . A new picture of history is developing. The conceptual penetration of the materials is the task of the philosopher today. The results of his analysis must be communicated to the general public and, if he happens to be a professor in a university, to the students. These chores, of keeping up with the problems, of analyzing the materials, and of communicating the results are the concrete actions through which the philosopher participates in the eschatological movement of history and conforms to the Platonic/Aristotelian practice of dying. (AM, 127)

22. Voegelin, "Wisdom and the Magic of the Extreme," 287.

Works by Eric Voegelin, 1922–1981

BOOKS

1928   *Ueber die Form des amerikanischen Geistes.* Tuebingen: J. C. B. Mohr (Paul Siebeck).

1933   *Rasse und Staat.* Tuebingen: J. C. B. Mohr (Paul Siebeck). *Die Rassenidee in der Geistesgeschichte von Ray bis Carus.* Berlin: Junker & Duennhaupt.

1936   *Der Autoritaere Staat.* Vienna: Springer.

1938   *Die politischen Religionen.* Vienna: Bermann-Fischer. Reprint ed., 1939, with new Foreword, Stockholm: Bermann-Fischer.

1952   *The New Science of Politics: An Introduction.* Chicago: University of Chicago Press.

1956   *Israel and Revelation.* Baton Rouge: Louisiana State University Press. Vol. I of *Order and History.*

1957   *The World of the Polis.* Baton Rouge: Louisiana State University Press. Vol. II of *Order and History.* *Plato and Aristotle.* Baton Rouge: Louisiana State University Press. Vol. III of *Order and History.*

1959   *Die Neue Wissenschaft der Politik/Eine Einfuehrung.* Munich: Pustet. (Translation of *The New Science of Politics.*) *Wissenschaft, Politik, und Gnosis.* Munich: Koesel.

1966   *Anamnesis: Zur Theorie der Geschichte und Politik.* Munich: R. Piper & Co., Verlag.

1968   *Science, Politics, and Gnosticism.* Chicago: Henry Regnery. (Translation of *Wissenschaft, Politik, und Gnosis* by William J. Fitzpatrick, with a Foreword to the American edition.) *La Nuova Scienza Politica.* Turin: Borla. (Translation of *The New Science of Politics,* with an introduction by A. Del Noce.)

1970   *Il Mito del Mondo Nuovo.* Milan: Rusconi. (Translation of *Wis-*

senschaft, Politik, und Gnosis by Arrigo Munari, with an introduction by Mario Marcolla.)

1972 Anamnesis: Teoria della Storia e della Politica. Milan: Guiffré. (Translation of Anamnesis.)

1974 The Ecumenic Age. Baton Rouge: Louisiana State University Press. Vol. IV of Order and History.

1975 From Enlightenment to Revolution. Edited by John H. Hallowell. Durham, N.C.: Duke University Press.

1978 Anamnesis. Notre Dame, Ind. and London: University of Notre Dame Press. (Translated and edited by Gerhart Niemeyer, with a new Chapter 1, "Remembrance of Things Past," for the American edition.)

1980 Conversations with Eric Voegelin. Edited by Eric O'Connor. S. J. Montreal: Thomas More Institute. (Transcript of four lectures and discussions held in Montreal in 1965, 1967, 1970, and 1976.)

ARTICLES AND ESSAYS

1922 "Die gesellschaftliche Bestimmtheit soziologischer Erkenntnis." Zeitschrift fuer Volkswirtschaft und Sozialpolitik. New series, II, 4–6, pp. 331–48.

1924 "Reine Rechtslehre und Staatslehre." Zeitschrift fuer Oeffentliches Recht. IV, 1/2, pp. 80–131.

1925 "Die Zeit in der Wirtschaft." Archiv fuer Sozialwissenschaft und Sozialpolitik. LIII, 1, pp. 186–211.

"Ueber Max Weber." Deutsche Vierteljahrsschrift fuer Literaturwissenschaft und Geistesgeschichte. III, pp. 177–93.

1926 "Die Verfassungsmaessigkeit des 18. Amendments zur United States Constitution." Zeitschrift fuer Oeffentliches Rechts. V, 3, pp. 445–64.

"Wirtschafts- und Klassengegensatz in America." Unterrichtsbriefe des Instituts fuer angewandte Soziologie. V, 6, pp. 6–11.

1927 "Zur Lehre von der Staatsform." Zeitschrift fuer Oeffentliches Recht. VI, 4, pp. 572–608.

"Kelsen's Pure Theory of Law." Political Science Quarterly. XLII, 2, pp. 268–76.

"La Follette und die Wisconsin-Idee." Zeitschrift fuer Politik. XVII, 4, pp. 309–21.

1928 "Konjunkturforschung und Stabilisation des Kapitalismus." Mitteilungen des Verbandes oesterreichischer Banken und Bankiers. IX, 9/10, pp. 252–59.

"Der Sinn der Erklaerung der Menschen- und Buergerrechte von

1789." *Zeitschrift fuer Oeffentliches Recht.* VIII, 1, pp. 82–120.

"Zwei Grundbegriffe der Humeschen Gesellschaftslehre." *Archiv fuer angewande Soziologie.* I, 2, pp. 11–16.

"Die ergaezende Bill zum Federal Reserve Act und Die Dollarstabilisation." *Mitteilungen des Verbandes oesterreichischer Banken und Bankiers.* X, 11/12, pp. 252–59.

"Die ergaenzende Bill zum Federal Reserve Act." *Nationalwirtschaft.* II, 2, pp. 225–29.

1929   "Die Souveraenitaetstheorie Dickinsons und die Reine Rechtslehre." *Zeitschrift fuer Oeffentliches Recht.* VIII, 3, pp. 413–34.

"Die Transaktion." *Archiv fuer angewandte Soziologie.* I, 4/5, pp. 14–21.

1930   "Die amerikanische Theorie vom Eigentum." *Archiv fuer angewandte Soziologie.* II, 4, pp. 165–72.

"Die amerikanische Theorie vom ordentlichen Rechtsverfahren und von der Freiheit." *Archiv fuer angewandte Soziologie.* III, 1, pp. 40–57.

"Die oesterreichische Verfassungsreform von 1929." *Zeitschrift fuer Politik.* XIX, 9, pp. 585–615.

"Max Weber." *Koelner Vierteljahreshefte fuer Soziologie.* IX, 1/2, pp. 1–16.

"Die Einheit des Rechts und das soziale Sinngebilde Staat." *Internationale Zeitschrift fuer Theorie des Rechts.* 1/2, pp. 58–59.

1931   "Die Verfassungslehre von Carl Schmitt/Versuch einer konstruktiven Analyse ihrer staatstheoretischen Prinzipien." *Zeitschrift fuer Oeffentliches Recht.* XI, 1, pp. 80–109.

"Das Sollen im System Kants." In Alfred Verdrosz, ed., *Gesellschaft, Staat und Recht.* Vienna: Springer. Pp. 136–73.

1932   "Nachwort." In Ernst Dimnet, ed., *Die Kunst des Denkens.* Freiburg: Herder. Pp. 279–96.

1935   "Le régime administratif. Avantages et inconvenients." *Mémoires de l'Academie Internationale de Droit comparé.* II, 3, pp. 126–49.

"Rasse und Staat." In Otto Klemm, ed., *Psychologie des Gemeinschaftslebens.* Jena: Fischer. Pp. 91–104.

1936   "Volksbildung, Wissenschaft und Politik." *Monatsschrift fuer Kultur und Politik.* I, 7, pp. 594–603.

"Josef Redlich." *Jur. Blaetter,* LXV, 23, pp. 485–86.

1937   "Das Timurbild der Humanisten/Eine Studie zur politischen Mythenbildung." *Zeitschrift fuer Oeffentliches Recht.* XVII, 5, pp. 545–82.

"Change in the Ideas on Government and Constitution in Austria since 1918." *Austrian Memorandum* No. 3. Paris: International Studies Conference on Peaceful Change.

1940 "Extended Strategy: A New Technique of Dynamic Relations." *Journal of Politics*, II, 2, pp. 189–200.

"The Growth of the Race Idea." *Review of Politics*. II, 3, pp. 283–317.

1941* "Some Problems of German Hegemony." *Journal of Politics*. III, 2, pp. 154–68.

"The Mongol Orders of Submission to European Powers, 1245–1255." *Byzantion*. XV, pp. 378–413.

1942 "The Theory of Legal Science: A Review." *Louisiana Law Review*. IV, pp. 554–72.

1944 "Nietzsche, the Crisis and the War." *Journal of Politics*. VI, 2, pp. 177–212.

"Siger de Brabant." *Philosophy and Phenomenological Research*. IV, 4, pp. 507–26.

"Political Theory and the Pattern of General History." *American Political Science Review*. XXXVIII, 4, pp. 746–54.

1946 "Bakunin's Confession." *Journal of Politics*. VIII, 1, pp. 24–43.

1947 "Zu Sanders 'Allgemeiner Staatslehre'." *Oesterreichische Zeitschrift fuer Oeffentliches Recht*. New Series, I, 1/2, pp. 106–35.

"Plato's Egyptian Myth." *Journal of Politics*. IX, 3, pp. 307–24.

1948 "The Origins of Scientism." *Social Research*. XV, 4, pp. 462–94. (Translated as "Wissenschaft als Aberglaube/Die Urspruenge des Scientifismus." *Wort und Wahrheit*. VI, 5, pp. 341–60.)

"Political Theory." In Ernest S. Griffith, ed., *Research in Political Science*. Chapel Hill: University of North Carolina Press. Pp. 190–201.

1949 "The Philosophy of Existence: Plato's *Gorgias*." *Review of Politics*. XI, 4, pp. 477–98.

1950 "The Formation of the Marxian Revolutionary Idea." *Review of Politics*. XII, 3, pp. 275–302. (Translated as "La formación de la idea revolucionaria marxista." *Hechos e Ideas*, XII [1951], pp. 227–50. Reprinted in M. A. Fitzsimons, T. McAvoy, Frank O'Malley, eds., *The Image of Man*. Notre Dame, Ind.: University of Notre Dame Press, 1959. Pp. 265–81.)

1951 "Machiavelli's Prince: Background and Formation." *Review of Politics*. XIII, 2, pp. 142–68.

"More's Utopia." *Oesterreichische Zeitschrift fuer Oeffentliches Recht*. New Series, III, 4, pp. 451–68.

1952 "Gnostische Politik." *Merkur*. IV, 4, pp. 301–17.

"Goethe's Utopia." In Carl Hammer, ed., *Goethe After Two Centuries*. Baton Rouge: Louisiana State University Press. Pp. 55–62.

1953 "The Origins of Totalitarianism." *Review of Politics*. XV, 1, pp. 68–85. With a reply by Hannah Arendt.

"The World of Homer." *Review of Politics*. XV, 4, pp. 491–523.

"The Oxford Political Philosophers." *Philosophical Quarterly*. III, 11, pp. 97–114. (Translated as "Philosophia der Politik in Oxford." *Philosophische Rundschau*. I, 1, pp. 23–48.)

1958 "Der Prophet Elias." *Hochland*. I, 4, pp. 325–39.

1959 "Diskussionsbereitschaft." In Albert Hunold, ed., *Erziehung zur Freiheit*. Erlenbach-Zurich and Stuttgart: Rentsch. Pp. 355–72. (Translated as "On Readiness to Rational Discussion." In Albert Hunold, ed., *Freedom and Serfdom*. Dordrecht-Holland: D. Reidel Publishing Co., 1961. Pp. 269–84.)

"Demokratie im neuen Europa." *Gesellschaft-Staat-Erziehung*. IV, 7, pp. 293–300.

1960 "El concepto de la 'buena sociedad.'" *Cuadrenos del Congresso por la Libertad de la Cultura*. Supplement 40, pp. 25–28.

"Religionsersatz/Die gnostischen Massenbewegunen unserer Zeit." *Wort und Wahrheit*. XV, 1, pp. 5–18. (Translated as "Ersatz Religion: The Gnostic Movements of Our Time," in Eric Voegelin, *Science, Politics, and Gnosticism*. Regnery, 1968. Pp. 81–114.)

"La Société industrielle à la recherche de la raison." In Raymond Aron, George Kennan, *et al.*, eds., *Colloques de Rheinfelden*. Paris: Calmann-Levy, 1960. Pp. 44–64. (Translated as "Die industrielle Gesellschaft auf der Suche nach der Vernunft," Das Seminar von Rheinfelden. *Die Gesellschaft und die drei Welten*. Zurich: EVZ-Verlag, 1961. Pp. 46–64. Also translated as "Industrial Society in Search of Reason." In R. Aron, ed., *World Technology and Human Destiny*. Ann Arbor: University of Michigan Press, 1963. Pp. 31–46.)

"Verantwortung und Freiheit in Wirtschaft und Demokratie." *Die Aussprache*. X, 6, pp. 207–13.

"Der Liberalismus und seine Geschichte." In Karl Forster, ed., *Christentum und Liberalismus: Studien und Bericht der Katholischen Akademie in Bayern*. Munich: Zink. Pp. 13–42. (Translated as "Liberalism and Its History." *Review of Politics*. XXXVI, 4, pp. 504–20.)

"Historiogenesis." *Philosophisches Jahrbuch*. LXVII, pp. 419–46. (Also in Max Mueller and Michael Schmaus, eds., *Philosophia Viva: Festschrift fuer Alois Dempf*. Freiburg/Munich: Alber, 1960. Pp. 419–46. Reprinted in Eric Voegelin, *Anamnesis*. Munich: Piper, 1966. Pp. 79–116. Translated and expanded in Eric Voegelin, *The Ecumenic Age*. Baton Rouge: Louisiana State University Press, 1974. Pp. 59–114.)

1961 "Toynbee's History as a Search for Truth." In Edward T. Gargan, ed., *The Intent of Toynbee's History*. Chicago: Loyola University Press, 1961. Pp. 181–98.

"Les Perspectives d'Avenir de la civilisation occidentale." In Raymond

Aron, ed., *L'Histoire et ses interprétations: Entretiens autour de Arnold Toynbee.* The Hague: Mouton, 1961. Pp. 133–51.

1962 "World Empire and the Unity of Mankind." *International Affairs.* XXXVIII, pp. 170–88.

1963 "Das Rechte von Natur." *Oesterreichische Zeitschrift fuer Oeffentliches Recht.* XIII, 1/2, pp. 38–51. (Reprinted in Eric Voegelin, *Anamnesis.* Munich: Piper, 1966. Pp. 117–33. Translated as "What Is Right by Nature?" in Gerhart Niemeyer, ed. and trans., *Anamnesis.* Notre Dame: University of Notre Dame Press, 1978. Pp. 55–70.)

"Hacia Una Nueva Ciencia del Orden Social." *Atlantida: Revista del pensamiento actual.* I, 2, pp. 121–37.

1964 "Ewiges Sein in der Zeit." In Erich Dinkler, ed., *Zeit und Geschichte: Dankesgabe an Rudolph Bultmann Zum 80. Geburtstag.* Tuebingen: J. C. B. Mohr. Pp. 591–614. (Reprinted in Eric Voegelin, *Anamnesis.* Munich: Piper, 1966. Pp. 254–80. Translated as "Eternal Being in Time," in Gerhart Niemeyer, ed. and trans., *Anamnesis.* Notre Dame: University of Notre Dame Press, 1978. Pp. 116–40.)

"Der Mensch in Gesellschaft und Geschichte." *Oesterreichische Zeitschrift fuer Oeffentliches Recht.* XIV, 1/2, pp. 1–13.

"Demokratie und Industriegesellschaft." In *Die Unternehmerische Verantwortung in unerer Gesellschaftsordnung,* Vol. IV of the Walter-Raymond-Stiftung meeting. Cologne and Opladen: Westdeutscher Verlag, n.d. Pp. 96–114.

"Metaphysik und Geschichte." In *Die Philosophie und die Frage nach dem Fortschritt.* Munich: Pustet.

1965 "Was ist Natur?" In H. Hantsch, F. Valsecchi, E. Voegelin, eds., *Historica: Festschrift fuer Friedrich Engel-Janosi.* Vienna: Herder. Pp. 1–18. (Reprinted in Eric Voegelin,. *Anamnesis.* Munich: Piper, 1966. Pp. 134–52. Translated as "What Is Nature?" in Gerhart Niemeyer, ed. and trans., *Anamnesis.* Notre Dame: University of Notre Dame Press, 1978. Pp. 71–88.)

1966 "Die deutsche Universitaet und die Ordnung der deutschen Gesellschaft." In *Die Deutsche Universitaet im Dritten Reich.* Munich: Piper. Pp. 241–82. (Reprinted as "Universitaet und Oeffentlichkeit: Zur Pneumopathologia der Deutschen Gesellschaft." *Wort und Wahrheit.* XXI, 8/9, pp. 497–518.)

"Was ist Politische Realitaet?" *Politische Vierteljahresschrift.* VII, 1, pp. 1–54. (Reprinted in Eric Voegelin, *Anamnesis.* Munich: Piper, 1966. Pp. 283–354. Translated as "What Is Political Reality?" in Gerhart Niemeyer, ed. and trans., *Anamnesis.* Notre Dame: University of Notre Dame Press, 1978. Pp. 143–213.)

1967 "On Debate and Existence." *Intercollegiate Review*. III, 4/5, pp. 143–52.

"Immortality: Experience and Symbol." *Harvard Theological Review*. LX, 3, pp. 235–79.

1968 "Configurations in History." In Paul Kuntz, ed., *The Concept of Order*. Seattle: University of Washington Press. Pp. 23–42.

"Zur Geschichte des Politischen Denkens." In *Zwischen Revolution und Restauration: Politisches Denken in England in 17. Jahrhundert*. Munich: Paul List Verlag. P. 181.

"Helvétius," with Peter Leuschner. In Arno Baruzzi, ed., *Aufklaerung und Materialismus im Frankreich des 18. Jahrhunderts*. Munich: Paul List Verlag. Pp. 63–97.

1969 "History and Gnosis." In Bernhard Anderson, ed., *The Old Testament and Christian Faith*. New York: Herder and Herder. Pp. 64–89.

1970 "Equivalences of Experience and Symbolization in History." In *Eternita è Storia, I valori permanenti nel divenire storico*. Florence: Valecchi. Pp. 215–34.

"The Eclipse of Reality." In Maurice Natanson, ed., *Phenomenology and Social Reality*. The Hague: Martinus Nijhoff. Pp. 185–94.

1971 "Henry James's 'The Turn of the Screw.'" With 1. Prefatory note by Robert Heilman, 2. A letter to Robert Heilman, 3. Postscript: "On Paradise and Revolution." *Southern Review*. New Series, VII, 1, pp. 3–48.

"The Gospel and Culture." In D. Miller and D. G. Hadidian, eds., *Jesus and Man's Hope*. Pittsburgh: Pittsburgh Theological Seminary Press. II, pp. 59–101.

"On Hegel: A Study in Sorcery." *Studium Generale*. No. 24, pp. 335–68. (Reprinted in J. T. Fraser, F. C. Haber, G. H. Mueller, eds., *The Study of Time*. Heidelberg and Berlin: Springer Verlag, 1972. Pp. 418–51.)

1973 "On Classical Studies." *Modern Age*. XVII, pp. 2–8.

"Philosophy of History: An Interview." *New Orleans Review*, No. 2 (1977), pp. 135–39.

1974 "Reason: The Classic Experience" *Southern Review*. New Series, X, 2, pp. 237–64. (Reprinted in Gerhart Niemeyer, ed. and trans., *Anamnesis*. Notre Dame: University of Notre Dame Press, 1978. Pp. 89–115.)

1975 "Response to Professor Altizer's 'A New History and a New but Ancient God?'" *Journal of the American Academy of Religion*. XLIII, 4, pp. 765–72.

1978 "Remembrance of Things Past." Chapter 1 in Gerhart Niemeyer, ed. and trans., *Anamnesis*. Notre Dame: University of Notre Dame Press. Pp. 3–13.

1981   "Wisdom and the Magic of the Extreme: A Meditation." *Southern Review.* New Series, XVII, 2, pp. 235–87. (Reprinted in *Eranos Jahrbuch*, No. 46. Frankfort: Insel Verlag, forthcoming.)

"Die Symbolisierung der Ordung." *Politische Studien*, vol. XXXII, no. 255 (January/February, 1981), 12–23. Translation by Peter J. Opitz of "Introduction: The Symbolization of Order," in *Order and History*, vol. 1 (1956), 1–11.

Index

Theophany: 200, 212, 225; and epoch,
232; God of noetic (philosophy) and
pneumatic (revelation) the same,
232–33; Paul's, 235–39; of Aristotle
and Paul, 236
Thibaudet, Albert, 40
Third Realm, 57, 66, 108–109. *See also*
Gnosticism; Ideology; Joachim of
Flora
Time, 193, 197, 248
Time of the Tale, 238
Totalitarianism, 62–69, 109–11. *See
also* Ideology; National socialism
Toynbeè, Arnold J., 8, 9, 10, 22, 85,
126*n*, 127–32
Transcendence: 138, 152–53, 166–67,
231; and immanence, 155; as decisive
problem of philosophy, 180–82
Transfiguration: 109–10; of reality
through metastatic faith, 134–35; of
history and the Whole, 228; in Paul's
Vision and its exegesis, 235–39; in
egophanic revolt as Gnosis of transmutation, 240–43
Truth: 93–94, 119–20, 184, 188–89;
tension between society's and philosopher's, 99; institutionalization of,
98; of soul as substance of historical
process, 101; transcendental, 102–
104; cosmological, anthropological,
and soteriological distinguished as
types of, 103–104, 104*n*; objectivity
of, 125; and untruth, 132–33, 235; of
being not affected by empirical defections, 140–41; represented in philosopher for Everyman, 142; etymology of
as *aletheia*, 145; search for, 149; as
unit of meaning in Truth-Experience-
Symbol, 221; and language of truth as
the truth of language, 225–26, 243.
See also Experiences-symbolisms
(symbolisations); Language

Unknown: symbol of divine beyond
beyond the Beyond (*epekeina*),
233–35
Unoriginality, 91

Valéry, Paul, 37, 40, 43
Values: and *wertbeziehende Methode* in
Rickert's value-free science, 46–47

Varro, 105
Vauvenargues, Marquise de, 41
Verdross, Alfred von, 35
Vico, Giambattista, 135
Vision: in philosophers' theophanic ex-
perience-symbolization, 212–13; and
Noesis in philosophy, contrasted with
logic, 217; in Voegelin's thought,
218–25; in Plato (*opsis, hora*), 212,
222, 235, 250; Hellenic and Judaic-
Christian compared, 249–50; and
Voegelin's Saving Tale, 251
Voegelin, Elisabeth Ruehl (mother), 33
Voegelin, Eric (Erich Hermann
Wilhelm): revolution in thought of,
1–2, 11–12; obscurity of, 1, 9, 10–12;
and common sense, 4; and new science of human affairs, 4; language a
central concern of, 5, 15; estimates of
his stature, 6–12; and philosophy of
history, 8; and political science, 9–11;
an independent thinker, 12–13; as
philosopher and political scientist, 13,
19, 24; and derailment of philosophy
after Aristotle, 14; and conception of
science, 14; and Christianity, 16; and
dogmatism, 16; originality of, 16; on
modernity, 17; and Gnosticism,
17–18; centrality of common sense
and ordinary experience to his
thought, 19; and Whitehead, 19; and
William James's "radical" empiricism,
23, 171–77; "unoriginality" of his
theory, 25–26; and Marx's thought,
27–29; and systems, 29–30; and constants in history, 30–31; and study of
Greek and Christian philosophy, 60;
and political views in 1930s, 60–62;
regarded as a Jew by Nazis, 63–64;
and sum of work as a new science of
human affairs or *Principia Noetica*,
188–216 *passim*; and Vision at center
of thought, 218–25; and postulate of
balance, 232–43; radical empiricism
and his ontology, 243–45; and Vision
of the Whole, 249–51; and Vision and
Saving Tale, 251
—biography: Lippincott Award, 9–10;
Henry Salvatori Distinguished
Scholar at Stanford, 10, 87–88; escape
from Austria and emigration, 12–13,

68–70; Laura Spellman Rockefeller Memorial Fellowship for study in America and France, 20; at Columbia, Harvard, Wisconsin, 20, 37; discovers Scottish common sense school of philosophy, 20; political circumstances in 1920s, 28; chronology of his life, 33, 71; childhood, 33–34; early education, 33–34; university student in Vienna, 34–35; activities, studies, membership in *Geistkreis* (Intellectual Circle), 35–37; major influences in intellectual development, 37–41; and Max Weber, 38–40; year in France, 40; learns Russian, 41; study of French thinkers, 41–42; introduction to alchemy, astrology, and Gnosticism, 42; Medieval and Renaissance studies, 43; membership in Stefan George Circle and influence of Karl Kraus, 43–44; relationship with Hans Kelsen, 45–46; interest in Classical philosophy, 45; beginnings of a new political science, 46, 60; early teaching career in Vienna, 48; dismissed by Nazis, 49; analysis of totalitarian politics, 50–60; analyses of the problem of scientism and its dogmas, 54–55; appointments at Harvard, Bennington, Alabama, and Louisiana State University, 71–77; learns Hebrew and Chinese, 72, 74; daily regimen, 76; effect as a teacher, 74–75; Walgreen Lectures at Chicago, 77; at the University of Munich, 10, 84–87; retirement from Munich and return to Stanford, 87–88
—writings: "Autobiographical Memoir," 3; quoted, 12–13, 17, 18, 20–22, 38, 39, 40; on Bodin's significance, 42; on Karl Kraus and problem of language, 44–45, 47, 48, 49, 51; on Austrian politics, 60–62, 63, 64, 65; on escape from Austria, 68–70, 72, 76; on *The New Science of Politics*, 77–79; on transition from "History of Political Ideas" to *Order and History*, 80–84; on Marx, 86; on Hitler, 87; on philosophy of history, 91; on metastatic faith, 134–35; on theory of consciousness, 168–71; on philosophy as the

practice of dying, 251; *Order and History*, 4, 6–8, 10, 60, 81–84, 87–88, 116–42, 149–56 *passim*, 189–200, 226–51 *passim*; *The New Science of Politics*, 9, 14, 17, 62, 77–79, 90–116 *passim*, 143; *Anamnesis*, 17, 84, 144, 152, 157–87 *passim*; "Equivalences of Experience and Symbolization," 17, 26, 30–32, 88, 91, 195–96, 198, 209; *Ueber die Form des amerikanischen Geistes*, 21, 44, 48, 169, 171, 172, 173, 175, 180; *From Enlightenment to Revolution*, 27–28, 76–77; *Wechselwirkung und Gezweiung* (doctoral dissertation), 38; "History of Political Ideas," 41, 43, 60, 72–74, 76–77, 80–84, 168; *Die Rassenidee in der Geistesgeschichte von Ray bis Carus*, 44, 50–53, 56–60; *Der Autoritaere Staat*, 48, 62–64; *Rasse und Staat*, 50, 54–56, 57; *Die politischen Religionen*, 64–68; *Science, Politics, and Gnosticism*, 78–79, 86; "Remembrance of Things Past" (*Anamnesis*, ed. Niemeyer, Chap. 1), 189n, 223–24; "Reason: The Classic Experience," 191, 213–16; *The Beginning and the Beyond*, 214, 225; "Wisdom and the Magic of the Extreme: A Meditation," 218n, 242, 250–51
Voegelin, Lissy Onken (wife), 33, 69–70, 72
Voegelin, Otto Stefan (father), 33
Voegelinian revolution: 1, 2, 89; and new political science, 90–91, 96, 116, 144, 188–216 *passim*, 217–51 *passim*

Waelder, Robert, 36
Warren, Robert Penn, 75, 76
Weber, Alfred, 40
Weber, Max: 10, 22, 37, 38–40, 167; and ethics of responsibility, 38; value-free science in, 39; empirical horizon and comparative knowledge, 39–40
Weininger, Otto, 36
Weiser, Friedrich, 35
Wellesz, Egon, 36
Wesley, John (Columbia University economist), 20
Whitehead, Alfred North, 14, 19, 21, 201
Whole: as symbol of comprehensive re-

ality, 198; and Question of truth, 243–45; truth of symbolized as "visionary revelation-struggle-salvation," 250
Wilde, Johannes, 36

Wilhelmsen, Frederick D., 16
Windelband, Wilhelm, 39, 46
Wiser, James L., 7
Wittgenstein, Ludwig, 35